THE PENGUIN CLASSICS

FOUNDER EDITOR (1944–64): E. V. RIEU

HENRIK IBSEN was born at Skien, Norway, in 1828. His family went bankrupt when he was a child, and he struggled with poverty for many years. His first ambition was medicine, but he abandoned this to write and to work in the theatre. Of his early verse plays, *The Vikings at Helgeland* is now best remembered. In the year of its publication (1858) he married Susannah Thoresen, a pastor's daughter.

A scholarship enabled Ibsen to travel to Rome in 1864. In Italy he wrote *Brand* (1866), which earned him a state pension, and *Peer Gynt* (1867), for which Grieg later wrote the incidental music. These plays established his reputation. Apart from two short visits to Norway, he lived in Italy and Germany until 1891.

From *The League of Youth* (1869) onwards, Ibsen renounced poetry and wrote prose drama. Though a timid man, he supported in his plays many crucial causes of his day, such as the emancipation of women. Plays like *Ghosts* (1881) and *A Doll's House* (1879) caused critical uproar. Other plays included *The Pillars of the Community, The Wild Duck, The Lady From the Sea, Hedda Gabler, The Master Builder, John Gabriel Borkmann* and *When We Dead Wake*.

Towards the end of his life Ibsen, one of the world's greatest dramatists, suffered strokes which destroyed his memory for words and even the alphabet. He died in 1906 in Kristiania (now Oslo).

PETER WATTS was born in 1900 and went to school in Canada. He originally trained as a doctor at Cambridge and St Thomas's Hospital, but then turned to journalism and the theatre. In the twenties he stage managed the Old Vic for eight years. He then travelled about Europe and the Middle East and after a period as a literary agent and then as a wine merchant he returned to the theatre in 1938 as a producer. When the theatre closed at the beginning of the war, he went to the Admiralty as a King's Courier, but left in 1941 when the BBC offered him a post as a drama producer. He remained with them for nearly twenty years, working both in radio and television. He produced most of his translations of Ibsen and Strindberg on the Third Programme. Peter Watts died in 1972.

Henrik Ibsen

———— * ————

GHOSTS
A PUBLIC ENEMY
WHEN WE DEAD WAKE

———— * ————

TRANSLATED BY
PETER WATTS

PENGUIN BOOKS

Penguin Books Ltd, Harmondsworth, Middlesex, England
Penguin Books Inc., 7110 Ambassador Road, Baltimore, Maryland 21207, U.S.A.
Penguin Books Australia Ltd, Ringwood, Victoria, Australia
Penguin Books Canada Ltd, 41 Steelcase Road West, Markham, Ontario, Canada
Penguin Books (N.Z.) Ltd, 182–190 Wairau Road, Auckland 10, New Zealand

—

This translation first published 1964
Reprinted 1966, 1967, 1969, 1970, 1971, 1973, 1974, 1976

—

Copyright © the Estate of Peter Watts, 1964

—

Made and printed in Great Britain
by Hazell Watson & Viney Ltd,
Aylesbury, Bucks
Set in Linotype Pilgrim

All applications to perform the plays in this volume
should be made to A. P. Watt & Son, 26/28 Bedford Row,
London WC1R 4HL

CONTENTS

INTRODUCTION

———————— * ————————

THE plays in this book show three very different aspects of Ibsen's work; they are a realistic drama, a comedy, and a piece of symbolism. People who know Ibsen only from the great social dramas of his middle period may be surprised that the 'Great Realist' should have written a symbolic play in the manner of Strindberg. Many more will not have realized that he also wrote comedies. Indeed, seeing that he is one of the half-dozen greatest dramatists that the world has known, Ibsen is surprisingly misunderstood even by the well-informed. Not long ago, even on the B.B.C. programme 'The Critics', a woman could state that 'Ibsen was famous for his well-made plays', without any of her male colleagues joining issue with her; and this when most of Ibsen's life was a struggle to free the European theatre from the *pièce bien faite* of Scribe and his followers.

Probably the greatest general misconception about Ibsen is the popular idea that he is dull and stodgy. Even though today most of the causes that he fought for so passionately have long ago been won, the plays are still exciting reading and superb 'theatre'. Part of the blame for this reputation for stuffiness must lie, unfortunately, with William Archer's translation. The last thing I want to do is to belittle that brilliant achievement or the devotion that brought Ibsen before the English-speaking world. Archer had spent much of his youth in Norway and knew the language intimately; all his work is studded with felicities of translation that have never been bettered, and his handling of the more difficult passages is brilliant. The trouble is that, naturally, he translated the plays into the accepted theatrical language of his period – the ponderous stilted dialogue that makes Henry Arthur Jones and Pinero such an effort to read today – and our idea of Ibsen has suffered by it.

Even those who have a fairly accurate mental picture of the tetchy secretive little Doktor Ibsen might find it hard to reconcile with that of the lonely sixteen-year-old chemist's assistant fathering a child by a servant-girl ten years his senior. Still less can they see him failing as a stage manager at the Bergen theatre because he was too diffident to correct the actors – and particularly the actresses. That one of his Danish colleagues at that theatre could describe him as 'a tight-lipped little Norwegian with an observant eye' may not surprise us, but it seems strange that the woman who later became his mother-in-law should have seen him as 'a small shy woodchuck'. We certainly think of him as fiercely nationalistic, yet he could assert (without much regard for truth) that he hadn't a drop of Norwegian blood in his veins. At the same time, he spent nearly thirty of the most productive years of his life in a self-imposed exile, in disgust at Norway's neutrality in the Prusso–Danish war – an attitude that might endear him to many Englishmen who remember the days of Munich.

How, too, do we reconcile our picture with that of the middle-aged poet striding about Rome in a sombrero decorated with a tuft of blue feathers, so that the Italians nicknamed him 'The Hat'? There is, again, something endearing about the way he so jealously collected decorations and orders, and wore them all whenever he possibly could – particularly resenting the fact that Norway was almost the last European country to award him one.

He was well called 'the spirit of contradiction', this irascible little man with the tremendous sense of fun, who loved cafés and bars and who even admitted of *Peer Gynt* that 'wine did this', yet who kept such a jealous and accurate eye on his book sales and royalties. Even at the last when, at his deathbed, Fru Ibsen suddenly said, 'Look, the Doktor is getting better!' he opened his blazing blue eyes almost for the last time to say 'On the contrary!'

These three plays are all later works. *Ghosts* and *A Public Enemy* belong to the great middle period of his social plays, written when he was in his early fifties. *When We Dead Wake* is his last play, when he was over seventy – an author taking stock of his life and work, weighing his triumph and bitterly deploring what he takes to be his failure.

Success came late to Ibsen. It was not until he was nearly forty that he wrote that essentially youthful play *Peer Gynt* that brought him fame. He was at that time primarily a poet, and though this first great success was also in verse – and exciting, vital, galloping verse at that – it was after this that he suddenly and strangely decided that verse was the enemy of drama. Some years later, he crystallized this attitude in a letter to a great Norwegian actress:

Verse has done incalculable damage to the art of acting, and any actor who goes in for modern drama should be particularly on his guard against delivering even a single line of it. I'm sure that in the drama of the future verse will hardly be used at all. Being quite impossible to reconcile with the aims of that drama, it will fall into disuse. Art-forms become extinct, just as the preposterous animal-forms of prehistoric times died out when they had had their day. . . .

For the past seven or eight years, I myself have hardly written a single line of verse. Instead, I have disciplined myself to the much more difficult art of writing truthfully in the fluent speech of everyday life . . .

From *The League of Youth*, his next play, onwards, all his plays were in prose – indeed he was soon to find that he had quite lost the power to write verse. It is this deliberate renunciation and the subsequent loss of his talent that is the key to the enigma of *When We Dead Wake*.

*

Ghosts is one of a group of plays on a theme that obsessed Ibsen all his life: the way that we are dominated by the past. 'We sail,' he wrote, 'with a corpse in the cargo.' Here its particular aspect is the sins of the fathers. In a sense it follows logically from *A Doll's House* written two years earlier; Osvald carries the problem of Dr Rank a stage further, while Mrs Alving is a Nora who stayed at home.

Ibsen seems to have felt a particularly strong compulsion to write this play. Years later, in 1898, at a reception in his honour at the royal palace in Stockholm, King Oscar II of Sweden said, '. . . But you should never have written *Ghosts*, Ibsen; it's not a good work – not like *Lady Inger of Østråt*!' Ibsen remained silent and embarrassed while Queen Sophie tried to cover the awkward situation, and finally burst out, 'Your Majesty, I *had* to write *Ghosts*.'

He had mulled over the idea during a wet summer in Berchtesgaden, and then came back to Rome, and later to Sorrento, to get it on paper. In Sorrento he stayed at the same hotel as Ernest Renan, but was so absorbed in his work that he never met him. In the past he had found it particularly difficult to start writing each day, and he used to end a day's work with a sizeable block of dialogue ready in his head so that he had something to put on paper at once; sometimes he would even leave a speech half-finished. But *Ghosts* he wrote quickly and fluently; the first act took him only ten days between late September and early October 1881. Act Two he wrote in the third week of October, and he started the last act four days later and had finished it by the 28th. In this play particularly he was aiming at complete naturalism: 'I want the reader to feel,' he wrote, 'that, as he reads, he is sharing in an actual experience.'

After two or three weeks for revision, he sent the MS. to Hegel his publisher in mid-November, so that, like most of his great plays, it could be in the bookshops in time for the Christmas rush. It seems strange that, though Ibsen was a practical man of the theatre who had worked for many years behind the scenes as stage manager and 'Resident Poet', he always thought of his plays primarily as books to be read. We must realize though that, in the Scandinavian theatre of his day, half a dozen performances meant a great success, and that it was from the book sales that the royalties came. Even when he became internationally famous, with plays continually performed all over Europe, he never outgrew the habit.

When he had sent off the manuscript to Hegel, he began to have doubts, and a few days later he wrote to him again:

Ghosts will probably cause some disquiet in certain quarters, but if it weren't to do so, I shouldn't have needed to write it.

Hegel had no such qualms, and printed an extra large edition – only to be left with many of the 10,000 copies unsold, and a catastrophic drop in the sales of all Ibsen's other books. In those days it was still possible for a book to be called filthy and yet be remaindered.

The uproar against Ghosts was the most violent of all the many storms that Ibsen raised. None of the Scandinavian theatres would stage it, and it was not till 1884 that anyone dared to translate it into German. In fact its first performance was not in Europe at all, but was given by a touring company in Chicago. When at last it was staged in London, the critics labelled it 'putrid', 'naked loathsomeness', and 'an open sewer', and they dubbed Ibsen 'an egoist and a bungler – a crazy cranky being'. The Pall Mall Gazette even ended its review with 'Old Ibsen is as dead as a doornail'. Few people now remember the *Pall Mall Gazette*.

*

Ibsen was naturally hurt and angered by this unreasonable reaction to his intensely moral play. He turned his anger to good use with *A Public Enemy*, which he dashed off in half the time that it usually took him to conceive and write a play. It appeared within a year of *Ghosts*, making almost the only exception to the regular two-year interval between his plays at this period.

In January 1882, a month after *Ghosts* appeared, he wrote to Georg Brandes:

Never in any circumstances shall I be able to belong to a party that has the majority on its side. . . . The minority is always right – that is to say, the minority that is leading the way towards some point at which the majority has not yet arrived.

That might be called the germ of *A Public Enemy*, though actually Ibsen had a rough idea for a play on some such theme in 1879 after *A Doll's House*, but nothing came of it. It was only the shock of this sudden unpopularity that gave him the drive to start work on it a mere three months after *Ghosts* appeared. By the middle of February 1882 he was writing to his publisher:

Just now I'm extremely busy on the early stages of a new play. This time it'll be a very harmless one that can safely be read by politicians and rich businessmen – and their wives. Theatres won't have to shy away from it. It'll be easy to write, and I'm going to try to have it ready for you by the autumn of this year.

Will you once again be so good as to lend me 1,000 kroner?

In casting about for a plot to illustrate his theme, Ibsen hit on two true incidents. He remembered a friend from

Munich, the poet Alfred Meissner, who had once told him how, in the 1830s, his father had been Medical Officer at a health resort at Teplitz in Bohemia when cholera broke out there. Dr Meissner felt that it was his duty to warn the public, whereupon all the guests took fright and left. The angry townspeople stoned his house and in the end he had to leave the district. The other incident dated from only the year before, when a Christiania chemist, Harald Thaulow, had a resounding quarrel with a local steam kitchen, in which the whole capital took sides. There was a public meeting very like that in Act Four of the play. There is a good deal of Thaulow in Dr Stockmann, but Ibsen claimed that he also used both Bjørnson and Jonas Lie as models; from Lie came Stockmann's 'abruptness and his joyous virtue', while his strength of will came from Bjørnson.

This is the only one of Ibsen's major plays where we have no notes or first draft. Archer suggests that he wrote the play so quickly that he needed no notes and made no revision, but in a letter to Hegel in August 1882, a month before he sent him the finished play, Ibsen said that he had rewritten the play twice. Perhaps for once he destroyed all his rough work; certainly we know that he was furious when it leaked out, from an envelope covered with notes that he dropped in a train, that his hero was to be a doctor.

By September the play was finished, and in his covering letter to Hegel, Ibsen wrote: 'I've enjoyed writing it, and now that it's off my hands I feel quite lost and lonely.' This enjoyment shows itself in the rollicking vitality of the writing, and the play became a great popular success. Commenting on it six months later, Ibsen wrote to Brandes from Rome:

In ten years' time, the majority will probably come round to the point of view that Dr Stockmann held at the meeting. . . .

But the Doctor himself won't have been standing still all those ten years – once again he'll be at least ten years ahead of the majority. . . . Nowadays there's a reasonably compact crowd standing at the point where I stood when I wrote each of my plays, but *I*'m not there any longer, I'm further ahead again, I hope.

*

When We Dead Wake was Ibsen's last play, written when he was over seventy, as 'the epilogue to a life's work'. It is an intensely personal statement – an artist assessing his art – and in it Ibsen, the 'Great Realist', became a symbolist. As he grew older he found it more difficult than ever to write, and he began to look back longingly to those early days when verse had flowed so freely from his pen. (Incidentally, it is hard for us to realize now that Ibsen wrote much more verse, bulk for bulk, than he did prose.) Eventually he must have come to feel guilty at having renounced verse, though that renunciation had seemed so right in the days when he called verse 'the enemy of the drama', and could write to Edmund Gosse (January 1874):

You feel that the play would have been better if I'd written it in verse; I can't agree. You must have seen that this is a realistic play . . . and I wanted to make the reader feel that he was looking at something that had actually happened. . . . It isn't as if we were still living in the days of Shakespeare. . . . I wanted to draw ordinary human beings, so how could I let them speak 'the language of the gods'?

Now, twenty-five years later, he bitterly reproached himself for having buried his talent, and blamed that for his present sterility. This terrible and difficult play should be read with that guilt always in mind. In Professor Rubek, Ibsen draws a man who has renounced his true love; he has sacrificed Irena, his inspiration, for the sake of what he convinces himself is his Art.

Ibsen found *When We Dead Wake* the most difficult of all his plays to bring to birth. Ever since *Pillars of Society* in 1877, he had turned out a new play regularly every two years, breaking the rhythm only in 1882, when he wrote *A Public Enemy* in a single year. Now he found his new play so difficult to get on paper that, though he started work on it only a few months after he had sent off *John Gabriel Borkmann*, it was three years before he could finish it.

In the summer of 1897 he wrote that he had '. . . a new dramatic something in my mind, but it hasn't taken shape yet'. On his seventieth birthday, the following March, he said that he certainly didn't mean to stop writing:

I still have various whimsies in hand that I haven't been able to put down yet. It'll be only after I've got them thoroughly out of my system that perhaps the time will come to stop.

'Getting them out of his system' may be something more than a mere cliché; it could well hark back to something that he had written years before:

When I was working on *Brand*, I kept a scorpion in a tumbler on my desk. From time to time the insect would become ill, and then I would drop a juicy piece of fruit into the glass, whereupon the creature would pounce on it furiously and squirt its poison into it. After this, it would become well again. . . . Surely there's a parallel between this and the writing of poetry!

which is good psychology, if rather shaky natural history.

It was not until February 1899 (after he had written to Archer that he had 'put his characters out to grass, where he hoped they would thrive'), that he was able really to start work on his first draft. After this he was able to make himself write quickly, feeling perhaps that this was to be his last play. Even so, he wrote it in prose, although here at last was a play that would have been well-suited to verse; for in his later years he had somewhat softened his inflexible attitude, and had even gone so far as to say that he had thought of returning to verse for his last play – 'if only one could tell which would be the last'.

Probably Ibsen never meant *When We Dead Wake* to be staged. He was too much a practical man of the theatre not to see that it would hardly be feasible to have a stream on the stage where his characters could sail leaves and petals, still less a group of children playing in the distance. And what theatre could provide convincingly a thickening mist through which actors could climb up into the sunlight, or an avalanche that would sweep them away? Though Ibsen invariably visualized his plays in the clearest detail in the theatre of his own mind, here particularly he thought primarily of reaching not an audience but a reader.

Ibsen had only just finished his 'Epilogue' when, early in 1900, he had a stroke that affected his walking. A year later, a second stroke wiped out his memory for words. He lived on in this state till 1906. One day his son found him with a pencil struggling to form letters:

'Look what I'm doing,' he said, 'I'm sitting here trying to learn the alphabet – and I was once an author.'

*

In working on these plays I have tried to render the text faithfully and at the same time to achieve dialogue that would sound as natural now as Ibsen's original must have done to the audiences of his day – dialogue that would be easy for actors to speak, and acceptable to modern readers and theatregoers.

The problem was to arrive at language that would be in keeping with the period of the action and yet not seem stilted. I felt it particularly important not to try to wrench the plays out of their time. Such things as Pastor Manders's views on life belong so definitely to the end of the last century that they would sound hopelessly unreal in modern colloquial speech, just as they would seem incredible in the mouths of players dressed in the clothes of the 1960s. And in a world without electric light, telephones, or chain-smoking it would have been incongruous to use, as some recent translators have done, such expressions as 'make it snappy'.

Just as the plays belong irrevocably to the late nineteenth century, so, too, do they have a quality that is essentially Norwegian; nowhere else could people act and speak as Ibsen's characters do, and a translation that was virtually a transplantation would continually bring the reader up against subtle improbabilities. I soon found this in *A Public Enemy*, a play full of provincialisms which I was tempted to render into the dialect of Lancashire, where the story seemed most at home, but this, far from clarifying the story, merely made the characters and their actions seem improbable. In the end I had to compromise by trying to give the dialogue a slight unlocalized provincial tang.

To help this essential Norwegian feeling, I have tended to keep the original spelling of the proper names, though I have sometimes rendered them phonetically where they might suggest a too familiar English pronunciation. For example I have written 'Irena', where the Norwegian spelling, being the same as ours, might have tempted the reader to see the word as 'Irene' – or perhaps even 'I-reen'.

I have taken liberties, too, with the modes of address. Where an accurate translation would give a specifically Norwegian flavour, I have kept to it, but I have dropped altogether such things as the Scandinavian habit of calling people by their trade – Carpenter Engstrand, Editor Hovstad, Printer Aslaksen – which might not strike an English reader as particularly Norwegian, but merely as rather outlandish and even irritating.

I have also tried to make the characters speak to each other in the form that would be used in a like situation by English people of roughly the same walk of life, preferring to be illogical rather than create a false impression. I have put in a 'Mr' or two where the bare surname, especially where a woman is speaking to a man, would sound odd. I have also deviated from the custom that makes a wife call her husband by his surname, though this causes a difficulty in *When We Dead Wake*, where Ibsen differentiates between Maia, who always addresses her husband as 'Rubek', and Irena, who calls him 'Arnold'; here I have kept to the original forms.

There is one other point where I have taken liberties with the original. All the Scandinavian languages tend to use words in pairs; our own Norse ancestors have left traces of the habit in English, and we talk of 'law and order', 'free and easy', 'this day and age', and so on, but to nothing like the same extent as the Norwegians do. I have rendered these 'doublets' accurately when their effect was not too long-winded or tautological, but I have tended to telescope them, especially when I could find a single English word that conveyed the whole sense.

P.W.

GHOSTS

A Domestic Drama in Three Acts

CHARACTERS

———— * ————

MRS HELENA ALVING, widow of Captain Alving, late
  Court Chamberlain[1]
OSVALD ALVING, her son, an artist
PASTOR MANDERS
ENGSTRAND, a carpenter
REGINA ENGSTRAND, in service with Mrs Alving

*The action takes place in Mrs Alving's country house
by a large fjord in Western Norway*

ACT ONE

———— * ————

A large garden-room, with one door in the left wall and two in the wall to the right.
In the middle of the room is a round table; at it there are chairs, and on it are books, newspapers, and magazines.
In the foreground to the left is a window, with a small sofa and a work-table in front of it.
At the back, the room opens on a conservatory, rather smaller, and walled with large panes of glass. From the right of this conservatory a door leads into the garden.
Through the glass, a view of a gloomy fjord, half-hidden by continual rain, can be made out.[2]

> [ENGSTRAND, *the carpenter, is standing at the garden door. His left leg is rather deformed, and the sole of his boot is built up with wood.* REGINA, *with an empty garden syringe in her hand, is barring his way in.*]

REGINA [*lowering her voice*]: What do you want? Stay where you are, you're dripping wet!

ENGSTRAND: It's God's good rain, my girl.

REGINA: It's the devil's rain, that's what it is!

ENGSTRAND: Lor', what a way to talk, Regina. [*He limps a step or two into the room.*] What I wanted to say was –

REGINA: Don't clump about with that foot, man! The young master's asleep upstairs.

ENGSTRAND: Asleep? At this hour of the day?

REGINA: That's no business of yours.

ENGSTRAND: Now *I* was out on the spree last night –

REGINA: I can well believe it!

ENGSTRAND: Well, my girl, we all have our weaknesses –

REGINA: We certainly have.

ENGSTRAND: – and the snares of this world are manifold, you know . . . but all the same, I swear I was at work by half past five this morning.

REGINA: All right, all right, but get along now. I'm not going to stand here and have a *rendezvous* with you.

ENGSTRAND: You're not having a *what*?

REGINA: I'm not having anyone find you here. So go on – get out!

ENGSTRAND [*coming a little nearer*]: Damned if I'm going before I've had a little talk with you. I'll have finished my job down at the school this afternoon, so I'll be off back to town by tonight's steamer.

REGINA [*under her breath*]: Pleasant journey!

ENGSTRAND: Thank you, my girl. You see, tomorrow'll be opening day at the Orphanage and there's bound to be a great to-do and plenty of liquor – and I'm not having anyone say Jakob Engstrand can't resist temptation when it comes his way.

REGINA: Ha!

ENGSTRAND: Besides, there'll be a lot of smart people here tomorrow. And they're expecting Pastor Manders to come from town.

REGINA: As a matter of fact, he's coming today.

ENGSTRAND: Well, there you are, you see; I'm damned if I'll give him a chance to say anything against me.

REGINA: Oh, so *that's* it!

ENGSTRAND: What is?

REGINA [*giving him a shrewd look*]: What are you trying to diddle Mr Manders out of now?

ENGSTRAND: Sh! Are you off your head? Now, would *I* diddle Mr Manders out of anything? Oh no, Mr Manders

has been far too good to me for that. But that's what I
wanted to talk to you about; you see, I'm going back
home tonight –

REGINA: The sooner the better, *I* say!

ENGSTRAND: – and I want you to come with me, Regina.

REGINA [*open-mouthed*]: What? You want *me* . . . ?

ENGSTRAND: I said I wanted you back home with me.

REGINA [*scornfully*]: You're never getting me back home
with you!

ENGSTRAND: Oh? We'll see about that!

REGINA: We'll see, all right! What, *me*? When I've been
brought up by a lady like Mrs Alving? – treated almost
like one of the family here? *Me* go back with you – to a
place like that? Tcha!

ENGSTRAND: What the devil . . . ? Are you setting yourself
up against your father, you little slut?

REGINA [*under her breath, not looking at him*]: You've
always said I was none of yours.

ENGSTRAND: Pooh, why worry about that?

REGINA: Just think of all the times you've sworn at me
and called me a . . . *Fi donc!*[3]

ENGSTRAND: I'm damned if I ever used a dirty word like
that.

REGINA: You needn't tell *me* what word you used!

ENGSTRAND: Well, that was only when I'd had a drink
or two . . . the snares of this world are manifold,
Regina –

REGINA: Ugh!

ENGSTRAND: – or when your mother started making a
scene, and I had to find some way of getting even with
her. Always giving herself airs, she was. [*Mimicking her*]
'Let me be, Jakob, let me go! I was three years in service
with the Alvings at Rosenvold, and he was a Chamberlain!' [*Laughing*] Lord help us, she could never forget

that the Captain was made a Chamberlain while she was working here.

REGINA: Poor Mother, you certainly drove her to an early grave.

ENGSTRAND [*with a shrug*]: That's right – blame it all on me!

REGINA [*under her breath, turning away*]: And then that leg – ugh!

ENGSTRAND: What's that you say, my girl?

REGINA: *Pied de mouton!*

ENGSTRAND: That's English, I suppose?

REGINA: Yes!

ENGSTRAND: Ah, you've had education out here, Regina; that'll come in handy now.

REGINA [*after a moment*]: Just what do you want me in town for?

ENGSTRAND: Need you ask why a father wants his only child? Aren't I a poor lonely widower?

REGINA: Don't you come to me with that tale! What do you want me for?

ENGSTRAND: Well, I'll tell you: I've been thinking of going in for something new.

REGINA [*with a snort*]: Oh, you're always doing that, and it never comes to anything!

ENGSTRAND: Ah, but this time, Regina, you'll see – devil take me if –

REGINA [*stamping her foot*]: None of that language!

ENGSTRAND: Sh! Sh! You're quite right, my girl. All I wanted to say was this: I've put by quite a bit of money, working on this new Orphanage.

REGINA: Have you? That's nice for you.

ENGSTRAND: After all, what's there to spend anything on out here in the country?

REGINA: Well?

ENGSTRAND: Well you see, I thought of putting the money into something that'd pay – a sort of lodging-house for seamen.

REGINA: Ugh!

ENGSTRAND: A really high-class lodging-house, you know – not some sort of pigsty for common sailors. No, damn it, it'll be a place for ships' captains and mates and – and really high-class people, you know.

REGINA: And what should I –?

ENGSTRAND: You'd give a hand, of course. Just for the look of the thing, you see. You wouldn't have a hell of a lot of work; you could do just what you felt like.

REGINA: Oh? Well?

ENGSTRAND: Because there'll have to be some women about the place – that's as clear as daylight. We'll have to cheer things up a bit in the evenings, with singing and dancing and so on. Remember these are wayfaring men, from the seven seas. [*Coming nearer*] Now don't be a fool and stand in your own way, Regina. What future is there for you out here? All this education that your mistress has paid for – is it going to be any good to you? I hear you'll be looking after the children in this new Orphanage. What's the use of that to *you*, eh? Are you all that keen to go and work yourself to the bone for a lot of dirty kids?

REGINA: No. If things go the way I want . . . and they *might* – they very well might. . . .

ENGSTRAND: What might?

REGINA: Never you mind. Have you saved a lot of money up here?

ENGSTRAND: What with one thing and another, it must be seven or eight hundred kroner.

REGINA: That's not bad.

ENGSTRAND: Enough to make a start with, my girl.

REGINA: You didn't think of giving *me* any of it?

ENGSTRAND: No, by God, I didn't.

REGINA: You didn't even think of sending me a length of stuff for a dress?

ENGSTRAND: Just you come down to the town with me and you'll have plenty of dresses.

REGINA: Pooh! I could get them for myself if I wanted.

ENGSTRAND: Ah, but you'd be all the better for a father's guiding hand, Regina. There's a nice little house I can get in Little Harbour Street; they're not asking too much down, and it could be like a sort of Seaman's Home, you know.

REGINA: But I don't want to go with you – I don't want to have anything to do with you. So clear out!

ENGSTRAND: You wouldn't be with me all that damned long, my girl – no such luck – not if you know the ropes. You've turned into a pretty little thing this last year or two.

REGINA: Well?

ENGSTRAND: It wouldn't be long before some ship's officer came along – a captain, even . . .

REGINA: I'm not marrying anyone like that. Sailors have no *savoir vivre*.

ENGSTRAND: Haven't got *what*?

REGINA: I know what sailors are, I tell you. They're not the ones to marry.

ENGSTRAND: Well then, *don't* marry – that can pay just as well. [*More confidentially*] That Englishman – the one with the yacht – he gave three hundred dollars, he did . . . and she wasn't any prettier than you.

REGINA [*advancing on him*]: Get out!

ENGSTRAND [*retreating*]: Now, now – you wouldn't hit me!

REGINA: I would! Just you talk about my mother again

and I'll hit you. Get out, I tell you! [*She drives him towards the garden door.*] And don't bang the doors – young Mr Alving –

ENGSTRAND: – is asleep, *I* know! It's funny how anxious you are about young Mr Alving. [*Softly*] Aha! Now it couldn't be *him*, could it?

REGINA: Outside – and quick about it! You're a fool! No, not that way – here comes Pastor Manders. Off with you down the back stairs.

ENGSTRAND [*going to the right*]: All right, all right! Now you talk to *him* when he comes; he's the man to tell you what a child owes its father. Because I *am* your father, you know; I can prove it by the Parish Register.

[*He goes out by the farther door which* REGINA *has opened for him.* REGINA *takes a quick look at herself in the glass, fans herself with a handkerchief and straightens her collar, then busies herself with the flowers.*

PASTOR MANDERS, *wearing an overcoat, carrying an umbrella, and with a little travelling satchel on a strap over his shoulder, comes through the garden door into the conservatory.*]

PASTOR MANDERS: Good morning, Miss Engstrand.[4]

REGINA [*turning in pleased surprise*]: Why, good morning, Pastor. Is the steamer in already?

PASTOR MANDERS: It's just arrived. [*He comes into the room.*] What terrible weather we've been having lately.

REGINA [*following him*]: But it's good for the farmers, Pastor.

PASTOR MANDERS: Yes, of course you're right; we towns-people don't think of them. [*He begins to take off his overcoat.*]

REGINA: Let me help you. . . . There! Oh it *is* wet! I'll just hang it in the hall. Give me your umbrella too – I'll open it so that it can dry.

[*She takes the things out through the farther door on the right.* PASTOR MANDERS *takes off his satchel and puts it and his hat on a chair. Meanwhile* REGINA *comes back.*]

PASTOR MANDERS: Ah, it's good to get indoors! And is everything going well out here?

REGINA: Yes, thank you very much.

PASTOR MANDERS: Rather busy though, I expect, getting ready for tomorrow.

REGINA: Yes, there's a lot to do.

PASTOR MANDERS: Mrs Alving's at home, I hope?

REGINA: Oh yes; she's just gone upstairs with a cup of chocolate for the young master.

PASTOR MANDERS: Ah yes, tell me – I heard down at the quay that Osvald should be here –

REGINA: Yes, he came the day before yesterday. We weren't expecting him till today.

PASTOR MANDERS: Fit and well, I hope?

REGINA: Yes, quite well, thank you – but terribly tired after the journey. He came all the way from Paris in one trip. . . . I mean, he made the whole journey without a break. I think he's having a little sleep now, so we ought to talk a bit quieter.

PASTOR MANDERS: Sh! We'll be very quiet!

REGINA [*moving an armchair up to the table*]: Do please sit down, Pastor, and make yourself at home. [*He sits, and she puts a footstool under his feet.*] There! Is that comfortable?

PASTOR MANDERS: Excellent, thank you. [*Looking at her*] Do you know, Miss Engstrand, I really do believe you've grown since I saw you last!

REGINA: Do you think so, Pastor? Madam says I've filled out, too.

PASTOR MANDERS: Filled out? Well, yes, I think you *have*, a little . . . but very becomingly.

[*A short pause.*]

REGINA: Shall I go and tell Madam?

PASTOR MANDERS: Oh, there's no hurry, thank you, my dear child. Tell me, Regina, how has your father been getting on out here?

REGINA: Oh, pretty well, thank you, Pastor.

PASTOR MANDERS: He came to see me the last time he was in town.

REGINA: Did he? He's always so pleased when he can have a talk with you.

PASTOR MANDERS: And you're a good girl and go down and see him every day?

REGINA: I? Oh yes, I do – whenever I have the time. . .

PASTOR MANDERS: Your father isn't a very strong character, Miss Engstrand; he badly needs a guiding hand.

REGINA: Yes, I know he does.

PASTOR MANDERS: He needs someone by him whom he can cling to – someone whose judgement he can rely on. The last time he was at my house, he admitted that himself, quite frankly.

REGINA: Yes . . . he said something of the sort to me. But I don't know if Mrs Alving could do without me – especially now, when we'll have the new Orphanage to manage. Besides, I should be terribly sorry to leave Mrs Alving – she's always been so kind to me.

PASTOR MANDERS: But my good girl, a daughter's duty . . . Naturally we should have to get your mistress's consent first.

REGINA: But I don't know if it would be quite right for me, at my age, to keep house for a single man.

PASTOR MANDERS: What? But my dear Miss Engstrand, we're speaking of your own father!

REGINA: Yes, maybe, but all the same . . . now if it were in a good house, with a real gentleman –

PASTOR MANDERS: But my dear Regina –

REGINA: – someone that I could like and respect, and be like a daughter to. . . .

PASTOR MANDERS: But my dear good child . . . !

REGINA: Because I'd like to go back to the town; it's terribly lonely out here, and you know yourself, Pastor, what's it's like to be all alone in the world. I can honestly say that I'm able and willing. Don't you know of a place like that for me, Pastor?

PASTOR MANDERS: Who, me? No, I certainly do not.

REGINA: But dear, dear Pastor, you will think of me, won't you, if ever . . .?

PASTOR MANDERS [getting up]: Yes, Miss Engstrand, I will.

REGINA: Yes, because if I –

PASTOR MANDERS: Perhaps you'll be kind enough to let Mrs Alving know I'm here.

REGINA: I'll fetch her at once, sir. [She goes out to the left.]
    [PASTOR MANDERS walks up and down the room once or twice, then stands for a while at the back, with his hands behind him, looking out into the garden. Then he comes back to the table, picks up a book, and looks at the title page. He gives a start, then looks at several more.]

PASTOR MANDERS: Well . . . really!
    [MRS ALVING comes in from the left, followed by REGINA who immediately goes out again by the nearer door to the right.]

MRS ALVING: Ah, Pastor, I'm very glad to see you.

PASTOR MANDERS: How do you do, Mrs Alving. Here I am, as I promised.

MRS ALVING: Punctual as ever!

PASTOR MANDERS: It wasn't easy to get away, though, you know. All those blessed committees and boards that I'm on....

MRS ALVING: All the kinder of you to come so early; now we can get our business settled before luncheon. But where's your luggage?

PASTOR MANDERS [*hastily*]: My things are down at the village shop; I'm staying there tonight.

MRS ALVING [*suppressing a smile*]: Can't you really be persuaded to stay the night here this time?

PASTOR MANDERS: No, no, Mrs Alving, thank you very much all the same. I shall stay down there as usual – it's so convenient for catching the boat.

MRS ALVING: Well, you must do as you like. All the same, I do think a couple of old people like us . . .

PASTOR MANDERS: Good gracious, what a thing to say! Still, you're naturally in particularly good spirits today, what with the celebrations tomorrow, and having Osvald home, too.

MRS ALVING: Yes, isn't it lucky for me? It's over two years since he was home last, and now he's promised to stay the whole winter with me.

PASTOR MANDERS: Has he indeed? That's very nice and dutiful of him; because I should think life in Rome or Paris must offer many more attractions.

MRS ALVING: Ah, but you see, here he has his mother. He's a dear good boy, and he still has a soft spot for his mother.

PASTOR MANDERS: It would be very distressing if leaving home and taking up such things as Art were to blunt his natural feelings.

MRS ALVING: Yes, I agree; but there's no danger of that with him, I'm sure. It'll be interesting to see if you know him again. He'll be down soon; he's just resting for a bit on the sofa upstairs. But do sit down, my dear Pastor.

PASTOR MANDERS: Thank you. Now would this be a convenient time . . . ?

MRS ALVING: Yes certainly. [*She sits at the table.*]

PASTOR MANDERS: Good; then I'll show you. . . . [*He goes to the chair where his satchel is, and takes a bundle of papers from it. Then he sits at the opposite side of the table and tries to find a space to put the papers.*] Now, to begin with, we have . . . [*breaking off*] Tell me, Mrs Alving, how did these books get *here*?

MRS ALVING: These books? *I*'m reading them.

PASTOR MANDERS: Do you read that sort of thing?

MRS ALVING: Of course I do.

PASTOR MANDERS: Do you feel any better or happier for reading this sort of book?

MRS ALVING: I think it makes me somehow more – confident.

PASTOR MANDERS: Extraordinary! How is that?

MRS ALVING: Well, they seem to explain – or confirm – a lot of things that I've been thinking myself. Yes, that's the extraordinary thing, Mr Manders – there's really nothing particularly new in these books – nothing more than what most people think and believe already. It's just that most people either don't take much account of these things, or won't admit it.

PASTOR MANDERS: But good heavens, do you seriously believe that most people . . . ?

MRS ALVING: Yes, I really do.

PASTOR MANDERS: But surely not in this country? Not among us here?

MRS ALVING: Oh, yes, among us too.

PASTOR MANDERS: Well really, I must say . . . !

MRS ALVING: Besides, what have you actually got against these books?

PASTOR MANDERS: What have I –? You surely don't imagine I waste my time examining that sort of publication?

MRS ALVING: Which means that you know nothing at all about the thing you're denouncing.

PASTOR MANDERS: I've read quite enough about such books to disapprove of them.

MRS ALVING: Yes, but your own opinion. . . .

PASTOR MANDERS: My dear lady, there are many occasions in life when one must rely upon the opinions of others. That is the way of this world. And rightly too – how else could society continue?

MRS ALVING: Oh well, you may be right.

PASTOR MANDERS: Apart from that, naturally I don't deny that there may be a considerable fascination about such works. Nor can I blame you for wishing to make yourself acquainted with the intellectual trends which, I'm told, prevail out in the great world – where you have allowed your son to wander for so long. But . . .

MRS ALVING: But . . .?

PASTOR MANDERS [lowering his voice]: But one doesn't talk of it, Mrs Alving. One is really not obliged to account to all and sundry for what one reads and thinks within one's own four walls.

MRS ALVING: Of course not – I quite agree.[5]

PASTOR MANDERS: You must realize, too, that you owe some consideration to this Orphanage – which you decided to found at a time when, so far as I can judge, your opinions on intellectual matters were very different from what they are now.

MRS ALVING: Yes, I fully admit that. But it was about the Orphanage –

PASTOR MANDERS: It was about the Orphanage that we were going to talk, yes. Still – discretion, dear lady . . .! And now to business. [*He opens an envelope and takes out some papers.*] You see these?

MRS ALVING: The deeds?

PASTOR MANDERS: All of them, and in perfect order. I don't mind telling you, it wasn't easy to get them ready in time – I even had to bring a certain amount of pressure to bear; the authorities are almost painfully conscientious when it's a matter of documents! But here they are. [*He goes through the pile.*] This is the Conveyance of the plot known as Solvick, being a part of the Rosenvold estate, together with the buildings newly erected thereon, namely the Schoolhouse, the Staff Quarters, and the Chapel. And this is the legal Authorization for the endowment, and for the rules of the Institution. Here, you see: [*reads*] 'Regulations for the Captain Alving Memorial Children's Home'.

MRS ALVING [*after a long look at the documents*]: So, here it is!

PASTOR MANDERS: I've chosen 'Captain' rather than 'Chamberlain' for the title; 'Captain' seemed less pretentious.

MRS ALVING: Oh yes, whatever you think best.

PASTOR MANDERS: And here's the account of the capital in the Savings Bank, that will provide the interest to cover the running expenses of the Orphanage.

MRS ALVING: Thank you; but it'd be more convenient if you'd be kind enough to look after that.

PASTOR MANDERS: Willingly. To begin with, I think, we'll leave the money in the Savings Bank. Certainly the interest's not very attractive: four per cent and six months' notice of withdrawal. Later on, if we could find a good mortgage – it would have to be a first mortgage, of course, with unimpeachable security – we could re-consider the matter.

MRS ALVING: Yes, you know best about all that sort of thing, dear Pastor Manders.

PASTOR MANDERS: I'll keep my eyes open, anyhow. And now there's one other thing that I've been meaning to ask you about for some time.

MRS ALVING: What is that?

PASTOR MANDERS: Shall the Orphanage buildings be in-sured or not?

MRS ALVING: Of course they must be insured.

PASTOR MANDERS: Ah, but just a moment, Mrs Alving; let's look into the matter rather more closely.

MRS ALVING: I always have everything insured – build-ings, contents, crops, and stock.

PASTOR MANDERS: Naturally, on your own estate. I do the same, of course. But this, you see, is quite different; the Orphanage is, as it were, to be consecrated to a higher purpose.

MRS ALVING: Yes, but even so. . . .

PASTOR MANDERS: Speaking entirely personally, I cer-tainly shouldn't see the least objection to our covering ourselves against all eventualities –

MRS ALVING: No, I quite agree.

PASTOR MANDERS: – but what would be the general feel-ing in the neighbourhood? You'd know that better than I should.

MRS ALVING: Hm, the general feeling. . . .

PASTOR MANDERS: Would there be any considerable body of opinion – really responsible opinion – that might be shocked at it?

MRS ALVING: What exactly do you mean by really re-sponsible opinion?

PASTOR MANDERS: Well, I'm thinking particularly of

men of independent means in such responsible positions
that one cannot help attaching a certain weight to their
opinions.

MRS ALVING: Yes, there are a good many people like that
here, who might well be shocked if –

PASTOR MANDERS: There, you see! We have plenty of
them in the town, too – all my fellow-pastors' congrega-
tions, for a start. They might so very easily come to the
conclusion that neither you nor I had a proper trust in
Divine Providence.

MRS ALVING: But my dear Pastor, you must know yourself that you're –

PASTOR MANDERS: Oh, I know, I know. My conscience
is clear – that's perfectly true; but all the same we
shouldn't be able to escape grave misrepresentation, and
that could very easily hinder the work of the Orphanage.

MRS ALVING: Ah well, if it's going to do *that*, then . . .

PASTOR MANDERS: Nor can I entirely shut my eyes to
the difficult – I might even call it the *painful* position that
I might find myself in. Influential people in the town are
taking a great interest in the Orphanage. Indeed, it is
intended partly for the benefit of the town as well,
and it is hoped that it will have a not inconsiderable
effect in lowering our Poor Rate. And since I've been your
adviser, and have looked after the business side, I fear
that the more fanatical might well blame *me*, first and
foremost.

MRS ALVING: Oh no, you mustn't risk that.

PASTOR MANDERS: Not to mention the attacks that
would certainly be made on me by certain papers and
periodicals which –

MRS ALVING: Say no more about it, my dear Pastor
Manders – that settles it completely.

PASTOR MANDERS: Then you won't have it insured?

MRS ALVING: No, we'll leave it.

PASTOR MANDERS [*leaning back in his chair*]: But if there *did* happen to be an accident – you never know – would you be able to make good the damage?

MRS ALVING: No, I can tell you quite definitely I shouldn't do anything of the sort.

PASTOR MANDERS: Well, you know, Mrs Alving, we're taking a great responsibility on ourselves.

MRS ALVING: But what else *can* we do, do you think?

PASTOR MANDERS: No, that's just it – there's nothing else we can do. We mustn't lay ourselves open to misrepresentation, and we've no right to offend public opinion.

MRS ALVING: Certainly not you, as a clergyman.

PASTOR MANDERS: And I really think, too, that we may take it that an Institution like this has good fortune on its side – that it's under a Special Protection.

MRS ALVING: Let's hope so, Mr Manders.

PASTOR MANDERS: Then shall we leave it at that?

MRS ALVING: Yes, certainly.

PASTOR MANDERS: Good. Just as you wish. [*Making a note*] No insurance, then.

MRS ALVING: It's odd that you should happen to mention that today. . . .

PASTOR MANDERS: I've been meaning to ask you about it for some time.

MRS ALVING: – because we nearly had a fire down there yesterday.

PASTOR MANDERS: Really?

MRS ALVING: Oh, it wasn't anything much – some shavings caught fire in the carpenter's shop.

PASTOR MANDERS: Where Engstrand works?

MRS ALVING: Yes, they say he's often very careless with matches.

PASTOR MANDERS: He has a lot on his mind, poor man

– so many temptations. Thank God, I hear he's now trying to live a blameless life.

MRS ALVING: Oh? Who told you that?

PASTOR MANDERS: He told me so himself. And he's certainly a very good workman.

MRS ALVING: Yes – as long as he's sober.

PASTOR MANDERS: Ah, it's a sad failing. But he tells me
he's often driven to it by his bad leg. The last time he
was in town, I was really very touched; he came and
thanked me so sincerely for having found him work up
here where he could be near Regina.

MRS ALVING: He doesn't really see much of her.

PASTOR MANDERS: Oh yes, he has a word with her every
day – he told me so himself.

MRS ALVING: Oh well, perhaps he does. . . .

PASTOR MANDERS: He feels so strongly that he needs
someone to restrain him when temptation comes. That's
what's so likeable about Jakob Engstrand; he comes to
you quite helplessly to confess his failings and to re-
proach himself. The last time he was talking to me –
Look, Mrs Alving, if it should ever be really necessary for
him to have Regina living at home with him again –

MRS ALVING [*rising suddenly*]: Regina?

PASTOR MANDERS: – you mustn't try to stand in his way.

MRS ALVING: But I most certainly shall stand in his way.
Besides, Regina is to be on the Staff at the Orphanage.

PASTOR MANDERS: But remember, he's her father.

MRS ALVING: I know exactly what sort of a father he's
been to her. No, she's never going back to him with my
consent.

PASTOR MANDERS [*getting up*]: But my dear Mrs Alving,
there's no need to be so vehement about it. It's sad the
way you misjudge Engstrand; one would almost think
you were afraid –

MRS ALVING [*more calmly*]: Be that as it may, I've taken Regina into my house, and there she shall stay. [*Listening*] Sh! Don't say any more about it, my dear Mr Manders. [*Radiant with happiness*] Listen, there's Osvald on the stairs; now we'll think about nothing but him.

> [OSVALD ALVING, *in a light overcoat* [6] *with his hat in his hand, smoking a large meerschaum pipe, comes in through the door on the left.*]

OSVALD [*stopping in the doorway*]: Oh, I'm sorry – I thought you were in the study. [*Coming in*] Good morning, Pastor.

PASTOR MANDERS [*staring*]: Extraordinary!

MRS ALVING: Well, what do you think of him, Mr Manders?

PASTOR MANDERS: I – I – No, can it really be . . .?

OSVALD: Yes, it's really the Prodigal Son, Pastor.

PASTOR MANDERS: Oh, my dear boy . . .!

OSVALD: Well, the son come home again, then.

MRS ALVING: Osvald's thinking of the time when you were so set against the idea of his becoming an artist.

PASTOR MANDERS: Many a step that seems unwise to our human judgement turns out afterwards to be – [*Grasping his hand*] Anyhow, welcome home! Well my dear Osvald – may I still call you Osvald?

OSVALD: Of course, what else should you call me?

PASTOR MANDERS: Good. What I was going to say, my dear Osvald, was this: you mustn't imagine that I condemn the artistic life unreservedly; I'm sure there are many people who can keep their souls unspotted even in those surroundings.

OSVALD: Let's hope so.

MRS ALVING [*beaming with pleasure*]: I know someone who's kept both his soul and body unharmed. Just look at him, Pastor Manders.

OSVALD [*pacing across the room*]: All right, Mother dear, all right!

PASTOR MANDERS: Ah, certainly – that's undeniable. And you've begun to make a name for yourself already. The papers have often mentioned you – most favourably, too. Though I must admit, I don't seem to have seen it so often recently.

OSVALD [*up by the conservatory*]: No, I haven't been painting so much lately.

MRS ALVING: Even an artist must have a rest now and then.

PASTOR MANDERS: Yes, I can see that – so that he can collect his forces and prepare himself for something great.

OSVALD: Yes . . . Will lunch be ready soon, Mother?

MRS ALVING: In less than half an hour. He's got a good appetite, thank heaven.

OSVALD: I found Father's pipe in my room, so –

PASTOR MANDERS: Ah, so *that* was it!

MRS ALVING: What?

PASTOR MANDERS: When Osvald came in at the door with the pipe in his mouth, it was like seeing his father in the flesh.

OSVALD: Oh, really?

MRS ALVING: No, you can't say that! Osvald takes after me.

PASTOR MANDERS: Yes, but there's a look about the corners of his mouth – something about the lips – that definitely reminds me of Alving. Especially now he's smoking.

MRS ALVING: I don't agree. *I* think Osvald has much more of a clergyman's mouth.

PASTOR MANDERS: Yes – yes – several of my colleagues have just that expression.

MRS ALVING: But put your pipe away, my dear boy; I won't have smoking in here.

OSVALD [*putting the pipe down*]: Of course. I only wanted to try it – I smoked it once before, as a child.

MRS ALVING: You?

OSVALD: Yes, it was when I was quite small; I remember I went up to Father's study one evening when he was in a particularly good mood . . .

MRS ALVING: Oh, you don't remember anything of those days.

OSVALD: Yes, I remember it distinctly – he picked me up and put me on his knee and let me smoke his pipe. 'Smoke it, boy,' he said, 'go on, boy, smoke away!' And I smoked as hard as I could, till I felt myself turning pale, and great drops of sweat broke out on my forehead. Then he burst out laughing.

PASTOR MANDERS: How extraordinary.

MRS ALVING: My dear Pastor, it's only something Osvald must have dreamed!

OSVALD: No, I'm sure I didn't dream it, Mother. Because, don't you remember, you came in and carried me off to the nursery. Then I was sick, and I saw that you were crying. Did Father often play tricks like that?

PASTOR MANDERS: When he was young, he was full of high spirits. . . .[7]

OSVALD: And yet he managed to achieve so much in the world – so much that was good and useful – although he died so young.

PASTOR MANDERS: Yes, you've certainly inherited a worthy name from an industrious man, my dear Osvald Alving. Let's hope it'll be an inspiration to you.

OSVALD: It certainly ought to be.

PASTOR MANDERS: Anyhow, it was good of you to come home for the celebrations in his honour.

OSVALD: That was the least I could do for my father.

MRS ALVING: But best of all is that I shall have him here for so long.

PASTOR MANDERS: Yes, I hear that you're going to stop at home for the winter.

OSVALD: I'm staying here indefinitely, Pastor. Oh it's good to be home again!

MRS ALVING [*beaming*]: Yes, isn't it?

PASTOR MANDERS [*looking at him with sympathy*]: You went out into the world very young, my dear Osvald.

OSVALD: I did – I sometimes wonder if it wasn't too early....

MRS ALVING: Oh, not in the least; it's the best thing for a healthy boy – especially when he's an only child; he shouldn't stay at home with his father and mother and get spoilt.

PASTOR MANDERS: That's a very moot point, Mrs Alving; a child's proper place must always be his father's house.

OSVALD: Yes, I agree with you there, Pastor.

PASTOR MANDERS: Look at your own son – oh yes, we can say it to his face – what has it done to *him*? At twenty-six or twenty-seven years old, he's never had a chance of knowing what a real home is like.

OSVALD: Oh no, I'm sorry, Pastor, but you're quite wrong there.

PASTOR MANDERS: Oh? I thought you'd been living almost entirely in artistic circles.

OSVALD: So I have.

PASTOR MANDERS: And chiefly among the younger artists.

OSVALD: Yes.

PASTOR MANDERS: Well, I shouldn't think most of those people could afford to set up a home and support a family.

OSVALD: Many of them certainly can't afford to marry, Pastor.

PASTOR MANDERS: That's exactly what I'm saying.

OSVALD: But they can still have a home; and several of them have – very pleasant, comfortable homes, too.

[MRS ALVING, *who has been listening intently, nods but does not speak.*]

PASTOR MANDERS: Ah, but I'm not talking about bachelor establishments. By a home, I mean family life, where a man lives with his wife and children.

OSVALD: Yes, or with his children and his children's mother.

PASTOR MANDERS [*with a start, clasping his hands*]: But good heavens . . . !

OSVALD: Well?

PASTOR MANDERS: Lives with – with his children's mother?

OSVALD: Yes. Would you rather he abandoned his children's mother?

PASTOR MANDERS: So these are illicit relationships you're referring to? What are known as 'irregular unions'.

OSVALD: I've never noticed anything particularly irregular about these people's lives together.

PASTOR MANDERS: But how could a young man or a young woman with any sort of decent upbringing bear to live like that – and quite openly, too?

OSVALD: But what else can they do – a poor young artist or a young girl? It costs a good deal of money to get married. What are they to do?

PASTOR MANDERS: What are they to do? Well, Mr Alving, I'll tell you what they can do. They should keep away from each other from the beginning, that's what they should do.

OSVALD: That sort of advice wouldn't get you very far with warm-blooded young lovers.

MRS ALVING: No, it wouldn't.

PASTOR MANDERS [*continuing*]: And to think that the authorities permit such things – allow them to go on quite openly! [*To Mrs Alving*] How right I was to be so deeply concerned about your son! In circles where open immorality is accepted – and even honoured –

OSVALD: Let me tell you something, Pastor: I often used to spend Sunday at some of these 'irregular' homes –

PASTOR MANDERS: On Sunday, too!

OSVALD: Yes, the day when one should relax – but I've never heard an objectionable word, and certainly never seen anything that could be called immoral. No, but do you know when I *have* come across immorality in artistic circles?

PASTOR MANDERS: No, thank heaven!

OSVALD: Let me tell you, then: I've met it when one or two of your model husbands and fathers have come abroad to have a little look round on their own account, and have done the artists the honour of calling on them in their humble lodgings. Then we learned a thing or two; those gentlemen could tell us about places and things we'd never dreamed of.

PASTOR MANDERS: What? Do you mean to tell me that respectable men from home here would . . .

OSVALD: Haven't you ever heard these respectable men, when they got home again, holding forth about how rampant immorality is abroad?

PASTOR MANDERS: Yes, of course.

MRS ALVING: I have, too.

OSVALD: Well, you can take their word for it – some of them are experts! [*Clasping his head*] Oh, I can't bear to hear the wonderful, free life over there degraded like that!

MRS ALVING: You mustn't get so excited, Osvald, it only upsets you.

OSVALD: No, you're right, Mother, it isn't good for me. It's because I'm so infernally tired, you see. I'll go out and have a little walk before lunch. Forgive me, Mr Manders; I know you can never agree with me about it, but I had to speak out. [*He goes out by the farther door on the right.*]

MRS ALVING: My poor boy!

PASTOR MANDERS: You may well say that! So this is what he's come to! [MRS ALVING *looks at him without speaking;* PASTOR MANDERS *paces up and down.*] He called himself the Prodigal Son . . . oh, the pity of it – the pity of it! [MRS ALVING *continues to look at him.*] And what have you to say to all that?

MRS ALVING: I say that Osvald was right in every single word.

PASTOR MANDERS: Right? Right to have standards like that?

MRS ALVING: Living all alone here, I've come to think along those same lines, Mr Manders, though I've never had the courage to put it into words. Now, thank goodness, my boy can speak for me.

PASTOR MANDERS: You are much to be pitied, Mrs Alving. But now I must have a serious talk with you. I'm not here now as your man of business and adviser, nor even as your late husband's old friend. I stand here as a priest; just as I stood before you at the most critical moment of your life.

MRS ALVING: And what has the priest to say to me?

PASTOR MANDERS: First let me refresh your memory. This is an appropriate moment – tomorrow is the tenth anniversary of your husband's death. Tomorrow a memorial is to be unveiled in his honour; tomorrow I shall have to speak to all the assembled company. But today I want to speak to you alone.

MRS ALVING: Well, Pastor, go on.

PASTOR MANDERS: Do you remember how, after less than a year of married life, you stood on the brink of a precipice? How you left your home, how you ran away from your husband? Yes, Mrs Alving, ran away – ran away and refused to go back to him in spite of all his prayers and entreaties.

MRS ALVING: Have you forgotten how utterly miserable I was in that first year?

PASTOR MANDERS: Craving for happiness in this life is the sign of an unruly spirit. What right have we mortals to happiness? No, we have our duty to do, Mrs Alving; and it was your duty to cleave to the man you had chosen, and to whom you were joined in holy matrimony.

MRS ALVING: You know perfectly well the sort of life my husband was leading in those days, and the excesses he was guilty of.

PASTOR MANDERS: I know only too well the rumours about him that were going round, and – if those rumours were true – I should be the last to approve of such conduct in a young man. But it's not a wife's place to judge her husband. When a Higher Power had laid a cross on you for your own good, it should have been your duty to bear it with patience. Instead of which, you rebelled – you cast off the cross, you deserted the sinner whom you should have helped; you went away risking your good name – and imperilling other people's reputations into the bargain.

MRS ALVING: Other people's? You mean one other person's.

PASTOR MANDERS: It was grossly inconsiderate of you to seek refuge with me.

MRS ALVING: With our priest? Our great friend?

PASTOR MANDERS: For that reason above all. Yes, you can thank God that I had the necessary strength of mind to dissuade you from your outrageous plan; and that it was vouchsafed to me to lead you back to the path of duty – and home to your rightful husband.

MRS ALVING: Yes, Pastor Manders, *that* was certainly your doing.

PASTOR MANDERS: I was only the poor instrument of a Higher Power. And haven't you been increasingly thankful, all the days of your life since then, that I made you submit, in all obedience, to your duty? Didn't it all happen as I foretold? Didn't Alving turn his back on his dissolute ways as a husband should, and didn't he live an irreproachable and affectionate life with you from then on till the end of his days? Didn't he become a great benefactor in the district, and didn't he encourage you so much by his example that in the end you came to be his helper in all his enterprises – and a very capable helper, too. . . . Yes, I know you did, Mrs Alving – I give you your due for *that*. But now I come to the second great mistake in your life.

MRS ALVING: What do you mean?

PASTOR MANDERS: Just as you failed once in your duty as a wife, you have since failed in that of a mother.

MRS ALVING: Oh . . . !

PASTOR MANDERS: All your life, you've been ruled by your deplorable wilfulness; your entire energy has been devoted to indiscipline and lawlessness – you would never tolerate the slightest restraint. Without scruple or remorse, you've evaded everything in your life that was difficult – as if it were a load that you could shrug off at will. It didn't suit you to be a wife any longer, so you left your husband; you found it tedious to be a mother, so you sent your child to live among strangers.

MRS ALVING: Yes, it's true I did that.

PASTOR MANDERS: So that now you've become a stranger to him yourself.

MRS ALVING: No no, that I'm certainly not.

PASTOR MANDERS: You are; you must be. And look how he's come back to you! Think carefully, Mrs Alving . . . you did your husband a great wrong – that memorial down there is an admission of it – now admit that you wronged your son, too. There may still be time to turn him from his sinful ways. Mend your own ways, and save what is left to be saved in him. For the truth is, Mrs Alving [*raising his forefinger*], you have failed as a mother, and I consider it my duty to tell you so.

[*Pause.*]

MRS ALVING [*slowly, and with self-control*]: You've spoken your mind, Pastor Manders, and tomorrow you'll make a speech in my husband's memory. I don't mean to speak tomorrow, but I'm going to speak to you now for a moment, just as you've been speaking to me.

PASTOR MANDERS: Naturally you want to make excuses for your conduct.

MRS ALVING: No, only to state facts.

PASTOR MANDERS: Well?

MRS ALVING: Of all that you've been saying about me and my husband, and of our life together after you brought me back to what you call the path of duty – of all that, you know absolutely nothing at first hand. From that moment, you, who had been our greatest friend, never set foot in our house again.

PASTOR MANDERS: You and your husband moved away from town directly afterwards.

MRS ALVING: Yes, and all the time my husband was alive, you never once came out here to see us. It was only because you had to deal with the business affairs of the Orphanage that you were finally forced to come and visit me.

PASTOR MANDERS [*in a low, diffident voice*]: Helena, if that's meant as a reproach, I can only beg you to remember –

MRS ALVING: – the respect that you owe to your cloth, yes! I'd been a runaway wife; one can never be too careful with loose women like that!

PASTOR MANDERS: My dea— er – Mrs Alving, that is a gross exaggeration.

MRS ALVING: Yes, perhaps it is. But what I wanted to say was that when you pass judgement on my married life, you have nothing more to go on than common gossip.

PASTOR MANDERS: Perhaps – but what of it?

MRS ALVING: Now, Mr Manders, I'm going to tell you the truth. I'd promised myself that you should hear it one day . . . and no one but you.

PASTOR MANDERS: What is the truth?

MRS ALVING: The truth is this: that my husband was just as dissolute when he died as he had been all his life.

PASTOR MANDERS [*reaching for a chair*]: What do you mean?

MRS ALVING: After nineteen years of married life, he was as dissolute – in his desires, at any rate – as he was when you married us.

PASTOR MANDERS: You call those youthful indiscretions, those irregularities – excesses, if you like – a dissolute life?

MRS ALVING: It was our doctor who used the expression.

PASTOR MANDERS: I don't understand. . . .

MRS ALVING: It doesn't matter.

G.P.—3

PASTOR MANDERS: It almost makes my head reel. . . . Do you mean that the whole of your married life – all those years with your husband – was nothing but a whited sepulchre?

MRS ALVING: That was all. Now you know.

PASTOR MANDERS: I – I don't seem able to take it in – I can't grasp it. . . . How could you possibly –? How could a thing like that be kept quiet?

MRS ALVING: That was my continual struggle – day in and day out. After Osvald was born, I thought he re-formed a little, but it didn't last. After that, I had to fight twice as hard – a desperate battle so that no one should know the sort of man my child's father was. Well, you know how charming Alving was – no one could bring themselves to believe anything but good of him. He was one of those men whose life had no effect on his reputa-tion. . . . But at last, Mr Manders – there came something else that you must know about – the most abominable thing of all.

PASTOR MANDERS: More abominable still?

MRS ALVING: I'd put up with him, although I knew only too well what sort of life he was secretly leading out-side. . . . But when it came to debauchery in this very house –

PASTOR MANDERS: What? Here?

MRS ALVING: Yes, in our own home. [*She points to the nearer door on the right.*] It was in the dining-room that I first came across it. I was doing something or other out there, and the door was ajar. I heard our housemaid come up from the garden with some water for the plants over there. . . .[8]

PASTOR MANDERS: Well?

MRS ALVING: After a little while I heard my husband come in too. I heard him say something to her softly, and then I heard [*with a short laugh*] – oh, I can still hear it, it was so distressing and yet so ridiculous at the same time – I heard my own housemaid whisper: 'Leave go, sir – let me be!'

PASTOR MANDERS: A piece of unseemly high spirits on his part, Mrs Alving. . . . It can't have been more than high spirits, believe me.

MRS ALVING: I knew what to believe soon enough, Pastor Manders. My husband had his way with the girl, and the affair had its consequences.

PASTOR MANDERS [*as though turned to stone*]: And all in this house! In this house. . . .

MRS ALVING: I've endured a great deal in this house. To keep him at home in the evenings – and at night – I've had to force myself to join in his secret drinking bouts up in his room. I've had to sit alone with him – clinking glasses and drinking with him, and listening to his lewd stupid talk. I've had to fight with him, physically, to get him to go to bed.

PASTOR MANDERS [*shaken*]: You had to endure all that?

MRS ALVING: I had to endure it for my little boy's sake . . . until there was this final humiliation, with my own servant-girl. Then I vowed to myself: 'This is the end!' I took over the control of the house – complete control, over him and over everything else. He didn't dare to protest, you see, now that I had a weapon against him. That was when I sent Osvald away. He was seven then, and beginning to notice things and ask questions, as children do. I thought he might be poisoned just by the unwholesome atmosphere of this house . . . and *that*, Mr Manders, I would not endure. That's why I sent him away. And now you see why I couldn't let him set foot in this house as long as his father was alive. No one knows what it cost me.

PASTOR MANDERS: It must have been a terrible life for you!

MRS ALVING: I could never have gone through with it if I hadn't had my work. Yes, I honestly claim to have worked: all the improvements on the estate – all the modern equipment that my husband got so much credit for – do you imagine that he had the energy for anything of the sort – lying all day on the sofa reading an old Court Circular? No, and I'll tell you something else: it was I who encouraged him when he had his few good days; and it was I who was left to manage everything when he went back to his debauchery, or when he relapsed into whining self-pity.

PASTOR MANDERS: And this is the man whom you're building a memorial to!

MRS ALVING: There you see the power of a bad conscience.

PASTOR MANDERS: A bad . . . What do you mean?

MRS ALVING: I always felt that the truth must come out one day, and that everyone would believe it. The Orphanage was to refute all the rumours and dispel any doubts.

PASTOR MANDERS: You've certainly succeeded there, Mrs Alving.

MRS ALVING: There was one other reason: I didn't want Osvald, my own son, to inherit anything whatever from his father.

PASTOR MANDERS: Then it was from Alving's estate that . . .

MRS ALVING: Yes. The sums that I've set aside, year by year, for this Orphanage, make up the amount – I've reckoned it out very carefully – the amount that made Lieutenant Alving a good match in his day.

PASTOR MANDERS: I don't see –

MRS ALVING: That was my purchase price. I don't want that money to go to Osvald. Whatever my son inherits shall come from me and no one else.

[OSVALD ALVING *comes through the farther door on the right, having left his hat and overcoat in the hall.* MRS ALVING *goes to meet him.*]

My darling boy, are you back already?

OSVALD: Yes. What is there to do out of doors in this everlasting rain? But I gather lunch is just ready — that's fine.

REGINA [*coming from the dining-room with a parcel*]: A parcel's just come for you, Madam. [*She gives it to her.*]

MRS ALVING [*glancing at Pastor Manders*]: The music for the choir tomorrow probably.

PASTOR MANDERS: Hm...

REGINA: And lunch is ready.

MRS ALVING: Thank you — we'll come in a moment, I just want to ... [*She starts to undo the parcel.*]

REGINA [*to Osvald*]: Would you like red wine or white, Mr Osvald?

OSVALD: Both, please, Miss Engstrand.

REGINA: *Bien.* Very good, Mr Osvald. [*She goes into the dining-room.*]

OSVALD: I may as well help you to open it. [*He follows her into the dining-room; the door swings half-open again after him.*]

MRS ALVING: Yes, I thought so, it's the song for the choir, Pastor.

PASTOR MANDERS [*clasping his hands*]: How shall I ever be able to make my speech tomorrow with a clear conscience?

MRS ALVING: Oh, you'll manage.

PASTOR MANDERS [*quietly, so as not to be heard in the dining-room*]: Yes — we mustn't have any scandal.

MRS ALVING: And then this long hideous farce will be over. From tomorrow onwards, I shall feel as if my late husband had never lived in this house; there will be no one here but my son and his mother.

[*From the dining-room comes the noise of a chair falling, and* REGINA'S *voice in a sharp whisper*:]

REGINA: Stop it, Osvald! Don't be silly! Let me go!

MRS ALVING [*with a start of horror*]: Ah!

[*She stares wildly at the half-open door.* OSVALD *can be heard coughing and humming inside. A bottle is opened.*]

PASTOR MANDERS [*upset*]: What's happening? Mrs Alving – what is it?

MRS ALVING [*hoarsely*]: Ghosts! The couple in the conservatory – walking again.

PASTOR MANDERS: What do you mean? Regina . . .? Is *she* . . .?

MRS ALVING: Yes. Come – not a word! [*She takes Pastor Manders by the arm and walks unsteadily with him to the dining-room.*]

ACT TWO

———————— ✳ ————————

*The same room. The wet mist still hangs over the land-
scape.*

[PASTOR MANDERS *and* MRS ALVING *come out of
the dining-room.*]

MRS ALVING [*in the doorway*]: Let's sit here, Mr Manders.[9]
[*Calling into the dining-room*] Aren't you coming too,
Osvald?

OSVALD [*off*]: No thank you; I think I'll go out for a bit.

MRS ALVING: Yes, do; it's clearing a little now. [*She shuts
the dining-room door, then goes to the hall door and
calls*]: Regina!

REGINA [*off*]: Yes, Madam?

MRS ALVING: Go down to the wash-house and help them
with the decorations.

REGINA: Very good, Madam.
[MRS ALVING *makes sure that she has gone, then
shuts the door.*]

PASTOR MANDERS: You're sure he can't hear us in there?

MRS ALVING: Not with the door shut. Besides, he's just
going out.

PASTOR MANDERS: I'm still upset; I can't think how I
managed to swallow a mouthful of that excellent
luncheon.

MRS ALVING [*walking up and down, controlling her agitation*]: Nor can I. But what's to be done?

PASTOR MANDERS: Yes, what's to be done? I don't know,

I really don't. I've had no experience at all of this sort
of thing.

MRS ALVING: I'm quite sure that nothing . . . unfortunate
has happened yet.

PASTOR MANDERS: Heaven forbid. All the same, it's
shocking behaviour.

MRS ALVING: It's all just a passing fancy on Osvald's
part, you can be sure of that.

PASTOR MANDERS: Well, as I said, I don't know much
about these things, but it certainly seems to me –

MRS ALVING: She must leave this house – and at once,
too. That's as clear as daylight.

PASTOR MANDERS: Yes, I agree.

MRS ALVING: But where to? We can't really –

PASTOR MANDERS: Where to? Back to her father, of
course.

MRS ALVING: Where did you say?

PASTOR MANDERS: To her – Oh, but Engstrand isn't . . .
Good heavens, Mrs Alving, that can't be true. There
must be some mistake.

MRS ALVING: There's no mistake at all, I'm afraid. Johanna
had to confess the whole thing to me, and my husband
couldn't deny it. So the only thing to do was to hush
it up.

PASTOR MANDERS: Yes, that was all you could do.

MRS ALVING: The girl went at once, with quite a reasonable sum of money to make her hold her tongue. She
looked after the rest for herself when she got back to
the town. She renewed an old acquaintance with Engstrand – probably dropping a hint about all the money
she had – and told him a tale about some foreigner or
other who'd put in here on a yacht that summer. So she
and Engstrand got married in a hurry. Why, you married
them yourself.

PASTOR MANDERS: But how could –? I distinctly remember Engstrand coming to arrange about the wedding. He was utterly repentant, reproaching himself bitterly for the folly that he and his fiancée had been guilty of.

MRS ALVING: Naturally he had to take the blame himself.

PASTOR MANDERS: But how dishonest of him – and to *me*, too! I'd never have believed it of Jakob Engstrand – he can be quite sure he'll get a good talking to from me. And then the immorality of a marriage like that – just for the money! How much was the girl given?

MRS ALVING: Three hundred dollars.

PASTOR MANDERS: Just think! For a miserable three hundred dollars to go and marry a fallen woman!

MRS ALVING: Then what do you think of me? I went and married a fallen man.

PASTOR MANDERS: But good heavens – what do you mean? A fallen man?

MRS ALVING: Do you really think that when I went to the altar with Alving, he was any purer than Johanna was when Engstrand married her?

PASTOR MANDERS: Ah, but there's all the difference in the world between . . .

MRS ALVING: Not so much difference really. Of course there was a big difference in the price. A miserable three hundred dollars, and a whole fortune.

PASTOR MANDERS: But you can't compare the two cases – you had consulted your own heart, you had discussed it with your parents.

MRS ALVING [*not looking at him*]: I thought you realized where my heart, as you call it, had strayed in those days.

PASTOR MANDERS [*with difficulty*]: If I'd realized anything of the sort, I couldn't have gone on coming to your husband's house almost every day.

MRS ALVING: Well, the fact remains that I certainly didn't consult myself at all.

PASTOR MANDERS: Your nearest relations, then – that would have been only right – your mother and your two aunts.[10]

MRS ALVING: Yes, that's true – those three arranged it all for me. Oh, you'd never believe how clear they made it that it'd be sheer madness to refuse an offer like that. If my mother could only see me now, and know what all that splendid promise has come to!

PASTOR MANDERS: No one's to blame for the way things have turned out. And at least one thing's certain: your marriage was solemnized in full accordance with law and order.

MRS ALVING [at the window]: Oh, law and order! Yes, I often think they're the cause of all the trouble in the world.

PASTOR MANDERS: Mrs Alving, that's very wicked of you.

MRS ALVING: Perhaps. But I'm not putting up with all those duties and obligations any longer. I simply can't. I must somehow free myself.

PASTOR MANDERS: What do you mean by that?

MRS ALVING [tapping on the pane]: I should never have hushed up the truth about my husband's life. But in those days, I dared not do anything else – I was too much of a coward.

PASTOR MANDERS: A coward?

MRS ALVING: Yes, if people had got to know about it, they'd have said: 'Poor man, it's only natural he should kick over the traces, when he has a wife who runs away from him.'

PASTOR MANDERS: They'd have had a certain amount of right to say that.

MRS ALVING [*looking fixedly at him*]: If I were the woman I ought to be, I should take Osvald on one side and say: 'Listen, my boy, your father was a dissolute man –'

PASTOR MANDERS: Heaven forbid!

MRS ALVING: And then I should have told him everything that I've told you – word for word.

PASTOR MANDERS: Mrs Alving, I'm really shocked at you.

MRS ALVING: Yes, I know; I know perfectly well how you feel – when I think about it, I'm shocked at myself. [*Coming away from the window*] I'm such a coward.

PASTOR MANDERS: Do you call it cowardice to do your plain duty? Have you forgotten that a child should love and honour his father and mother?

MRS ALVING: Don't let's generalize; let us ask 'Should Osvald love and honour Captain Alving?' [11]

PASTOR MANDERS: Don't you, as a mother, hear a voice in your heart forbidding you to destroy your son's ideals?

MRS ALVING: But the truth …

PASTOR MANDERS: But his ideals …

MRS ALVING: Oh, ideals – ideals! If only I weren't the coward that I am!

PASTOR MANDERS: Don't reject ideals, Mrs Alving – they can take a cruel revenge. Take Osvald's case in particular: I'm afraid that Osvald hasn't very many ideals, but I can see already that his father is something of an ideal to him.

MRS ALVING: Yes, you're right.

PASTOR MANDERS: And this picture of his father is something that you yourself have fostered and encouraged in him by your letters.

MRS ALVING: Yes, thanks to my regard for duty, I've been lying to my boy for years on end. What a coward – what a coward I've been!

PASTOR MANDERS: You've planted a beautiful illusion in your son's mind, Mrs Alving – and that's something to be proud of.

MRS ALVING: Hm; I wonder if it was really such a good thing after all. Anyhow, I won't have any carrying on with Regina – he's not going to ruin that poor girl's life.

PASTOR MANDERS: Good heavens no, that would be terrible.

MRS ALVING: If I thought he was in earnest, and that it would make him happy . . .

PASTOR MANDERS: Well? What?

MRS ALVING: But it wouldn't do; I'm afraid Regina's not up to it.

PASTOR MANDERS: But . . . but what do you mean?

MRS ALVING: If I weren't such a miserable coward, I'd say: 'Marry her, or anything else you like – so long as there's no more deceit.'

PASTOR MANDERS: God forbid! A legal marriage? That would be unheard-of – monstrous!

MRS ALVING: Do you call it unheard-of? Honestly, Pastor Manders, do you really believe there aren't plenty of married couples out here in the country who are just as closely related?

PASTOR MANDERS: I simply don't understand you.

MRS ALVING: I think you do.

PASTOR MANDERS: Oh, you're thinking of cases where possibly . . . Yes, I'm afraid family life is certainly not always as pure as it should be. But with the sort of thing that you're hinting at, one can't really know – at least, not with any certainty. But in this case, for you, a mother, to be willing to allow your –

MRS ALVING: But I'm not willing to allow it. I wouldn't allow it for anything in the world – that's just what I was saying.

PASTOR MANDERS: No, because you're a coward, as you put it. But if you weren't a coward – Great God! such a revolting union!

MRS ALVING: Yet they say we all spring from some such union. And who was it who arranged the world like that, Pastor Manders?

PASTOR MANDERS: I refuse to discuss such questions with you, Mrs Alving – not while you're in such an unsuitable state of mind. But what do you mean by calling yourself a coward just because –

MRS ALVING: I'll tell you what I mean by it. I'm timid and frightened because I can never really be free of the ghosts that haunt me.

PASTOR MANDERS: What do you mean by that?

MRS ALVING: I'm haunted by ghosts. When I heard Regina and Osvald out there, it was just as if there were ghosts before my very eyes. But I'm inclined to think that we're all ghosts, Pastor Manders; it's not only the things that we've inherited from our fathers and mothers that live on in us, but all sorts of old dead ideas and old dead beliefs, and things of that sort. They're not actually alive in us, but they're rooted there all the same, and we can't rid ourselves of them. I've only to pick up a newspaper, and when I read it I seem to see ghosts gliding between the lines. I should think there must be ghosts all over the country – as countless as grains of sand.[12] And we are, all of us, so pitifully afraid of the light.

PASTOR MANDERS: Ah! So there we have the fruits of your reading – and fine fruits they are, upon my word! Oh, these terrible, subversive, free-thinking books!

MRS ALVING: You're wrong, my dear Pastor, it was you yourself who started me thinking, and I'm most grateful for it.

PASTOR MANDERS: I?

MRS ALVING: Yes, when you led me back to what you called the path of duty and obedience – when you praised as right and proper something that my whole soul revolted against as an abomination – then I began to look closely at the stuff your teaching was made of. I only wanted to unpick a single stitch, but once I'd got that undone, the whole thing unravelled. Then I realized that it was just chain-stitch! [13]

PASTOR MANDERS [*quietly moved*]: And is that the outcome of the hardest struggle in my life?

MRS ALVING: Call it rather your most pitiful defeat.

PASTOR MANDERS: It was my life's greatest victory, Helena – victory over myself.

MRS ALVING: It was a crime against us both.

PASTOR MANDERS: Because when you were out of your senses, and came to me crying, 'Here I am, take me,' and I said, 'Woman, go home to your lawful husband' – was that a crime?

MRS ALVING: *I* think so.

PASTOR MANDERS: We don't understand each other, you and I.

MRS ALVING: Not any more, certainly.

PASTOR MANDERS: I have never – even in my most secret dreams – thought of you except as another man's wife.

MRS ALVING: Do you really believe that?

PASTOR MANDERS: Helena!

MRS ALVING: It's so easy to forget how one felt.

PASTOR MANDERS: Not for me – I'm the same as I always was.

MRS ALVING [*with a sudden change of mood*]: Well, well, well, don't let's talk any more about the old days. You're up to your eyes in committees and boards, and here am I struggling with ghosts, both inside me and out.

PASTOR MANDERS: At any rate, I can help you to conquer the external ones. After all the shocking things that I've heard from you today, I can't in all conscience let a defenceless girl stay on in your house.

MRS ALVING: Don't you think it would be best if we could get her settled – suitably married, I mean?

PASTOR MANDERS: There's no doubt about that – I think it would be the best thing for her from every point of view. Regina has now reached an age when – well, I don't know much about these things, but . . .

MRS ALVING: Regina matured very early.

PASTOR MANDERS: Yes she did, didn't she? I seem to remember that she was particularly well developed physically when I was preparing her for confirmation.[14] But first, whatever happens, she must go home, where she'll be under her father's eye. Oh . . . but Engstrand isn't –! To think that he, of all people, could hide the truth from me like that!

[*There is a knock on the door.*]

MRS ALVING: Who can that be? Come in!

ENGSTRAND [*at the door, in his Sunday clothes*]: I humbly beg pardon, but –

PASTOR MANDERS: Ah! Hm –

MRS ALVING: Oh, it's you, Engstrand.

ENGSTRAND: – there weren't any servants about, so I made so very bold as to knock.[15]

MRS ALVING: Oh, well, come in. Did you want to see me about something?

ENGSTRAND: No, thank you all the same – it was the Pastor I wanted to have just a word with.

PASTOR MANDERS [*pacing up and down*]: Oh, indeed? You want to speak to me, do you?

ENGSTRAND: Yes, if you'd be so kind. . . .

PASTOR MANDERS [*stopping in front of him*]: Well, what is it, may I ask?

ENGSTRAND: Well, it's this, Pastor: now that we've been paid off down there – thank you very much, Ma'am – and now that it's all finished, it seemed to me that it'd be only right and proper if all of us who've been united in honest toil for so long . . . well, it seemed to me we ought to end up with a little service this evening.

PASTOR MANDERS: A service? Down at the Orphanage?

ENGSTRAND: Yes. But of course, sir, if you don't think it fitting. . . .

PASTOR MANDERS: Oh, I do, but –

ENGSTRAND: I've been saying a prayer or two down there of an evening, myself.

MRS ALVING: Have you?

ENGSTRAND: Yes, ever so often . . . a little edification, as you might say. But I'm just a plain ordinary man, God help me, with no proper gift for it; so I thought with Pastor Manders happening to be here . . .

PASTOR MANDERS: Look here, Engstrand, there's a question I must ask you first. Are you in a proper state of mind for such a service? Do you feel that you have a clear conscience?

ENGSTRAND: Oh, God help us, Pastor, don't let's talk about conscience.

PASTOR MANDERS: But that's just what we must talk about. What do you say to my question?

ENGSTRAND: Well . . . we can all have a bad conscience at times.

PASTOR MANDERS: Ah, you admit that, at any rate. Now tell me – truthfully – what is your relationship to Regina?

MRS ALVING [quickly]: Mr Manders –

PASTOR MANDERS [reassuringly]: Leave this to me.

ENGSTRAND: With Regina? Lor' you gave me a scare.

[*Looking at Mrs Alving*] There isn't anything wrong with Regina, is there?

PASTOR MANDERS: Let us hope not. I mean, what is the position between you and Regina? You're supposed to be her father. Well?

ENGSTRAND [*uncertainly*]: Well, Pastor – er – you know how it was with me and poor Johanna.

PASTOR MANDERS: Stop twisting the truth. Your late wife told Mrs Alving the whole story before she left her service.

ENGSTRAND: Well I'll be – So she did, eh?

PASTOR MANDERS: So you've been found out, Engstrand.

ENGSTRAND: And after she's promised – given me her Bible oath –

PASTOR MANDERS: Her Bible oath?

ENGSTRAND: Well, she only swore – but very solemnly.

PASTOR MANDERS: And you've been concealing the truth from me all these years. From *me*, who've always had such complete faith in you.

ENGSTRAND: I'm very sorry to admit I have.

PASTOR MANDERS: Engstrand – have I deserved that from you? Haven't I always been ready to help you, both in word and deed, to the very best of my ability? Answer me – haven't I?

ENGSTRAND: Many's the time I'd have been in a very bad way, but for you, sir.

PASTOR MANDERS: And this is how you repay me! Causing me to make false entries in the Parish Register; and then, all these years, keeping back the information that you owed, not only to me, but to the cause of truth. You've behaved abominably, Engstrand, and from now on I shall have nothing further to do with you.

ENGSTRAND [*with a sigh*]: Yes, I can see that is how it must be.

PASTOR MANDERS: Yes, because there's no excuse for you, is there?

ENGSTRAND: But how could she go and add to her shame by talking about it? Just suppose, sir, that you were in the same trouble as poor Johanna –

PASTOR MANDERS: Me!

ENGSTRAND: Oh, Lor', I don't mean exactly the same. What I mean is, if you had something to be ashamed of in the eyes of the world, as the saying goes. We men didn't ought to judge a poor woman too hard, sir.

PASTOR MANDERS: But I'm not; it's you I'm reproaching.

ENGSTRAND: Might I be allowed, sir, to ask you one little question?

PASTOR MANDERS: Well, what is it?

ENGSTRAND: Isn't it right and proper for a man to help the fallen?

PASTOR MANDERS: Certainly.

ENGSTRAND: And isn't he bound to keep his word of honour?

PASTOR MANDERS: Yes, of course he is, but –

ENGSTRAND: Well – that time Johanna got into trouble thanks to that Englishman – or he might have been an American or a Russian, as they call them – well, she came back to town. . . . Poor girl, she'd turned me down once or twice before, because she wouldn't look at anyone who wasn't handsome, she wouldn't, and I had my bad leg. *You* remember, sir, the way I forced myself to go into a dance-hall where the sailors were carrying on with drink and debauchery, as the saying goes – and when I was trying to persuade them to lead a better life –

MRS ALVING [*over at the window*]: Hm!

PASTOR MANDERS: I know, Engstrand – the ruffians threw you downstairs. You've told me about it already. Your affliction is a credit to you.

ENGSTRAND: I'm not one to boast about it, sir. But what I wanted to say was that when she came and confessed to me with weeping and gnashing of teeth, I can tell you, Pastor, it broke my heart to hear it.

PASTOR MANDERS: Yes, I'm sure it did. Well?

ENGSTRAND: Well, I said to her: this American's roaming about on the high seas, he is; and you, Johanna, I said – you've committed a sin, and you're a fallen woman. But here stands Jakob Engstrand on his own two feet – well, in a manner of speaking, that is, sir. . . .

PASTOR MANDERS: I quite understand; go on.

ENGSTRAND: Well, that's how I raised her up and made an honest woman of her, so that folks shouldn't know she'd gone astray with foreigners.

PASTOR MANDERS: That was all very noble of you; but what I can't forgive is your stooping to take money.

ENGSTRAND: Money? Me? Not a farthing!

PASTOR MANDERS [referring it to Mrs Alving]: But . . . ?

ENGSTRAND: Oh yes, wait a minute, I remember now, Johanna did have a few shillings, but I wouldn't have anything to do with that. 'Pah,' I said, 'that's filthy lucre, that's what that is – the wages of sin. We'll throw this tainted gold – or notes, or whatever it was – back to the American!' I said. But, Pastor, he was off and away across the stormy seas.

PASTOR MANDERS: Yes, my good Engstrand, I suppose he was.

ENGSTRAND: Yes. So Johanna and I agreed that the money should go towards the child's upbringing – and so it did, and I can account for every penny of it.

PASTOR MANDERS: But this alters the whole thing!

ENGSTRAND: That's how it was, sir. And I may be so bold as to claim that I've been a good father to Regina so far as lay in my power – for I'm sorry to say I'm a poor weak man.

PASTOR MANDERS: There, there, my good Engstrand. . . .

ENGSTRAND: But I may be so bold as to say that I brought up the child and was a good husband to poor Johanna, and I made a home for them, like the Scripture says. But I'd never have dreamed of going to you, sir, and boasting and bragging that I'd done some good in the world for once, too. No, when anything like that happens to Jakob Engstrand, he holds his tongue about it. . . . Not that it happens all that often, I know that. No, when I come to Pastor Manders, it's always because I have my weakness and folly to talk about . . . because I tell you – like I was saying just now – conscience can be very hard on us sometimes.

PASTOR MANDERS: Jakob Engstrand – give me your hand.

ENGSTRAND: Oh Lor', Pastor. . . .

PASTOR MANDERS: No excuses, now! [*Grasping his hand*] There!

ENGSTRAND: And if I might humbly beg your forgiveness, sir –

PASTOR MANDERS: You? No, on the contrary, it's I who should ask forgiveness of *you*. . . .

ENGSTRAND: Oh *no*!

PASTOR MANDERS: Yes indeed; and I do so with all my heart. Forgive me for having misjudged you . . . and if there's anything I could do to show my sincere regret and my goodwill towards you . . .

ENGSTRAND: Do you mean that, sir?

PASTOR MANDERS: It would give me the greatest pleasure.

ENGSTRAND: Because it so happens there *is* something. With the good money I've put aside up here, I'm thinking of starting a sort of Seaman's Home in the town.

MRS ALVING: *You?*

ENGSTRAND: Yes, *it* could be a sort of Orphanage, too, in a manner of speaking.[16] There are such manifold temptations for a seaman when he's on shore; but in this house of mine, I thought he could be under a fatherly eye, in a way.

PASTOR MANDERS: What do you say to that, Mrs Alving?

ENGSTRAND: I haven't got much to start it with, Lord knows, but if only I could find someone to give me a helping hand. . . .

PASTOR MANDERS: Yes, yes, we must look into it; your plan interests me enormously. But now, go down and get everything ready, light the candles and make the place cheerful . . . and then, my dear Engstrand, we'll spend an edifying hour together – I feel that you're in just the right frame of mind.

ENGSTRAND: Yes, I believe I am. Good-bye, then, Ma'am, and thank you. Take good care of Regina for me. [*He wipes a tear from his eye.*] Poor Johanna's child . . . it's strange, but she's grown to be very close to my heart, she has indeed. [*He bows and goes out through the hall.*]

PASTOR MANDERS: There! What do you think of him now, Mrs Alving? That was a very different explanation he gave us.

MRS ALVING: It certainly was.

PASTOR MANDERS: So you see how particularly careful one must be in judging one's fellow men. Yet it's very pleasant to find one has been mistaken. . . . What do *you* say?

MRS ALVING: I say that you're a great baby, Pastor, and always will be.

PASTOR MANDERS: *I?*

MRS ALVING [*putting both hands on his shoulders*]: And I say that I should like to give you a big hug!

PASTOR MANDERS [*recoiling hastily*]: No no – heaven forbid! What an idea!

MRS ALVING [*with a smile*]: Oh, you needn't be afraid of me.

PASTOR MANDERS [*by the table*]: You have a most extravagant way of expressing yourself sometimes. Now first I'll just collect all the documents together and put them in my case. [*He does so.*] There! And now, good-bye for the present. Keep an eye on Osvald when he comes back. I'll look in again later. [*He takes his hat and goes out into the hall.*]

[MRS ALVING *gives a sigh, looks out of the window for a moment, tidies the room a little, and is about to go into the dining-room, but stops in the doorway with a stifled cry:*]

MRS ALVING: Osvald! Are you still sitting there?

OSVALD [*in the dining-room*]: I'm just finishing my cigar.

MRS ALVING: I thought you'd gone for a stroll up the road.

OSVALD: In weather like this?

[*A glass clinks; leaving the door open,* MRS ALVING *sits down on the sofa by the window with her knitting.*] Was that Pastor Manders going just now?

MRS ALVING: Yes, he went down to the Orphanage.

OSVALD: Hm.

[*The decanter clinks against the glass again.*]

MRS ALVING [*looking worried*]: Osvald dear, you ought to be careful with that liqueur, it's strong.

OSVALD: It keeps the damp out.

MRS ALVING: Won't you come in here with me?

OSVALD: I can't smoke in there.

MRS ALVING: You know perfectly well you can smoke cigars.

OSVALD: All right, then, I'll come. Just one more little drop. . . . There! [*He comes in with his cigar, shutting the door after him. After a short silence*:] Where has the Pastor gone?

MRS ALVING: Down to the Orphanage – I told you.

OSVALD: Oh, yes, so you did.

MRS ALVING: You oughtn't to sit at the table so long, Osvald.

OSVALD [*holding his cigar behind his back*]: But I think it's so nice, Mother. [*Stroking and fondling her*] Just think what it means to me to be at home, sitting at my mother's own table in my mother's room, eating my mother's delicious meals.

MRS ALVING: My darling boy.

OSVALD [*walking about rather irritably, and smoking*]: What else is there for me to do? I can't settle down to anything. . . .

MRS ALVING: Can't you?

OSVALD: In this wretched weather – without a glimpse of the sun all day?[17] [*Pacing the floor*] And not being able to work . . . !

MRS ALVING: Perhaps it wasn't a good idea, your coming home.

OSVALD: Yes, Mother, I had to.

MRS ALVING: Because I'd ten times rather give up the pleasure of having you with me, than that you should –

OSVALD [*stopping at the table*]: Tell me, Mother – does it really make you so very happy to have me home?

MRS ALVING: Make me happy?

OSVALD [*screwing up a newspaper*]: I shouldn't have thought it could make much difference to you whether I was here or not.

MRS ALVING: Osvald! How can you have the heart to say that to your mother?

OSVALD: You've managed to live without me all this time.

MRS ALVING: Yes, I *have* lived without you – that's true. [*A pause. Dusk falls gradually.* OSVALD, *who has put his cigar down, walks backwards and forwards across the room.*]

OSVALD [*stopping beside Mrs Alving*]: Mother, may I sit by you on the sofa?

MRS ALVING [*making room for him*]: Yes, my dear boy, do.

OSVALD [*sitting*]: There's something I've got to tell you, Mother.

MRS ALVING [*anxiously*]: What?

OSVALD [*staring straight in front of him*]: You see, I can't bear it any longer.

MRS ALVING: Bear what? What is it?

OSVALD [*as before*]: I couldn't bring myself to write to you about it – and since I've been home . . .

MRS ALVING [*clutching his arm*]: Osvald! What is it?

OSVALD: I've been trying, all yesterday and today, to avoid thinking about it – to get free from it. . . . But I couldn't.

MRS ALVING [*rising*]: Now you can tell me everything, Osvald.

OSVALD [*drawing her back on to the sofa*]: Sit down again, and I'll try to tell you. . . . I've been complaining of tiredness after my journey –

MRS ALVING: Yes, well?

OSVALD: But that's not what's wrong with me – not just ordinary tiredness.

MRS ALVING [*trying to rise*]: You're not ill, Osvald?

OSVALD [*pulling her down again*]: Sit still, Mother – just take it calmly. No, I'm not really ill, either . . . not what's usually called ill. [*Holding his head in his hands*] Mother, my mind's gone – broken down – I shall never be able to work again. [*Covering his face with his hands, he buries his head in her lap and bursts into bitter tears.*]

MRS ALVING: Osvald! Look at me! It can't be true.

OSVALD [*looking up with despair in his eyes*]: Never to be able to work again . . . never – never! It'll be a living death. Mother, can you think of anything more dreadful?

MRS ALVING: My poor boy! How could such a terrible thing happen to you?

OSVALD [*sitting up*]: That's just what I simply can't understand. I've never led a dissolute life at all – not in any way. You mustn't think that of me, Mother – I've never done that.

MRS ALVING: I'm sure you haven't, Osvald.

OSVALD: And yet this has happened to me – this appalling thing.

MRS ALVING: But it'll get better, my own darling boy. It's nothing but overwork – believe me, that's all it is.

OSVALD [*sadly*]: That's what I thought at first, but it isn't.

MRS ALVING: Tell me the whole thing, from beginning to end.

OSVALD: That's what I want to do.

MRS ALVING: When did you notice it first?

OSVALD: It was directly after the last time I was home. I'd just got back to Paris, when I began to get the most violent headaches – they seemed to be mostly at the back of my head. It was as if a ring of iron, from my neck upwards, were being screwed tight.

MRS ALVING: And then?

OSVALD: At first I thought they were only the ordinary headaches that I used to get so badly when I was small. . . .

MRS ALVING: Yes – yes . . .

OSVALD: But they weren't – I soon realized that. I couldn't work any longer. I wanted to start on a big new picture, but it was as if my skill had failed me – all my powers were paralysed, I couldn't collect my thoughts, my head seemed to swim and everything spun round. Oh, it was terrible. At last I sent for the doctor – and I learned the truth from him.

MRS ALVING: How do you mean?

OSVALD: He was one of the best doctors there. I had to tell him just how I felt, and then he began to ask me a whole lot of questions that didn't seem to me to have anything to do with it. I couldn't see what the man was driving at. . . .

MRS ALVING: Well?

OSVALD: At last he said: 'You have been more or less riddled from your birth.' The actual word he used was 'vermoulu'.[18]

MRS ALVING [anxiously]: What did he mean by that?

OSVALD: I didn't understand either, and I asked him to explain. Then the old cynic said – [He clenches his fists.] Oh . . . !

MRS ALVING: What did he say?

OSVALD: He said, 'The sins of the fathers are visited on the children. . . .'

MRS ALVING [rising slowly]: The sins of the fathers –!

OSVALD: I nearly hit him in the face.

MRS ALVING [walking across the room]: The sins of the fathers. . . .

OSVALD [smiling sadly]: Yes, what do you think of that? Of course I assured him that anything like that was quite impossible. But do you think he'd give way? No, he stood firm, and it was only when I produced your letters and translated all the bits about Father for him . . .

MRS ALVING: And then . . . ?

OSVALD: Well then, of course, he had to admit that he was on the wrong track. That was when I learned the truth – the incredible truth: I ought never to have joined in that gloriously happy life with my friends; it's been too much for my strength. It's all been my own fault!

MRS ALVING: No, Osvald – you mustn't think that.

OSVALD: According to him, there was no other possible explanation. *That*'s what's so terrible: my whole life ruined – irreparably ruined – and all through my own thoughtlessness. All the things I meant to do in the world . . . I daren't think about them again – I *can't* think about them. Oh, if only I could start afresh and have my life over again.

[*He throws himself face downwards on the sofa.* MRS ALVING *wrings her hands and paces backwards and forwards in silence, wrestling with herself. After a while,* OSVALD *looks up and raises himself on one elbow.*]

If only it *had* been something I'd inherited – something I wasn't to blame for. . . . But this! It's so shameful to have thrown away my health and happiness – everything in the world – so thoughtlessly, so recklessly. . . . My future – my life itself!

MRS ALVING: No, no, my dearest boy, that isn't possible. [*Bending over him*] It's not as terrible as you think.

OSVALD: Oh, you don't know. . . . [*Springing up*] And then look at all the pain I'm giving you, Mother. Often I've almost wished that you didn't really care about me so much.

MRS ALVING: Osvald! You're the only thing I care about! My only child – the one thing I have in the world.

OSVALD [*seizing her hands and kissing them*]: Yes, I see that. Now that I'm at home, I can see it plainly – and that's the worst thing of all for me. But you know it all now, and we won't talk about it any more today. I can't bear to think about it for long. [*Crossing the room*] Get me something to drink, Mother.

MRS ALVING: A drink? What do you want to drink now?

OSVALD: Oh, anything you like – there's surely some cold punch in the house.

MRS ALVING: Yes, but Osvald dear –

OSVALD: Don't deny me that, Mother – be nice about it. I must have something to drown all these thoughts that keep gnawing at me so. [*Going into the conservatory*] Besides, it's so gloomy here.

[MRS ALVING *pulls the bell-rope on the right.*[19]]

And this continual rain! It can go on week after week for months on end, without our ever getting a glimpse of the sun. All the times I've been home I can't remember ever having seen the sun.

MRS ALVING: Osvald – you're not thinking of leaving me?

OSVALD: Hm . . . [*Sighing deeply*] I'm not thinking of anything – I *can't* think of anything. [*Low*] I've given up thinking.

REGINA [*coming from the dining-room*]: Did you ring, Madam?

MRS ALVING: Yes, will you bring the lamp in?

REGINA: At once, Madam; I *have* lit it. [*She goes.*]

MRS ALVING [*going over to Osvald*]: Osvald, don't keep anything back from me.

OSVALD: I'm not, Mother. [*Going across to the table*] I've told you a great deal, I think.

[REGINA *brings the lamp and puts it on the table.*]

MRS ALVING: Regina, bring a half-bottle of champagne, will you please?

REGINA: Yes, Madam. [*She goes again.*]

OSVALD [*putting his arms round Mrs Alving's neck*]:

That's fine, Mother – I knew you wouldn't let your son go thirsty!

MRS ALVING: My poor darling Osvald, how can I refuse you anything now?

OSVALD [*eagerly*]: Is that true, Mother? Do you mean it?

MRS ALVING: Mean what?

OSVALD: That you can't refuse me anything.

MRS ALVING: But Osvald dear –

OSVALD: Sh!

REGINA [*bringing in a half-bottle of champagne and two glasses on a tray which she puts on the table*]: Shall I open it?

OSVALD: No thank you, I'll do it.

[REGINA *goes out again.*]

MRS ALVING [*sitting at the table*]: What were you thinking of that I mustn't refuse you?

OSVALD [*busy opening the bottle*]: First let's have a glass – or two. [*The cork pops; he fills one glass and is about to fill the other.*]

MRS ALVING [*putting her hand over the glass*]: No thank you – none for me.

OSVALD: Well, *I* will. [*He fills the glass, drains it, and refills it, then sits at the table.*]

MRS ALVING [*expectantly*]: Well?

OSVALD [*not looking at her*]: By the way, tell me – I thought you and Pastor Manders were looking very – well, *subdued*, at lunch.

MRS ALVING: Did you think so?

OSVALD: Yes. Er – [*After a short pause*] Tell me, what do you think of Regina?

MRS ALVING: What do I think?

OSVALD: Yes; isn't she wonderful?

MRS ALVING: Osvald dear, you don't know her as well as I do.

OSVALD: Oh?

MRS ALVING: I'm afraid Regina stayed at home for too long. I should have had her up here earlier.

OSVALD: Yes, but doesn't she look wonderful, Mother? [*He fills his glass.*]

MRS ALVING: Regina has a great many failings. . . .

OSVALD: Oh, well, what does that matter? [*He has another drink.*]

MRS ALVING: All the same, I'm fond of her, and I'm responsible for her. I wouldn't for the world have anything happen to her.

OSVALD [*jumping up*]: Mother, Regina is my only salvation.

MRS ALVING [*rising*]: What do you mean by that?

OSVALD: I can't go on enduring all this agony of mind alone.

MRS ALVING: But there's your mother to share it with you.

OSVALD: Yes, that's what I thought – that's why I came back home to you. But it won't do – I can see that it won't. I can't stand the life here.

MRS ALVING: Osvald!

OSVALD: I shall have to live a different sort of life, Mother. That's why I must leave you – I don't want you to have to watch it.

MRS ALVING: My poor boy! But Osvald, while you're as ill as this . . .

OSVALD: If it were only the illness, I'd stay here with you, Mother – you're the best friend I've got in the world.

MRS ALVING: Yes, that's true, Osvald, isn't it?

OSVALD [*pacing restlessly about*]: But it's all the torture of remorse – and then the great deadly fear – Oh, the terrible fear!

MRS ALVING [*following him*]: Fear? What do you mean? What fear?

OSVALD: Oh, you mustn't ask me any more. I don't know – I can't describe it to you.

[MRS ALVING *goes over to the right and rings the bell.*]

What do you want?

MRS ALVING: I want you to be happy, my dear, that's what I want. You mustn't go on brooding. [*To Regina, who has appeared at the door*] More champagne – a whole bottle!

[REGINA *goes.*]

OSVALD: Mother!

MRS ALVING: Do you think we don't know how to live, out here in the country?

OSVALD: Doesn't she look wonderful? What a figure! And so splendidly healthy.[20]

MRS ALVING [*sitting at the table*]: Sit down, Osvald, and let's talk this over quietly together.

OSVALD [*sitting*]: You don't know it, Mother, but there's something I've got to put right with Regina.

MRS ALVING: You?

OSVALD: A piece of thoughtlessness – call it what you like – quite innocent though. It was when I was last home . . .

MRS ALVING: Yes?

OSVALD: She was always asking me about Paris, and I used to tell her a few things about it. Then I remember I happened to say, 'Wouldn't you like to go there yourself?'

MRS ALVING: Well?

OSVALD: Then I saw that she was blushing scarlet. Then she said: 'Yes, I should love to.' 'All right,' I said, 'I daresay it could be arranged' – or something of the sort.

MRS ALVING: And then?

OSVALD: I naturally forgot all about it. Then, the day
before yesterday, I happened to ask her if she wasn't
glad that I was to be at home for so long –

MRS ALVING: Yes?

OSVALD: – then she looked at me rather oddly, and said:
'But what about my trip to Paris?'

MRS ALVING: *Her* trip!

OSVALD: And then it all came out that she'd taken it seriously. She'd been thinking about me all the time – and
she'd even started to learn French –

MRS ALVING: So *that* was why . . .

OSVALD: And when I saw that splendid girl standing there,
Mother, so fresh and lovely – I'd never really noticed her
before – but when she stood there looking as if her arms
were open ready for me –

MRS ALVING: Osvald!

OSVALD: – then I realized that my salvation lay in her
because I saw that she was filled with the joy of living.

MRS ALVING [*with a start*]: The joy of living . . .? Can
there be any salvation in *that*?

REGINA [*coming from the dining-room with a bottle of
champagne*]: I'm sorry to have been so long, but I had
to go down to the cellar. [*She puts the bottle on the
table.*]

OSVALD: And bring another glass.

REGINA [*looking at him in surprise*]: Madam's glass is
there, Mr Alving.

OSVALD: Yes, but bring one for yourself, Regina.
[REGINA *starts, and gives a quick shy glance at Mrs
Alving.*]
Well?

REGINA [*in a low voice, reluctantly*]: Does Madam . . . ?

MRS ALVING: Fetch the glass, Regina.

[REGINA *goes into the dining-room.*]

OSVALD [*following her with his eyes*]: Have you ever noticed her walk – so firm and confident?

MRS ALVING: Osvald – this is impossible!

OSVALD: It's all settled – you must see that. It's no good talking about it.

[REGINA *comes back with an empty glass which she keeps in her hand.*]

Sit down, Regina.

[REGINA *looks doubtfully at Mrs Alving.*]

MRS ALVING: Sit down.

[REGINA *sits on a chair by the dining-room door, still holding the empty glass.*]

Osvald, what was that you were saying about the joy of living?

OSVALD: Yes, the joy of living, Mother – it's something you don't know much about here at home. I've never felt it here.

MRS ALVING: Not even when you're with me?

OSVALD: Not when I'm at home. But you wouldn't understand that.

MRS ALVING: Yes I do – I think I'm beginning to understand it now.

OSVALD: That – and the joy of work, too. Well, actually they're the same thing. But you don't know anything about that, either.

MRS ALVING: Perhaps you're right, Osvald. Tell me more about it.

OSVALD: Well, what I mean is that people here are brought up to look on work as a curse, and a punishment for sin; and on life as a miserable business, something that the sooner we're done with the better.

MRS ALVING: A vale of tears, yes – and we do our best to make it one.

OSVALD: But people abroad won't stand for that; no one there really believes in that sort of doctrine any more. There you can feel that it's a joy and a delight merely to be in this world. Have you ever noticed, Mother, that everything that I've painted has been based on this joy of living? Always – without exception – on the joy of living. There's light and sunshine there, and a feeling of holiday, with faces radiating happiness. That's why I'm afraid to stay here at home with you.

MRS ALVING: Afraid? What are you afraid of here with me?

OSVALD: I'm afraid that everything that matters to me will be turned into something ugly here.

MRS ALVING [looking steadily at him]: Do you think that would happen?

OSVALD: I'm certain it would. Even if I lived the same life here as abroad, it still wouldn't be the same.

MRS ALVING [who has been listening intently, with her eyes large and thoughtful, rises and says]: I see how it all happened, now.

OSVALD: What do you see?

MRS ALVING: I see it now for the first time – and now I can speak.

OSVALD [getting up]: Mother – I don't understand.

REGINA [who has also risen]: Shall I go?

MRS ALVING: No, stay here. Now I can speak – now you shall hear everything, and then you can choose. Osvald – Regina –

OSVALD: Listen! Here's the Pastor.

PASTOR MANDERS [coming in from the hall]: Well, we've spent a most agreeable hour down there.

OSVALD: So have we.

PASTOR MANDERS: We must help Engstrand with his Sea-

man's Home – Regina must go and live there with him
and work for him.

REGINA: No thank you, sir.

PASTOR MANDERS [*noticing her for the first time*]: What
– you here! And with a glass in your hand?

REGINA [*quickly putting the glass down*]: Excuse me . . .

OSVALD: Regina is coming to live with me, Pastor.

PASTOR MANDERS: To – live with you?

OSVALD: Yes, as my wife – if she prefers that.

PASTOR MANDERS: But great heavens . . .!

REGINA: It's not my doing, sir.

OSVALD: Or she'll stay here – if I stay.

REGINA [*involuntarily*]: Here?

PASTOR MANDERS: Mrs Alving, I'm astonished at you!

MRS ALVING: It won't happen – either way. Because now
I can tell the truth.

PASTOR MANDERS: No, no! You mustn't do that!

MRS ALVING: I can, and I will. And without harming anyone's ideals.

OSVALD: Mother! What have you been hiding from
me?

REGINA [*listening*]: Madam – listen! There are people
down there shouting. [*She goes to the conservatory and
looks out.*]

OSVALD [*at the left-hand window*]: What's happening?
What's all that glare?

REGINA [*crying out*]: The Orphanage is on fire!

MRS ALVING [*at the window*]: On fire!

PASTOR MANDERS: On fire? Impossible! I was down
there just now.

OSVALD: Where's my hat? Oh, never mind. . . . Father's
Orphanage! [*He runs out into the garden.*]

MRS ALVING: My shawl, Regina. The whole place is
blazing!

PASTOR MANDERS: Terrible! Mrs Alving, that fire is a judgement on this wicked house!

MRS ALVING: Yes, yes, very likely. Come along, Regina. [*She and* REGINA *hurry out into the hall.*]

PASTOR MANDERS [*clasping his hands*]: And not insured! [*He follows them out.*]

ACT THREE

———— · ✳ ————

The room as before. All the doors are open; the lamp is still burning on the table. It is dark outside, except for a faint glow in the background to the left.

[MRS ALVING, *with a large shawl over her head, stands looking out from the conservatory.* REGINA, *also wearing a shawl, stands a little behind her.*]

MRS ALVING: Everything burnt – right to the ground.

REGINA: It's still burning in the basement.

MRS ALVING: Why doesn't Osvald come back? There's nothing to save.

REGINA: Shall I go down and take him his hat?

MRS ALVING: Hasn't he even got his hat?

REGINA [*pointing to the hall*]: No, it's still hanging there.

MRS ALVING: Leave it. He'd better come back now; I'll go and find him myself. [*She goes out into the garden.*]

PASTOR MANDERS [*coming in from the hall*]: Isn't Mrs Alving here?

REGINA: No, she's just gone down the garden.

PASTOR MANDERS: This is the most terrible night I've ever spent.

REGINA: Yes – a dreadful calamity, isn't it, sir? [21]

PASTOR MANDERS: Don't speak of it. I can hardly bear to think about it.

REGINA: But how can it have happened?

PASTOR MANDERS: Don't ask me, Miss Engstrand. How

should I know? Are *you* suggesting too . . . ? Isn't it enough that your father –?

REGINA: What about him?

PASTOR MANDERS: Oh, he's driving me out of my mind!

ENGSTRAND [*coming in from the hall*]: Pastor . . .!

PASTOR MANDERS [*turning round in horror*]: Have you followed me even here?

ENGSTRAND: Yes, God help me, but I *must*. . . . Oh Lor' this is a sad affair, sir!

PASTOR MANDERS [*pacing up and down*]: Terrible – terrible . . .!

REGINA: What's all this?

ENGSTRAND: Well, you see, it's all because of that service. . . . [*Under his breath*] We've got him now, my girl! [*Aloud*] And to think it was *my* fault that Pastor Manders is responsible for a thing like this.

PASTOR MANDERS: But, Engstrand, I assure you . . . !

ENGSTRAND: But nobody else touched the candles except you, sir.

PASTOR MANDERS [*standing still*]: Yes, so you keep saying. But I'm sure I don't remember ever having a candle in my hand.

ENGSTRAND: But I saw you, quite distinctly, sir, take a candle and snuff it in your fingers, and throw the wick away into the shavings.

PASTOR MANDERS: You watched me do it?

ENGSTRAND: Yes, I distinctly saw it.

PASTOR MANDERS: I simply can't understand it. You see, I never do snuff candles in my fingers.

ENGSTRAND: Yes, it did seem odd at the time. But is it really so dangerous, sir?

PASTOR MANDERS [*pacing restlessly to and fro*]: Oh, don't *ask* me!

ENGSTRAND [*walking with him*]: And you hadn't insured it either, had you, sir?

PASTOR MANDERS [*still walking*]: No no no – you heard me say so.

ENGSTRAND [*following him*]: Not insured! And then to go and set light to the whole place – oh Lord, oh Lord, what a calamity!

PASTOR MANDERS [*wiping the sweat from his forehead*]: You may well say so, Engstrand.

ENGSTRAND: And to think that a thing like that should happen to a charitable institution that was to have been a blessing to the whole neighbourhood, as they say. I shouldn't think the newspapers'll be very kind to you, sir.

PASTOR MANDERS: No, that's just what I've been thinking. That's almost the worst part of the whole thing . . . all the spiteful insinuations and attacks. Oh, it's terrible to think about!

MRS ALVING [*coming in from the garden*]: I can't get him away from the fire.

PASTOR MANDERS: Ah, there you are, Mrs Alving.

MRS ALVING: So you won't have to make your speech, Mr Manders.

PASTOR MANDERS: Oh, I should have been only too happy . . .

MRS ALVING [*quietly*]: It's just as well things have happened like this. That Orphanage would never have come to any good.

PASTOR MANDERS: Don't you think so?

MRS ALVING: Do you?

PASTOR MANDERS: It was a very great misfortune, all the same.

MRS ALVING: Let's discuss it simply as a matter of business. Are you waiting for the Pastor, Engstrand?

ENGSTRAND [*at the hall door*]: Yes, that's right.

MRS ALVING: Then sit down for a minute or two.

ENGSTRAND: I'd rather stand, thank you.

MRS ALVING [*to Pastor Manders*]: You'll be going back by the steamer, I suppose?

PASTOR MANDERS: Yes, it sails in an hour's time.

MRS ALVING: Would you mind taking all the papers back with you? I don't want to hear another word about it – I've got other things to think of.

PASTOR MANDERS: Mrs Alving –

MRS ALVING: Later on, I'll send you a Power of Attorney to deal with everything as you think best.

PASTOR MANDERS: I'll gladly undertake that. The original terms of the bequest will have to be completely altered now, I'm afraid.

MRS ALVING: Obviously.

PASTOR MANDERS: I think, in the first place, I shall arrange for the Solvik property to pass to the Parish. The land is clearly not without a certain value – it's sure to come in useful for something or other. As to the interest on the rest of the capital in the bank – perhaps I could best use it to help some scheme that might be of use to the town.

MRS ALVING: Just as you like. I'm simply not interested in it any more.

ENGSTRAND: Remember my Seaman's Home, sir.

PASTOR MANDERS: Yes indeed, that's a suggestion. Well, I shall have to consider it.

ENGSTRAND: To hell with 'consider' – Oh Lor' . . . !

PASTOR MANDERS [*with a sigh*]: And unfortunately I don't know how long I shall have any say in it – public opinion may force me to give the whole thing up. It all depends on the result of the official inquiry into the fire.

MRS ALVING: What's that you say?

PASTOR MANDERS: And there's no knowing what the result may be.

ENGSTRAND [*coming close to him*]: Ah, but there is! There's always Jakob Engstrand.

PASTOR MANDERS: But . . .?

ENGSTRAND: And Jakob Engstrand isn't the man to desert a noble benefactor in his hour of need, as the saying goes.

PASTOR MANDERS: Yes, but my dear fellow, how –?

ENGSTRAND: Jakob Engstrand is like a guardian angel, sir, that's what he is.

PASTOR MANDERS: No no, I certainly couldn't allow that.

ENGSTRAND: Ah, you will in the end. Someone I know has taken the blame for another man once before.

PASTOR MANDERS: Jakob! [*Grasping his hand*] You're a man in a thousand! Well, you shall have help with your Seaman's Refuge – you can rely on that.

[ENGSTRAND *tries to thank him, but is choked with emotion.* PASTOR MANDERS *puts his satchel over his shoulder.*]

And now, let us go. We will travel together.

ENGSTRAND [*at the dining-room door, softly to* REGINA]: You come with me, my girl – you'll live as snug as the yolk in an egg!

REGINA [*with a toss of her head*]: Merci! [*She goes out into the hall to fetch the Pastor's overcoat.*]

PASTOR MANDERS: Good-bye, Mrs Alving. And I trust that the spirit of law and order may soon return to this house.

MRS ALVING: Good-bye, Mr Manders. [*She goes out into the conservatory as she sees* OSVALD *coming in from the garden.*]

ENGSTRAND [*as he and* REGINA *help* PASTOR MANDERS

on with his coat]: Good-bye, my child. And if ever
you're in any trouble, you know where you can find
Jakob Engstrand. [*Softly*] Little Harbour Street. Ahem!
[*To Mrs Alving and Osvald*] And the house for seafaring
men shall be called 'The Captain Alving Home', that it
shall! And if I can run the house in my own way, I think
I can promise that it'll be worthy of his memory.

PASTOR MANDERS [*at the door*]: Hm . . . Come along,
my good Engstrand. Good-bye, good-bye. [*He and
ENGSTRAND go out into the hall.*]

OSVALD [*going to the table*]: What's this house he was
talking about?

MRS ALVING: It's some sort of Home that he and Pastor
Manders want to start.

OSVALD: It'll burn, just like this one.

MRS ALVING: Why do you say that?

OSVALD: Everything'll burn, till there's nothing left to
remind people of my father. Here am I burning up, too.
[*REGINA gives him a startled look.*]

MRS ALVING: Osvald, my poor boy, you shouldn't have
stayed out there so long.

OSVALD [*sitting at the table*]: I rather think you're right.

MRS ALVING: How wet you are, Osvald – let me wipe
your face. [*She wipes his face with her handkerchief.*]

OSVALD [*staring ahead indifferently*]: Thank you, Mother.

MRS ALVING: Aren't you tired, Osvald? Wouldn't you like
a sleep?

OSVALD [*distressed*]: Not a sleep – no! I never sleep, I
only pretend to. [*Sadly*] That'll come soon enough.

MRS ALVING [*watching him anxiously*]: My darling boy,
you really are ill!

REGINA [*tensely*]: Is Mr Alving ill?

OSVALD [*irritably*]: And do shut all the doors! This deadly
fear . . .

MRS ALVING: Shut them, Regina.

[REGINA *does so, and remains standing at the hall door*. MRS ALVING *takes her shawl off, and so does* REGINA. MRS ALVING *draws up a chair beside Osvald's, and sits by him.*]

There now, I'll come and sit by you.

OSVALD: Yes, do. And Regina must stay in here too – Regina must be with me always. You'll give me a helping hand, won't you, Regina?

REGINA: I don't understand. . . .

MRS ALVING: A helping hand?

OSVALD: Yes, when I need one.

MRS ALVING: But Osvald, haven't you got your mother to give you a helping hand?

OSVALD: You? [*Smiling*] No, Mother, you would never give me this sort of helping hand. [*With a sad laugh*] Ha! Not you! [*Looking earnestly at her*] All the same, you'd be the best one to do it. [*Impetuously*] Regina, why do you have to be so formal with me? [22] Why don't you call me Osvald?

REGINA [*quietly*]: I don't think Madam would like that.

MRS ALVING: You'll soon have every right to. Now come and sit here with us, too.

[*After some hesitation,* REGINA *sits down quietly at the other side of the table.*]

And now, you poor unhappy boy, I'm going to take a weight off your mind. . . .

OSVALD: You, Mother?

MRS ALVING: All that remorse and self-reproach that you spoke of.

OSVALD: Do you really think you can?

MRS ALVING: Yes, Osvald, I can now. You happened to speak of the joy of living, and it was as if I suddenly saw my whole life, and all that had happened, in a new light.

OSVALD [*shaking his head*]: I don't understand.

MRS ALVING: I wish you could have known your father when he was a young subaltern. *He* had the joy of living, all right.

OSVALD: Yes, I know.

MRS ALVING: He was so full of vitality and boundless energy that it did your heart good just to see him.

OSVALD: Well?

MRS ALVING: And then this boy, so full of the joy of living – because he was like a boy in those days – had to live here in a second-rate town where there were no pleasures, but only dissipations. He had no aim in life, only an official position. He had no work that he could throw himself into heart and soul, only routine. Not a single one of his friends knew what the joy of living really meant – they were just idlers and topers . . .

OSVALD: Mother!

MRS ALVING: And so the inevitable happened.

OSVALD: The inevitable?

MRS ALVING: You said yourself this evening what would happen to you if you stayed at home.

OSVALD: Do you mean to say that my father . . . ?

MRS ALVING: Your poor father could never find any outlet for this overwhelming joy of living that was in him. And I didn't bring any sunshine into his life, either.

OSVALD: Not even you?

MRS ALVING: They'd taught me a lot about duty and so forth, and I'd long ago come to believe it. So everything was based on duty – my duty and his duty . . . and I'm afraid I made his home unbearable for your poor father, Osvald.

OSVALD: Why didn't you ever tell me anything about this in your letters?

MRS ALVING: Until now, I never saw it as a thing that I could talk about to you – his son.

OSVALD: How did you see it, then?

MRS ALVING [*slowly*]: I saw only the one fact: that your father was a broken man before you were born.

OSVALD [*softly*]: Ah . . . ! [*He gets up and goes to the window.*]

MRS ALVING: And then there was one thing in my mind day in and day out: that in fact Regina had as much right here in this house as my own son.

OSVALD [*turning quickly*]: Regina?

REGINA [*rising, and asking in a strangled voice*] I . . . ?

MRS ALVING: Yes. Now you both know.

OSVALD: Regina . . . !

REGINA [*to herself*]: So my mother was like that.

MRS ALVING: In many ways your mother was a fine woman, Regina.

REGINA: Yes, but she was like that all the same. I sometimes thought so, but . . . Madam, may I go away at once, please?

MRS ALVING: Do you really want to, Regina?

REGINA: Yes, I really want to.

MRS ALVING: You must do as you like, of course, but –

OSVALD [*going to her*]: Go away now? When you belong here?

REGINA: *Merci*, Mr Alving. . . . Well, I suppose I can call you Osvald now – though this wasn't quite the way I'd expected.

MRS ALVING: Regina, I haven't been quite frank with you.

REGINA: No, you certainly haven't. If I'd known that Osvald was ill, then . . . And seeing that there can never

be anything serious between us now . . . Oh no, I'm certainly not staying out here in the country to wear myself
out nursing the sick!

OSVALD: Not even someone as close to you as I am?

REGINA: No, certainly not. A poor girl's got to make the
best of her youth, or before she knows it she'll be left
out in the cold. *I*'ve got the joy of living in me, too,
Madam.

MRS ALVING: I'm afraid you have. But don't throw yourself away, Regina.

REGINA: Oh well, if I do, I *do*. If Osvald takes after his
father, I expect I take after my mother. May I ask if
Pastor Manders knows this about me, Madam?

MRS ALVING: Pastor Manders knows it all.

REGINA [*busy putting on her shawl*]: Well then, the best
thing I can do is to get away by the steamer as soon as I
can. The Pastor's very nice to deal with, and it looks to
me as if I've got as much right to a bit of that money as
that dirty carpenter.

MRS ALVING: You're welcome to it, Regina.

REGINA [*with a hard look at her*]: You might have brought
me up as a gentleman's daughter – it would have been
more fitting. [*Tossing her head*] Oh well, it's all the same
to me! [*With a bitter glance at the unopened bottle*]
Anyway, I may drink champagne with gentlefolks yet!

MRS ALVING: If you ever need a home, Regina, come to
me.

REGINA: No thank you, Madam; Pastor Manders'll look
after me all right. And, if the worst comes to the worst,
I know one house where I shall be at home.

MRS ALVING: Where?

REGINA: At Captain Alving's Refuge!

MRS ALVING: Regina, you'll go to the bad, I know you
will!

REGINA: Pooh! *Adieu.* [*She bows and goes out into the hall.*]

OSVALD [*standing and looking out of the window*]: Has she gone?

MRS ALVING: Yes.

OSVALD [*muttering to himself*]: I think that was stupid.

MRS ALVING [*coming behind him and putting her hands on his shoulders*]: Osvald, my dear, has this upset you very much?

OSVALD [*turning to face her*]: All this about Father, do you mean?

MRS ALVING: Yes, about your poor father. I'm so afraid it may have been too much for you.

OSVALD: What makes you think that? Of course it came as a great shock, but after all I don't see that it can really matter so much to me.

MRS ALVING [*taking her hands away*]: Not matter? That your father was so desperately unhappy?

OSVALD: Of course I'm sorry for him – I should be for anyone – but . . .

MRS ALVING: Is that all? Your own father?

OSVALD [*impatiently*]: Oh, 'my father – my father'![23] I never knew anything about my father. All I remember about him is that he once made me sick.

MRS ALVING: That's a terrible thought! Surely whatever happens a child should feel some love for his father.

OSVALD: Even when the child has nothing to thank his father for – when he's never even known him? Can you really cling to an old superstition like that?[24] You're so intelligent about things as a rule.

MRS ALVING: You call it just a superstition . . . !

OSVALD: Yes, can't you see, Mother? It's only one of those current ideas that the world gets hold of, and –

MRS ALVING [*troubled*]: Ghosts!

OSVALD [*pacing the floor*]: Yes, you might call them ghosts.

MRS ALVING [*violently*]: Then, Osvald, don't you love me, either?

OSVALD: I do know you, at any rate.

MRS ALVING: Yes, you know me – but is that all?

OSVALD: And of course I know how fond of me you are, and naturally I'm grateful to you for that. And you can be particularly useful to me now that I'm ill.

MRS ALVING: Yes I can, can't I, Osvald? Oh, I'm almost thankful that this illness has sent you home to me, because it's easy to see that you're not really mine yet – I shall have to win you over.

OSVALD [*impatiently*]: Oh yes – yes . . . all that's just so much talk! You must remember, Mother, that I'm a sick man; I can't be bothered much with other people – I have enough to do to think about myself.

MRS ALVING [*gently*]: I'll be patient, and easily pleased.

OSVALD: And cheerful, too, Mother.

MRS ALVING: Yes my dear, you're quite right. [*Going to him*] Now have I taken away all your remorse and self-reproach?

OSVALD: Yes, you have. But now who's going to take away my fear?

MRS ALVING: Fear?

OSVALD [*pacing the room*]: Regina would have done it for a single kind word.

MRS ALVING: I don't understand . . . What is this about fear? And about Regina?

OSVALD: Is it very late, Mother?

MRS ALVING: It's almost morning. [*Looking out through the conservatory*] The dawn's beginning to break on the hills. It's going to be a fine day, Osvald – in a little while you'll see the sun!

OSVALD: I'm glad of that. Oh, perhaps there'll be lots of things for me to be glad about – and to live for . . .

MRS ALVING: I'm sure there will.

OSVALD: Even if I can't work?

MRS ALVING: Oh my dear boy, you'll soon be able to work again. Now that you haven't got to go on brooding over all those depressing ideas of yours.

OSVALD: Yes, it's a great relief that you could rid me of all that. And when I've settled one thing more . . . [*Sitting on the sofa*] Mother, we must have a talk together.

MRS ALVING: Yes, let's. [*She pushes an armchair over to the sofa and sits near him.*]

OSVALD: And then the sun'll be up. And then you'll know – and I shan't have this fear any longer.

MRS ALVING: What shall I know?

OSVALD [*not listening*]: Mother, you know you said earlier in the evening that there was nothing in the world that you wouldn't do for me if I asked you?

MRS ALVING: Yes, that's what I said.

OSVALD: And you still mean it, Mother?

MRS ALVING: You can rely on me, my own darling boy; I've nothing else to live for but you.

OSVALD: Very well then, I'll tell you. Now, Mother, I know you're strongwilled – so when I tell you this, I want you to take it very calmly.

MRS ALVING: What is it that's so terrible?

OSVALD: Now listen, you mustn't scream – promise me you won't. We'll sit and talk it over quite quietly. Promise me, Mother.

MRS ALVING: Yes yes, I promise – but what is it?

OSVALD: Well, you must understand that this tiredness of mine, and this not being able to think about my work – that's not the actual illness . . .

MRS ALVING: What is the actual illness, then?

OSVALD: This disease that I've inherited – [*he points to his forehead and goes on very softly*] – is seated here.

MRS ALVING [*almost speechless*]: Osvald! No, no!

OSVALD: Don't scream, I couldn't bear it. Yes, it sits here and waits. And it may break out any day – any minute.

MRS ALVING: But that's terrible . . . !

OSVALD: Now keep quiet. That's how things are with me.

MRS ALVING [*starting up*]: It isn't true, Osvald. It's not possible – it *can't* be!

OSVALD: I had one attack when I was abroad. It was soon over; but when I found out how it had been, I began to be haunted by this ghastly fear, and I hurried home to you as quickly as I could.

MRS ALVING: Then this is the fear –

OSVALD: Yes, you see, it's so unspeakably loathsome . . . Oh, if only it had been an ordinary fatal illness . . . because I'm not afraid to die, although I'd like to live as long as I can.

MRS ALVING: Yes, Osvald, you must.

OSVALD: But this is so horribly loathsome. To become like a helpless child again; to have to be fed; to have to – Oh, I can't speak of it!

MRS ALVING: My child will have his mother to look after him.

OSVALD [*springing up*]: No, never! That's just what I don't want. [*Simply*] I daren't think that perhaps I might linger on like that for years – until I'm old and grey. And perhaps you might die before me. [*He sits in Mrs Alving's chair.*] Because the doctor told me it might not be fatal at once. He called it a kind of softening of the brain, or something of the sort. [*With a wan smile*] I think it sounds such a nice expression; it always makes me think of cherry-coloured velvet curtains – something soft to stroke.

MRS ALVING [*screaming*]: Osvald!

OSVALD [*springing up and pacing the room*]: And now you've taken Regina away from me. If only I'd had her – I know she would have given me a helping hand.

MRS ALVING [*going to him*]: My darling boy – what do you mean? Is there any help in the world that I wouldn't be glad to give you?

OSVALD: When I got over the attack that I had in France, the doctor told me that when the next one came – and it *would* come – then there'd be no more hope.

MRS ALVING: How callous of him to –

OSVALD: I insisted on it. I told him I had arrangements to make. [*With a cunning smile*] And so I had. [*Bringing out a little box from his inside breast pocket*] Look at these, Mother.

MRS ALVING: What are they?

OSVALD: Morphia.

MRS ALVING [*looking at him in horror*]: Osvald . . . oh my dear!

OSVALD: I've managed to scrape together twelve tablets.

MRS ALVING [*snatching at it*]: Give me that box, Osvald!

OSVALD: Not yet, Mother. [*He puts the box back in his pocket.*]

MRS ALVING: I shall never get over this.

OSVALD: You must. If I'd had Regina here, and if I'd told her how things were with me and begged her to give me a helping hand at the last, she'd have helped me, I'm sure of that.

MRS ALVING: Never.

OSVALD: When the horror overtook me, and she saw me lying there helpless, like a little new-born baby – beyond help, lost, hopeless – past all cure –

MRS ALVING: Regina would never have done it – never in her life.

OSVALD: Regina would have done it. Regina was so wonderfully carefree – and she'd soon have got tired of
looking after an invalid like me.

MRS ALVING: Then thank heaven Regina isn't here.

OSVALD: So now it's you who'll have to give me the helping hand, Mother.

MRS ALVING [*with a great cry*]: I?

OSVALD: Who better than you?

MRS ALVING: I? Your mother?

OSVALD: For that very reason.

MRS ALVING: But I gave you your life!

OSVALD: I never asked you for life. And what sort of a
life have you given me? I won't have it – you can take
it back.

MRS ALVING: Help! Help! [*She runs out into the hall.*]

OSVALD [*following*]: Don't leave me! Where are you
going?

MRS ALVING [*in the hall*]: To fetch the doctor for you,
Osvald. Let me go out.

OSVALD [*also in the hall*]: You're not going out! And no
one's coming in.

[*A key is turned.*]

MRS ALVING [*returning*]: Osvald – Osvald, my child!

OSVALD [*following her in*]: Do you call this a mother's
love for me – to watch me suffering this unspeakable
terror?

MRS ALVING [*after a moment's silence – controlling her
voice*]: Here is my hand on it.

OSVALD: Will you . . . ?

MRS ALVING: If it's ever necessary. But it won't be necessary . . . no no, that's not possible.

OSVALD: Well . . . let's hope it isn't. And we'll live together
as long as we can. Thank you, Mother.

[*He sits in the armchair that Mrs Alving had moved*

*over to the sofa. Day is breaking. The lamp is still
alight on the table.*]

MRS ALVING: Do you feel easier now?

OSVALD: Yes.

MRS ALVING [*bending over him*]: This was just a terrible
delusion of yours, Osvald – only a delusion. All this
excitement has been too much for you, but now you
shall have a rest – at home with your own mother, my
dearest boy. You shall have everything you want, the
way you did when you were a little boy. There! It's all
over now. You see how simple it was – I knew it would
be. And look, Osvald, we're going to have a lovely day –
bright sunshine. Now you'll really be able to see your
home!

[*She goes to the table and puts out the lamp. The sun
rises; the glaciers and the peaks in the distance glow
in the morning light.*]

OSVALD [*sitting in the armchair with his back to the view,
suddenly speaks without moving*]: Mother, give me the
sun.

MRS ALVING [*at the table, looking at him with a start*]:
What did you say?

OSVALD [*again, dully and without expression*]: The sun
... the sun. ...

MRS ALVING [*going to him*]: Osvald – what's the matter?
[OSVALD *seems to shrink in the chair; all his muscles
go slack, his face is without expression, and his eyes
stare vacantly.*]

MRS ALVING [*shaking with fear*]: What is it? [*With a
loud scream*] Osvald – what's wrong? [*Falling on her
knees beside him and shaking him*] Osvald! Osvald, look
at me – don't you know me?

OSVALD [*still tonelessly*]: The sun, the sun ...

MRS ALVING [*springing up in despair, grasping her hair in*

both hands, screams]: I can't bear it! [*Whispering as though paralysed*] I can't bear it . . . never! [*Suddenly*] Where did he put them? [*Hurriedly feeling in his coat*] Here! [*She shrinks back a few paces and cries*] No no no . . . Yes! No no. . . .[25]

[*She stands a step or two away from him, with her hands twisted in her hair, staring at him in speechless horror.*]

OSVALD [*sitting motionless as before, says*]: The sun . . . the sun.

A PUBLIC ENEMY[26]

A Play in Five Acts

CHARACTERS

———————— ✱ ————————

DR TOMAS STOCKMANN, Medical Officer at the Baths [27]
MRS STOCKMANN, his wife
PETRA, their daughter, a teacher

EYLIF
MORTEN } their sons, aged thirteen and ten

PETER STOCKMANN, the Doctor's elder brother, Mayor and Chief of Police, Chairman of the Governors of the Baths

MORTEN KIIL, owner of a tannery, Mrs Stockmann's foster-father

HOVSTAD, Editor of the *People's Herald*

BILLING, his colleague on the paper

CAPTAIN HORSTER

ASLAKSEN, a printer [28]

The crowd at a public meeting: men of all walks of life, a few women, and a number of schoolboys

The action takes place in a seaside town in southern Norway

ACT ONE

———————— * ————————

The Doctor's living-room. It is evening.
The furniture and decorations are simple but neat. In the
side wall to the right there are two doors – the farther leads
to the hall, the nearer to the Doctor's study. In the opposite
wall, facing the hall door, is a door leading to the rest of
the house; the stove stands in the middle of this wall, and
farther forward is a sofa with a mirror hanging above it.
In the centre is an oval table with a cloth, and on it a
lighted lamp with a shade.
In the back wall, an open door leads to the dining-room,
where a table with a lamp on it is laid for supper.

> [BILLING *is sitting at the dining-table, with a napkin*
> *tucked under his chin;* MRS STOCKMANN *stands*
> *by the table, handing him a plate with a great*
> *slice of roast beef. The other places at the table are*
> *empty, and the table is untidy, as if supper were*
> *over.*]

MRS STOCKMANN: You've come an hour late, Mr Billing,
so you mustn't mind if it's cold.

BILLING [*eating*]: It's very good indeed – really delicious.

MRS STOCKMANN: You know how particular the Doctor
is about having his meals punctually.

BILLING: It doesn't matter a bit. I always think a meal
tastes better when I can sit and eat it all by myself, undisturbed.

MRS STOCKMANN: Oh well, as long as you enjoy it. . . .

[*Listening at the hall door*] And I expect this'll be Mr Hovstad coming now.

BILLING: Probably.

[PETER STOCKMANN, *the Mayor, comes in; he is wearing an overcoat, and has his mayoral hat and staff.*[29]]

THE MAYOR: Good evening, my dear sister-in-law.

MRS STOCKMANN [*coming into the living-room*]: Oh, it's you. Good evening; how nice of you to come and see us.

THE MAYOR: I just happened to be passing, so . . . [*Glancing into the dining-room*] Ah, but I see you have company.

MRS STOCKMANN [*rather embarrassed*]: No, not really – it just so happens . . . [*Quickly*] Won't you go in and have something too?

THE MAYOR: I? No thank you. Hot meat at night? [30] Good heavens, not with my indigestion!

MRS STOCKMANN: Oh, just for once. . . .

THE MAYOR: No no, thank you very much. I confine myself to my bread and butter and tea; it's a great deal more healthy in the long run – and also somewhat more economical.

MRS STOCKMANN [*smiling*]: Now, you mustn't think that Tomas and I are at all extravagant.

THE MAYOR: Not *you*, my dear sister-in-law – far be it from me to think *that*. [*Pointing to the Doctor's study*] Is he at home, by any chance?

MRS STOCKMANN: No, he went out for a little walk with the boys after supper.

THE MAYOR: I doubt if that could be good for him. [*Listening*] Here he comes now.

MRS STOCKMANN: No, he won't be back yet. [*A knock on the door*] Come in!

[HOVSTAD, *the editor, comes in from the hall.*]

Ah, here's Mr Hovstad.

HOVSTAD: Yes, do forgive me, I was held up by the printers. Good evening, Mr Mayor.

THE MAYOR [*bowing rather stiffly*]: Good evening. You're here on business, I presume?

HOVSTAD: Partly; there's something I want to put in the paper.

THE MAYOR: I thought as much. I hear that my brother has become quite a prolific contributor to the *People's Herald.*[31]

HOVSTAD: Yes, he's good enough to write for the *Herald* whenever he has anything he wants to say about this or that.

MRS STOCKMANN [*to Hovstad*]: But won't you . . . ? [*She points to the dining-room.*]

THE MAYOR: Mind you, I don't blame him in the least for writing for that circle of readers in which he feels he's most likely to obtain a sympathetic hearing. Not that I, personally, have cause to bear your paper any ill-will, Mr Hovstad.

HOVSTAD: No, I don't think you have.

THE MAYOR: Taken all in all, there's a splendid spirit of tolerance here in our town – a really good municipal spirit. And it all springs from our having a great common interest to unite us – an interest which is of equal concern to every right-minded citizen.

HOVSTAD: Yes, the Baths.

THE MAYOR: Precisely . . . we have our splendid, handsome new Bathing Establishment. Mark my words, Mr Hovstad, the Baths will become the very heart of our municipal life. There is no doubt of that.

MRS STOCKMANN: That's just what Tomas says.

THE MAYOR: It's quite extraordinary what strides the

town has made in these past few years. Money has been pouring in; there's life and movement everywhere; and land and house-property values are rising every day.

HOVSTAD: And unemployment is falling.

THE MAYOR: That is so, yes. There has been a most welcome reduction in the Poor Rate, which has taken a considerable burden from the landed classes. And there'll be a still greater reduction if we have a good summer this year to bring us a large influx of visitors – and plenty of invalids to spread the fame of the Baths.

HOVSTAD: I gather there's a reasonable chance of that.

THE MAYOR: It certainly appears highly promising. Inquiries about apartments and so forth are pouring in.

HOVSTAD: So the Doctor's article will come at just the right time.

THE MAYOR: Has he written something new?

HOVSTAD: It's something he wrote last winter – recommending the Baths and setting out our excellent health record here. I held it over for the time being.

THE MAYOR: Ah, something not quite satisfactory about it, perhaps?

HOVSTAD: No, nothing like that. I simply thought it'd be better to keep it till now, because the spring's the time when people think about their plans for the summer.

THE MAYOR: Very true. You were perfectly right, Mr Hovstad.

MRS STOCKMANN: Yes, Tomas never spares himself when it's to do with the Baths.

THE MAYOR: Well, seeing that he's on the staff . . .

HOVSTAD: Yes . . . And of course it was he who started the Baths in the first place.

THE MAYOR: He? Indeed? Yes, I have heard from time to time that there are certain people who hold that opinion.

But I certainly imagined that I, too, had a modest share in the enterprise.

MRS STOCKMANN: Yes, that's what Tomas always says.

HOVSTAD: Ah, nobody denies that, Mr Mayor; everyone knows that it was you who got the whole thing going, and put it on a practical footing. I only meant that the original idea came from the Doctor.

THE MAYOR: Oh yes, my brother has had a great many ideas in his time – unfortunately. But it takes a very different type of man to put a project on a practical basis. I should certainly have expected that in this house of all places –

MRS STOCKMANN: But my dear Peter –

HOVSTAD: Surely you don't think –

MRS STOCKMANN: Mr Hovstad, won't you go in and have something to eat? I'm sure my husband'll be back directly.

HOVSTAD: Thank you, perhaps I *will* just have a bite. [*He goes into the dining-room.*]

THE MAYOR [*dropping his voice a little*]: It's extraordinary how these people who come of peasant stock never seem to overcome their tactlessness.

MRS STOCKMANN: But surely it's not worth worrying about? Can't you and Tomas share the honour? You *are* brothers.

THE MAYOR: I should have thought we could, but apparently for some people a share is not sufficient!

MRS STOCKMANN: Oh, that's nonsense. You and Tomas get on very well together. [*Listening*] Here he is, I think. [*She goes and opens the hall door.*]

DR STOCKMANN [*laughing and talking boisterously outside*]: Look, here's another visitor for you, Katrina; isn't that splendid, eh? Come in, Captain Horster – hang your overcoat on that peg – Oh, no, of course you don't wear one, do you? [32] What do you think, Katrina — I met him in the street and I could hardly get him to come up here with me.

[CAPTAIN HORSTER *comes in and bows to Mrs Stockmann.* DR STOCKMANN *appears in the doorway.*] In you go, you boys! They're starving again, Katrina! Come along in, Captain Horster, you must have a slice of roast beef.

[*He pushes Horster into the dining-room;* EYLIF *and* MORTEN *follow them.*]

MRS STOCKMANN: But Tomas, haven't you noticed . . . ?

DR STOCKMANN [*turning in the doorway*]: Ah, Peter, it's you! [*Going to him with outstretched hand*] Well, this is really splendid!

THE MAYOR: Unfortunately I must be going in a moment.

DR STOCKMANN: Nonsense! There'll be some hot toddy any minute now. You haven't forgotten the toddy, Katrina?

MRS STOCKMANN: Of course not; the kettle's just on the boil. [*She goes into the dining-room.*]

THE MAYOR: Toddy, too?

DR STOCKMANN: Yes; now sit down and be comfortable.

THE MAYOR: Thank you, I never join in drinking-parties.

DR STOCKMANN: But this isn't a party.

THE MAYOR: It has that appearance to me. [*Looking towards the dining-room*] It's extraordinary how they can consume so much food!

DR STOCKMANN [*rubbing his hands*]: Yes, it does your heart good to see young people eat, doesn't it? They're always hungry — and so they should be! Plenty of meat to build up their strength. They're the ones who'll have to stir things up and keep them on the move for the future, Peter.

THE MAYOR: May I ask just what there is here that requires 'stirring up', as you term it?

DR STOCKMANN: You'll have to ask the young people about that – when the time comes. *We* obviously shan't see it – two old fogies like you and me.

THE MAYOR: Really! That's a most offensive expression!

DR STOCKMANN: Oh, you mustn't take me too literally, Peter; it's just that I'm in such excellent spirits today. I feel so indescribably happy at being a part of all this teeming, flourishing life. It's a wonderful age we're living in – it's as though a whole world were springing up around us!

THE MAYOR: Do you really think so?

DR STOCKMANN: Of course you wouldn't appreciate it as much as I do – you've lived in it all your life, and that blunts the impression. But after all those years stuck away in that wretched hole up north, hardly ever seeing a soul to exchange an intelligent word with, all this affects me as if I'd been transported into the heart of a teeming metropolis!

THE MAYOR: 'Metropolis?' Hm.

DR STOCKMANN: Of course I know there are plenty of places that make it look small – but there's *life* here, there's promise, there are innumerable causes to work and fight for – that's the thing that matters! [*Calling*] Katrina! Hasn't the postman been?

MRS STOCKMANN [*from the dining-room*]: No, nothing's come.

DR STOCKMANN: And then to be getting a good salary, Peter! That's something you learn to appreciate when you've been living, like us, on a starvation wage.

THE MAYOR: Oh, surely –

DR STOCKMANN: Yes, I don't mind telling you, things were often very hard for us up there. And now to be able to live like a lord . . . ! Take today: we had roast beef for luncheon, and we've had some for supper too. Won't you have a bit? Well, at any rate, let me show it to you. Come here.

THE MAYOR: No no, certainly not.

DR STOCKMANN: Well then, come over here. . . . Look, we've got a new tablecloth!

THE MAYOR: Yes, so I perceive.

DR STOCKMANN: And a lampshade, too. Look! All out of Katrina's savings. It makes the room look cosy, doesn't it? Just stand here . . . no no, not there, *here* . . . that's it! Now just look how all the light's concentrated in one place. I think it looks really lovely, don't you?

THE MAYOR: Yes – if one can afford such luxuries.

DR STOCKMANN: Oh, I can afford it now. Katrina says I'm earning almost as much as we spend.

THE MAYOR: 'Almost', yes.

DR STOCKMANN: But a man of science must live in a certain amount of style. I'm quite sure even an ordinary county magistrate spends more in a year than I do![33]

THE MAYOR: I should think so, indeed! A county magistrate is a most important person!

DR STOCKMANN: Well, a mere businessman, then. That sort of fellow spends much more –

THE MAYOR: These things are only relative.

DR STOCKMANN: And after all, Peter, I really don't squander my money. But I can't deny myself the pleasure of having people to the house – I insist on that, you know. I've lived without it for so long that it's the very breath of life for me to mix with bright, cheerful, hard-working, liberal-minded young fellows – and that's what they all are in there, sitting and eating so heartily. I wish you knew Hovstad a bit better. . . .

THE MAYOR: Yes, that reminds me: Hovstad was telling me that he means to print another article of yours.

DR STOCKMANN: An article of mine?

THE MAYOR: Yes, about the Baths. An article that you wrote last winter.

DR STOCKMANN: Oh, that one. Well, I'd rather that didn't appear for the time being.

THE MAYOR: Oh? This seems to me to be exactly the moment for it.

DR STOCKMANN: Yes, I'd agree with you – under ordinary circumstances. [*He paces about the room.*]

THE MAYOR [*following him with his eyes*]: What is un-usual about the present circumstances?

DR STOCKMANN [*coming to a halt*]: I can't really tell you for the moment, Peter – not this evening, at any rate. There could be a great deal that's very unusual about the circumstances . . . on the other hand, there may be nothing at all. Very likely it's just my imagination.

THE MAYOR: I must say it all sounds most mysterious. Is there something wrong – something that's being kept from me? As Chairman of the Board of Management of the Baths, I should have thought that *I* –

DR STOCKMANN: And I should have thought that *I* . . . Oh come, Peter, don't let's lose our hair with one another.

THE MAYOR: Heaven forbid! I'm not in the habit of 'losing my hair', as you term it. But whatever is going on, I must absolutely insist that it is carried out in a businesslike manner, through the properly constituted authorities for dealing with such matters. I cannot be a party to any crooked or underhand methods.

DR STOCKMANN: Now have I ever used crooked or underhand methods?

THE MAYOR: You have an ingrained tendency to go your own way, whatever the circumstances – and in a well-ordered community that is almost as reprehensible. The individual must subordinate himself to Society as a whole – or rather, to those authorities whose duty it is to watch over the welfare of Society.

DR STOCKMANN: Probably . . . but what the devil has it got to do with me?

THE MAYOR: That, my good Tomas, is precisely what you will never learn. Be careful, that's all; mark my words: one day, sooner or later, you'll have to pay for it. Good night.

DR STOCKMANN: Have you gone off your head? You're on the wrong track altogether.

THE MAYOR: I'm not in the habit of being wrong. And now you must excuse me. [*He bows towards the dining-room.*] Good night, Katrina; good night, gentlemen. [*He goes.*]

MRS STOCKMANN [*coming into the living-room*]: Has he gone?

DR STOCKMANN: Yes, and in a flaming temper, too!

MRS STOCKMANN: Oh Tomas, what have you been doing to him now?

DR STOCKMANN: Nothing at all! He really can't expect me to give him an account of things before they happen!

MRS STOCKMANN: What is there to give him an account of?

DR STOCKMANN: Aha – never you mind about that, Katrina. . . . It's odd that the postman hasn't been.

[HOVSTAD, BILLING, *and* HORSTER *have got up from the table and come into the living-room. After a moment,* EYLIF *and* MORTEN *follow them.*]

BILLING [*stretching*]: Ah! After a meal like that, you feel a new man, I'm hanged if you don't.

HOVSTAD: The Mayor wasn't in the best of tempers this evening.

DR STOCKMANN: It's his stomach – he has terrible indigestion.

HOVSTAD: What he found hard to stomach was us two from the *People's Herald*!

MRS STOCKMANN: I thought you seemed to be getting on quite well with him.

HOVSTAD: Oh yes, but it wasn't any more than a sort of temporary truce.

BILLING: That's it! That's exactly the word for it.

DR STOCKMANN: We mustn't forget that Peter's a lonely man, poor fellow. He doesn't have any private life or home comforts – only business, nothing but business. And then there's all that infernal weak tea he's always pouring down his throat! Now then, you boys, bring chairs up to the table! Aren't we going to have any toddy, Katrina?

MRS STOCKMANN [*on her way to the dining-room*]: I'm just bringing it.

DR STOCKMANN: Now, Captain Horster, you sit here on the sofa with me – we never see anything of you . . . Do sit down, everybody.

[*The men sit at the table;* MRS STOCKMANN *brings in a tray with a spirit-lamp, glasses, decanters, and so on.*]

MRS STOCKMANN: Here we are. This is arrack, this one's rum, and here's the brandy. Now you must all help yourselves.

DR STOCKMANN [*taking a glass*]: We certainly will! [*While the toddy is being prepared*] Now the cigars . . . Eylif, I'm sure you know where the box is – and, Morten, you can get my pipe. [*The boys go out to the study.*] I have a suspicion that Eylif sneaks a cigar from time to time, but I pretend not to notice.[34] [*Calls*] And my smoking cap, Morten! Katrina, you remember where I left it, don't you? . . . Ah, he's got it. [*The boys bring in the various things.*] Now, help yourselves, my dear fellows. I'll stick to my pipe – this one's seen me through a good many rough journeys up there in the north! [*They clink glasses.*] Skol! Ah, it's certainly better to be sitting snug and warm here!

MRS STOCKMANN [*settling down with her knitting*]: Will you be sailing soon, Captain Horster?

HORSTER: I'll be ready next week, I expect.

MRS STOCKMANN: And you're going to America?

HOVSTAD: Yes, that's the idea.

BILLING: So you won't be here to vote for the new Town Council?

HORSTER: Is there going to be another election?

BILLING: Didn't you know?

HORSTER: No, I don't bother with that sort of thing.

BILLING: But surely you take an interest in local politics?

HORSTER: No, I simply don't understand them.

BILLING: Still, everyone ought at least to vote.

HORSTER: Even people who don't understand what it's all about?

BILLING: Not understand? I don't see what you mean. Society's like a ship – every man must put his hand to the helm.

HORSTER: That might be all right on land, but it wouldn't work at sea.

HOVSTAD: It's odd how little interest sailors in general take in shore affairs.

BILLING: Quite extraordinary.

DR STOCKMANN: Sailors are like birds of passage – they feel just as much at home in the south as in the north . . . so the rest of us have to be all the more diligent. Will there be anything particularly interesting in tomorrow's *Herald*, Mr Hovstad?

HOVSTAD: No local news – but the day after tomorrow I thought I'd print your article –

DR STOCKMANN: Oh lord, that confounded article! Look, you'll have to hold it over.

HOVSTAD: Oh? We've got just the space for it, and it seems to me that this is exactly the right time –

DR STOCKMANN: Yes yes, I'm sure you're right; but you must hold it over all the same. I'll explain later.

[PETRA *comes in from the hall, in hat and cloak, and with a bundle of exercise books under her arm.*]

PETRA: Good evening.

DR STOCKMANN: Ah, good evening, Petra.

[*General greetings.* PETRA *leaves her things on a chair near the door.*]

PETRA: Here you all are sitting down and enjoying yourselves, while I've been out slaving!

DR STOCKMANN: Well, come along and enjoy yourself too!

BILLING: Let me mix you a little drink.

PETRA [*coming to the table*]: I'd better help myself, thank you – you always make it too strong. Oh, by the way, Father, I've got a letter for you. [*She goes to the chair where her things are.*]

DR STOCKMANN: A letter? Who from?

PETRA [*feeling in her coat pocket*]: I got it from the postman just as I was going out, and –

DR STOCKMANN [*getting up and going over to her*]: And you don't give it to me till now!

PETRA: I just hadn't time to run up again. Here it is.

DR STOCKMANN [*grabbing the letter*]: Let me see, child, let me see! [*Looking at the address*] Yes, this is it!

MRS STOCKMANN: Is it the one you've been wanting so much, Tomas?

DR STOCKMANN: Yes, it is! I must go to my room at once

and – I shall want a light, Katrina; I suppose, as usual, there's no lamp in my study!

MRS STOCKMANN: Yes, there's a lamp on your desk, and it's lit.

DR STOCKMANN: Splendid! Excuse me a moment. [*He goes out into the room on the right.*]

PETRA: What's all that about, Mother?

MRS STOCKMANN: I don't know; but these last few days he's been watching for the postman.

BILLING: Probably some patient out in the country.

PETRA: Poor Father; he'll soon have more work than he can manage. [*Mixing her drink*] There, that should be nice.

HOVSTAD: Have you been teaching in night-school again today?

PETRA [*sipping her drink*]: For two hours.

BILLING: And four hours at the Institute in the morning –!

PETRA [*sitting at the table*]: Five!

MRS STOCKMANN: And I see you have exercise books to correct this evening.

PETRA: A whole bundle, yes.

HORSTER: It looks as if you're quite a busy person, too.

PETRA: Yes, but I like it; you feel so delightfully tired at the end of it.

BILLING: Do you like that?

PETRA: Yes, then you get a good night's sleep.

MORTEN: You must be terribly wicked, Petra.

PETRA: Wicked?

MORTEN: Yes, because you work so hard. Mr Rørlund says that work is a punishment for our sins.

EYLIF [*snorting*]: Pooh! What a silly you are to believe a thing like that!

MRS STOCKMANN: Now, now, Eylif!

BILLING [*laughing*]: That's a good one!

HOVSTAD: So you wouldn't like to work so hard, Morten?

MORTEN: No, I wouldn't.

HOVSTAD: Well, what are you going to be when you grow up?

MORTEN: Most of all, I'd like to be a Viking – that's what I'd like.

EYLIF: But then you'd have to be a heathen.

MORTEN: Well then, I'd *be* a heathen.

BILLING: I quite agree, Morten, that's just what *I* say.

MRS STOCKMANN [*signalling to him*]: No no, Mr Billing; I'm sure you don't really.

BILLING: I'm hanged if I don't! I'm a heathen and proud of it. You wait, soon we'll all be heathens!

MORTEN: And then we'll be able to do anything we like, won't we?

BILLING: Yes, you see, Morten –

MRS STOCKMANN: Run along now, boys; I'm sure you must have some homework to do for tomorrow.

EYLIF: Oh, can't I stay a *bit* longer?

MRS STOCKMANN: No. Off you go, both of you.

[*The boys say good night, and go into the room on the left.*]

HOVSTAD: Do you really think it can hurt the boys to hear that sort of thing?

MRS STOCKMANN: I don't know. I just don't like it.

PETRA: Oh Mother, I think that's silly.

MRS STOCKMANN: Probably, but I don't like it – not in our own house.

PETRA: There seems to be nothing but hypocrisy, whether it's at school, or here at home! At home you have to hold your tongue, and at school you have to stand up and tell lies to the children!

HORSTER: Tell lies?

PETRA: Yes. Do you think we don't have to teach them all sorts of things that we don't believe in ourselves?

BILLING: Yes, that's very true.

PETRA: If only I had the money, I'd start a school of my own, and everything'd be very different *there*.

BILLING: Ah, the money. . . .

HORSTER: If you really mean it, Miss Stockmann, I'd willingly let you have room at my house. That huge old place of my father's is practically empty; there's an enormous dining-room on the ground floor —[35]

PETRA [*laughing*]: Oh, it's very kind of you . . . but it wouldn't really ever come to anything.

HOVSTAD: No, if you ask me, Miss Petra's much more likely to go over to journalism. By the way, have you had time to look at that English novel that you promised to translate for us?

PETRA: Not yet, but you shall have it in plenty of time.

[DR STOCKMANN *comes out of his room with the open letter in his hand.*]

DR STOCKMANN [*flourishing the letter*]: Well, here's some news that'll surprise the town, I can tell you!

BILLING: News?

MRS STOCKMANN: What sort of news?

DR STOCKMANN: A great discovery, Katrina!

HOVSTAD: Oh?

MRS STOCKMANN: A discovery of yours?

DR STOCKMANN: Yes, mine! [*Pacing up and down*] *Now* let them come, in their usual way, saying it's all imagina- tion – just a crazy idea! But they won't dare! Aha, I don't think they'll dare!

PETRA: But Father, do tell us what it is!

DR STOCKMANN: All right, all right – just give me time, and you'll hear all about it. If only Peter were still here!

It just shows how we can go about thinking we know everything, and yet be blinder than moles!

HOVSTAD: What do you mean, Doctor?

DR STOCKMANN [*coming to a stop by the table*]: This town's generally supposed to be a healthy place, isn't it?

HOVSTAD: Yes, everyone knows that.

DR STOCKMANN: A quite exceptionally healthy place, even? A place to be highly recommended not only for invalids, but for healthy folk too?

MRS STOCKMANN: But Tomas dear –

DR STOCKMANN: And we've been recommending it and praising it? I've written about it – in the *Herald* and in pamphlets – time and again.

HOVSTAD: Of course – but what . . . ?

DR STOCKMANN: These Baths, that are known as 'the main artery of the town', its 'chief nerve centre', and – and the devil only knows what else –

BILLING: 'The town's pulsating heart' I once called them in a convivial moment . . .

DR STOCKMANN: Yes, that too. But do you know what they really are – these splendid highly recommended Baths that have cost so much money? D'you know what they are?

HOVSTAD: No, what?

MRS STOCKMAN: Well, what are they?

DR STOCKMANN: The whole Baths are a pesthouse!

PETRA: The Baths, Father?

MRS STOCKMANN [*at the same time*]: Our Baths?

HOVSTAD [*also overlapping them*]: But Doctor . . . ?

BILLING: But that's incredible!

DR STOCKMANN: I tell you, the whole Baths are a poisonous whited sepulchre – the greatest possible danger to health! All that filth up at Mølledal – all that foul-smelling stuff – is polluting the water in the mains that lead to the Pump Room. What's more, the filthy infected muck seeps down to the beach —

HORSTER: Where the sea-bathing is?

DR STOCKMANN: Exactly.

HOVSTAD: But Doctor, how can you be so sure of all this?

DR STOCKMANN: I've made the most careful investigations I possibly could. Oh, I've had my suspicions of something of the sort for a long time. Last year there were some very strange cases of illness among the visitors — there were stomach upsets, and even typhoid . . .

MRS STOCKMANN: Yes, so there were.

DR STOCKMANN: At the time we thought the visitors must have brought the infection with them. But afterwards — last winter — I began to have other ideas, and I started to analyse the water as best I could.

MRS STOCKMANN: So *that* was what you were working at so hard!

DR STOCKMANN: Yes, Katrina, you may well say that I worked hard. But of course I hadn't the necessary scientific equipment here, so I sent samples of both our drinking-water and the sea water to the University for a complete analysis by an expert.

HOVSTAD: And now it's come?

DR STOCKMANN [showing the letter]: Here it is! This is proof that there's putrefying organic matter present in the water — millions of infusoria. This water, used either internally or externally, is a positive menace to health!

MRS STOCKMANN: What a blessing you've found it out in time!

DR STOCKMANN: You may well say so!

HOVSTAD: And what do you mean to do now, Doctor?

DR STOCKMANN: Why, put things right, of course.

HOVSTAD: Can that be done?

DR STOCKMANN: It must be done. Otherwise the whole

Baths will be useless – ruined! But there's no need for that! I'm quite clear about what must be done.

MRS STOCKMANN: But Tomas dear, why have you kept it all so secret?

DR STOCKMANN: You think I should have run round the town chattering about it before I had absolute proof? No thanks, I'm not quite as mad as that!

PETRA: Well, you might have told *us*. . . .

DR STOCKMANN: Not a living soul! But tomorrow you may run round to old Badger's –

MRS STOCKMANN: Now, Tomas –!

DR STOCKMANN: Well then, to your grandfather's. It'll give the old fellow quite a surprise; he thinks I'm not quite right in the head – yes, and I notice there are plenty of others who think the same. But now these good people are going to see – oh yes, they shall see, all right! [*He walks round rubbing his hands.*] There'll be such a commotion in the town, Katrina. Just think of it – all the conduits'll have to be relaid.

HOVSTAD [*rising*]: All the conduits?

DR STOCKMANN: Well, of course. The intake's too low – it'll have to be moved to a point much higher up.

PETRA: So you were right after all?

DR STOCKMANN: Ah, you remember, Petra: when it was first started, I wrote opposing the plan, but no one would listen to me then. Well, now I'm going to let them have it, you can be quite sure of that. Of course I've written a report to the Board of Governors – I've had it ready for a whole week; I've just been waiting for this. [*Holding up the letter*] Now it shall go off at once. [*He goes to his room, and comes back with a sheaf of papers.*] Look! Four closely written pages! And I'll put in this letter too. Give me something to wrap them in – a newspaper, Katrina. There, that's it. Give it to – to – [*Stamps his foot*] What the devil's her name? – give it to the maid, and tell her to take it straight to the Mayor. [MRS STOCKMANN *takes the packet and goes out through the dining-room.*]

PETRA: What do you think Uncle Peter'll say, Father?

DR STOCKMANN: What can he say? He's bound to be glad that such an important fact has been brought to light.

HOVSTAD: May I print a short article on your discovery in the *Herald*?

DR STOCKMANN: Yes, I should be very grateful if you would.

HOVSTAD: The public ought to hear about it as soon as possible.

DR STOCKMANN: I quite agree.

MRS STOCKMANN [*coming back*]: She's just gone with it.

BILLING: I'm hanged if this won't make you the most important man in the town, Doctor.

DR STOCKMANN [*pacing about with delight*]: Oh nonsense – After all, I haven't done any more than my duty. I've made a lucky find, that's all. But all the same . . .

BILLING: Hovstad, don't you think the town ought to get up a procession in Dr Stockmann's honour?

HOVSTAD: I shall certainly suggest it.

BILLING: And I'll have a word with Aslaksen about it.

DR STOCKMANN: No, my dear friends; don't let's have any of that sort of nonsense. I simply won't hear of anything of the kind. And if the Board should happen to raise my salary, I won't accept it. Do you hear, Katrina, I won't accept it.

MRS STOCKMANN: You're quite right, Tomas.

HOVSTAD and BILLING: Your health; your very good health, Doctor.

HORSTER [*touching glasses with the Doctor*]: I hope this'll bring you nothing but happiness.

DR STOCKMANN: Thank you, my dear friends, thank you! I'm so happy . . .! It's wonderful for a man to feel that he's done a service to his fellow citizens and his native town. Hurrah, Katrina!

[*He flings both arms round Mrs Stockmann's neck and whirls her round, while she screams and struggles. Everyone laughs, clapping and cheering the Doctor. The boys poke their heads in at the door.*]

ACT TWO

————— * —————

[*The Doctor's living-room; morning. The door to the dining-room is shut, till* MRS STOCKMANN *comes through it with a sealed letter in her hand. She goes to the nearest door on the right, and peeps in.*]

MRS STOCKMANN: Are you back, Tomas?

DR STOCKMANN [*off*]: Yes, I've just come in. [*Entering*] What is it?

MRS STOCKMANN: There's a letter from your brother. [*Giving it to him.*]

DR STOCKMANN: Ah, let's see. . . . [*He opens the envelope and reads*] 'I have received the enclosed communition, and return it herewith. . . .' [*He reads on under his breath.*] Hm . . .

MRS STOCKMANN: What does he say?

DR STOCKMANN [*stuffing the letter into his pocket*]: Nothing. Just that he's coming up here himself about noon.

MRS STOCKMANN: You must remember to stay at home, then.

DR STOCKMANN: That'll be all right; I've done all my visits for this morning.

MRS STOCKMANN: I shall be very interested to see how he takes it.

DR STOCKMANN: You'll find he won't like it that I made the discovery rather than him.

MRS STOCKMANN: Yes, I'm a bit worried about that, aren't you?

DR STOCKMANN: Oh, at heart he'll be quite glad, you know. All the same, Peter's always so confoundedly jealous when someone besides himself does anything for the good of the town.

MRS STOCKMANN: You know, Tomas, it'd be very nice of you if you'd share the honour with him. Couldn't you make it look as if it was he who put you on the trail?

DR STOCKMANN: Yes. It doesn't matter to me – not as long as I can get things put right.

[Old MORTEN KIIL *puts his head in through the hall door, and looks round inquisitively, chuckling to himself.*] [36]

KIIL [*slyly*]: Is it – is it true?

MRS STOCKMANN [*going to him*]: Oh, it's you, Father.

DR STOCKMANN: Ah, good morning, good morning.[37]

MRS STOCKMANN: Well, do come in.

KIIL: I will if it's true; if it isn't, I'm off again.

DR STOCKMANN: If what's true?

KIIL: All this ridiculous business about the waterworks. Well, is it true?

DR STOCKMANN: It certainly is; but how did you come to hear about it?

KIIL [*coming in*]: Petra ran in on her way to the school.

DR STOCKMANN: Ah, she did?

KIIL: Yes, and she told me. I thought perhaps she was just making a fool of me, but that isn't like Petra.

DR STOCKMANN: How could you think that?

KIIL: Well, you can never be sure of anyone. You can be made a fool of before you know where you are. So it's true after all?

DR STOCKMANN: It most certainly is. Do sit down, Father. [*Forcing him on to the sofa*] It's a lucky thing for the town, isn't it?

KIIL [*struggling not to laugh*]: Lucky for the town?

DR STOCKMANN: Yes — that I made this discovery in time.

KIIL [*still struggling*]: Yes, of course — of course. Well, I never thought you had it in you to play monkey tricks against your own brother.

DR STOCKMANN: Monkey tricks?

MRS STOCKMANN: But, Father dear . . .

KIIL [*resting his chin on his hands on the handle of his stick, and giving the Doctor a sly wink*]: What was it again? Some animals that had got into the water pipes?

DR STOCKMANN: Animalculae, yes. Infusoria.

KIIL: And according to Petra, a lot of these animals had got in — whole swarms of 'em.

DR STOCKMANN: Yes — hundreds of thousands, perhaps.

KIIL: But no one can see them! Wasn't that it?

DR STOCKMANN: Exactly; no one can see them.

KIIL [*with a quiet chuckle*]: Damme, if that isn't the best thing I've heard from you yet!

DR STOCKMANN: What do you mean?

KIIL: But you'll never get the Mayor to swallow a tale like that!

DR STOCKMANN: Well, we shall see.

KIIL: D'you really think he'd be fool enough?

DR STOCKMANN: I hope the whole town'll be fool enough.

KIIL: The whole town? Well, maybe they would . . . and it'd just serve them right — teach 'em a lesson. They think themselves so much cleverer than us old fellows. They hounded me off the Town Council . . . yes, they did — hounded me off like a dog, I tell you. But now they'll get their deserts. Just you keep on with your monkey tricks, Tomas.

DR STOCKMANN: Yes, but —

KIIL: Give 'em monkey tricks, that's what I say! [*Getting up*] If you manage it so that the Mayor and his cronies get their noses rubbed in it, I'll go right out and give a hundred kroner to the poor.

DR STOCKMANN: Well, that'd be very good of you.

KIIL: Yes. Mind you, I haven't got much to throw away, but if you can manage to do that, next Christmas I'll remember the poor to the tune of fifty kroner.

[HOVSTAD *comes in from the hall.*]

HOVSTAD: Good morning – [*He stops.*] Oh, I'm sorry. . . .

DR STOCKMANN: No, come in, come in!

KIIL [*chuckling again*]: Aha! Is he in this too?

HOVSTAD: What do you mean?

DR STOCKMANN: He certainly *is* in it.

KIIL: I might have known it – it'll be in the paper! You really are a caution, Tomas! Well, I'm off. Just you work the oracle!

DR STOCKMANN: No, don't go yet.

KIIL: Yes, I'm off. Play all the monkey tricks you can on 'em – you won't lose by it, I'm damned if you will.

[*He goes, and* MRS STOCKMANN *follows him out.*]

DR STOCKMANN [*laughing*]: What do you think . . .? The old chap doesn't believe a word of all this about the water supply.

HOVSTAD: Oh, was *that* it?

DR STOCKMANN: Yes, that's what it was. I suppose you've come about the same thing?

HOVSTAD: Yes, have you a minute to spare, Doctor?

DR STOCKMANN: Just as long as you like, my dear fellow.

HOVSTAD: Have you heard anything from the Mayor?

DR STOCKMANN: Not yet; he's coming here presently.

HOVSTAD: I've been thinking things over a good deal since last night.

DR STOCKMANN: Well?

HOVSTAD: To you, as a doctor and a man of science, this affair of the water supply seems to stand on its own – I mean, you haven't realized that a good many other things are involved.

DR STOCKMANN: Oh? In what way? Let's sit down, my dear fellow . . . no, you have the sofa.

[HOVSTAD *sits on the sofa, the* DOCTOR *in an easy chair on the far side of the table.*]

Now then . . . You think –?

HOVSTAD: You said yesterday that the pollution came from impurities in the soil?

DR STOCKMANN: Yes, there's not the slightest doubt that it all comes from that foul swamp up at Mølledal.

HOVSTAD: Excuse me, Doctor, but I think it comes from quite a different swamp.

DR STOCKMANN: What swamp is that?

HOVSTAD: The swamp in which our whole community lies rotting!

DR STOCKMANN: What the devil . . .? What are you driving at, Mr Hovstad?

HOVSTAD: All the affairs of this town have fallen, one after the other, into the hands of a pack of bureaucrats.

DR STOCKMANN: Oh come now, they're not all bureaucrats.

HOVSTAD: No, but the ones who aren't bureaucrats themselves are the friends and hangers-on of the bureaucrats. In this town, there's a clique of wealthy men of position and family, and they rule us completely.

DR STOCKMANN: Yes, but they are men of skill and ability.

HOVSTAD: Did they show skill and ability when they laid the water pipes where they did?

DR STOCKMANN: No, of course not – that was a great piece of stupidity on their part. But that's going to be put right now.

HOVSTAD: Do you think it'll be as simple as that?

DR STOCKMANN: Simple or not, it'll have to be done.

HOVSTAD: Yes, provided the Press takes a hand.

DR STOCKMANN: There'll be no need for that, my dear fellow; I'm quite sure my brother –

HOVSTAD: Excuse me, Doctor, but I must tell you that I mean to take the matter up.

DR STOCKMANN: In the paper?

HOVSTAD: Yes; when I took over the *People's Herald* my aim was to break this ring of obstinate old blockheads who've got all the power.

DR STOCKMANN: But you've told me yourself what came of that – you nearly ruined the paper.

HOVSTAD: Yes, it's true that *that* time we had to climb down; there was a danger that, without those men, the whole Baths project would fall through. But now, the Baths are established, and we can dispense with those high and mighty gentry.

DR STOCKMANN: Dispense with them, yes; but we still owe a great deal to them.

HOVSTAD: Oh, we shall acknowledge that, in all fairness. But no journalist with my democratic leanings could ever let slip an opportunity like this. This myth of official infallibility must be exploded. It must be rooted out like any other superstition.

DR STOCKMANN: That goes without saying. [*With sudden vehemence*] But still – but still . . .

HOVSTAD: You mustn't misjudge me – I'm no more self-seeking or ambitious than the next man –

DR STOCKMANN: But my dear fellow, who says you are?

HOVSTAD: I come of humble folk, as you know, and I've had plenty of opportunity of seeing what the lower classes really want; and *that*, Doctor, is to have a share in the direction of public affairs. That would be the way to develop their skill and ability and self-respect.

DR STOCKMANN: Yes, I can quite appreciate that.

HOVSTAD: And it seems to me that a journalist incurs a heavy responsibility if he fails to seize any favourable opportunity of emancipating the humble, down-trodden Masses! I know very well that the Powers-That-Be will call this anarchy and so forth, but they may call it what they please. If my conscience is clear, then . . .

DR STOCKMANN: Quite so, my dear Hovstad, quite so. But damn it, I still – [*There is a knock on the door.*] Come in! [ASLAKSEN, *the printer, appears at the hall door. He is poorly but respectably dressed in black, with a rather crumpled white tie. He has a silk hat, and gloves in his hand.*]

ASLAKSEN [*bowing*]: Beg pardon, Doctor, for making so bold . . .

DR STOCKMANN [*rising*]: Ah, if it isn't Aslaksen, the printer.

ASLAKSEN: Yes, that's right, Doctor.

HOVSTAD [*rising*]: Were you looking for me, Aslaksen?

ASLAKSEN: No, I didn't know I'd find you here. No, it was the Doctor . . .

DR STOCKMANN: Well, what can I do for you?

ASLAKSEN: Is it true what I hear from Mr Billing, sir, that you're going to get us a better water supply?

DR STOCKMANN: For the Baths, yes.

ASLAKSEN: Oh yes, I realize that. I only came to say that I'll support you as best I can.

HOVSTAD [*to the Doctor*]: You see . . .!

DR STOCKMANN: I'm very grateful to you, but –

ASLAKSEN: You might well find it useful to have us small tradesmen behind you. We make up what you might call a solid majority in the town, when we really want to. And it's always a good thing to have the majority with you, Doctor.

DR STOCKMANN: That's perfectly true; but I simply can't believe that we shall need any special measures over this. I should think that such a plain straightforward matter –

ASLAKSEN: Oh certainly. But it can be a good thing all the same. You see, I know our local authorities so well – those in power don't take kindly to suggestions from outsiders. So I thought it might not come amiss if we were to arrange a little demonstration.

HOVSTAD: A good idea, yes.

DR STOCKMANN: A demonstration, you say? But how would you demonstrate?

ASLAKSEN: Oh, very temperately, of course, Doctor. I always act temperately, because temperance is a citizen's highest virtue, to my way of thinking.[38]

DR STOCKMANN: You're known for your moderation, Mr Aslaksen.

ASLAKSEN: Yes, Doctor, I think I may safely lay claim to that. And this matter of the water supply is of great importance to us small tradesmen. The Baths look like being a little gold mine, as it were, to the town. The Baths will represent the livelihood of all of us – and of us householders most of all. That's why we wish to support your project as best we can; and as I'm Chairman of the Householders' Association . . .

DR STOCKMANN: Well?

ASLAKSEN: And as I'm an active worker for the Temperance Society – you know, Doctor, that I'm a Temperance worker –

DR STOCKMANN: Yes, that goes without saying.

ASLAKSEN: Then you'll realize that I come into contact with a great many people; and since I'm known to be a

sober, law-abiding citizen, as you said yourself, Doctor –
I have a certain influence in the town. And even a little
power, though I say it myself.

DR STOCKMANN: I'm quite sure of it, Mr Aslaksen.

ASLAKSEN: So you see, it would be quite simple for me to
get up a testimonial, if it came to the pinch.

DR STOCKMANN: A testimonial?

ASLAKSEN: Yes, a sort of vote of thanks from the townspeople, that you have brought to light this matter of
such importance to the community. It goes without saying that it must be worded very temperately, so as not
to offend the authorities and those in power. If only we
are careful about that, then no one could take it amiss,
I'm sure.

HOVSTAD: Well, even if they don't much like it . . .

ASLAKSEN: No no no! No offence to those in authority,
Mr Hovstad; no attacking the men who hold our whole
livelihood in their hands. I have done quite enough of
that in my time – no good ever comes of it. But a citizen's frank and sober opinion . . . no one can object to
that.

DR STOCKMANN [shaking him by the hand]: My dear
Mr Aslaksen, I can't tell you how pleased I am to find so
much support among my fellow-townsmen. I'm delighted
– really delighted. Now, what do you say to a little
sherry, eh?

ASLAKSEN: Thank you, no. I never touch any sort of
spirits.

DR STOCKMANN: A glass of beer, then – what do you say
to that?

ASLAKSEN: Thank you, Doctor, not that either; I never
take anything so early in the day. And now I shall go
round the town and have a word with some of the householders – to prepare the ground.

DR STOCKMANN: That's extremely kind of you, Mr Aslaksen. But I really can't believe that all these precautions are necessary; it seems to me that the thing would go ahead on its own momentum.

ASLAKSEN: The authorities always move slowly, Doctor – though heaven forbid that I should say a word against them. . . .

HOVSTAD: We'll stir 'em up in tomorrow's paper, Aslaksen!

ASLAKSEN: But no violence, Mr Hovstad! You'll get nowhere with them unless you proceed temperately. You can take that from me – and I got my experience in the school of life. And now I'll say good day, Doctor. You know now that at least you have us small tradesmen behind you – firm as a rock. You have the solid majority on your side, Doctor.

DR STOCKMANN: Thank you, my dear Mr Aslaksen. [*Holding out his hand*] Good-bye, good-bye.

ASLAKSEN: Are you coming my way – to the printers, Mr Hovstad?

HOVSTAD: I'll come later – I still have one or two things to settle.

ASLAKSEN: Very well.

[*He bows and goes.* DR STOCKMANN *follows him into the hall.*]

HOVSTAD [*as the Doctor comes back*]: Well, what do you say to that, Doctor? Don't you think it's time we blew away all this slackness – gave those half-hearted cowards a good shaking up?

DR STOCKMANN: Do you mean Aslaksen?

HOVSTAD: Yes, I do. He's one of the ones who're stuck in the swamp – decent enough fellow though he may be, apart from that. He's just like most of the people around here – always shilly-shallying and wavering from one side to the other; so full of scruples and misgivings that they never dare to make any definite move.

DR STOCKMANN: But Aslaksen seems to me to be a thoroughly well-meaning fellow.

HOVSTAD: I think it's more important for a man to have some confidence and self-reliance.

DR STOCKMANN: Oh, I agree absolutely.

HOVSTAD: That's why I want to seize this opportunity, and see if I can't for once put a little life into their good intentions. All this reverence for authority must be stamped out in our town. This gross and inexcusable blunder over the water supply must be brought home to every voter in the place.

DR STOCKMANN: Very well. If you think it's for the good of the community, then so be it. But not until I've spoken to my brother.

HOVSTAD: Anyhow, I'll have a leading article ready in the meantime; then, if the Mayor won't take the matter up . . .

DR STOCKMANN: But surely you don't think he —

HOVSTAD: It's on the cards. And *then* . . .?

DR STOCKMANN: Yes, then I promise you — Look, in that case you can print my report — exactly as it stands.

HOVSTAD: May I? You give me your word?

DR STOCKMANN [*handing him the manuscript*]: Here it is. Take it with you; there's no reason why you shouldn't read it through, then you can give it back to me afterwards.

HOVSTAD: Very well, I will. Good-bye, Doctor.

DR STOCKMANN: Good-bye, good-bye. You'll see, it'll all be plain sailing, Mr Hovstad — absolutely plain sailing.

HOVSTAD: Well, we shall see. [*He bows, and goes out through the hall.*]

DR STOCKMANN [*going to the dining-room and looking in*]: Katrina! Ah, so you're back, Petra.

PETRA [*coming in*]: Yes, I'm just back from the school.

MRS STOCKMANN [*coming in*]: Hasn't he been yet?

DR STOCKMANN: Peter? No. But I've been having a long talk with Hovstad; he's quite excited about this discovery of mine. Do you know, it's much more important than I thought at first; and he's put his paper at my disposal if I need it.

MRS STOCKMANN: But do you think you will?

DR STOCKMANN: I'm certain I shan't; but all the same, it's flattering to have the liberal-minded, independent Press on one's side. And just imagine – I've had a visit from the Chairman of the Householders' Association!

MRS STOCKMANN: Oh? And what did he want?

DR STOCKMANN: To support me too. They'll all support me if it comes to the pinch. Katrina, d'you know what I have behind me?

MRS STOCKMANN: Behind you? No, what?

DR STOCKMANN: The solid majority.

MRS STOCKMANN: Oh? Is that a good thing for you, Tomas?

DR STOCKMANN: Good? I should think so indeed! [*Rubbing his hands as he paces up and down*] Ye gods! What a splendid thing it is to be in complete agreement with one's fellow-townsmen!

PETRA: And to be doing something of such great practical value, Father.

DR STOCKMANN: Especially when it's for one's own town!

MRS STOCKMANN: There's the bell.

DR STOCKMANN: That'll be Peter. [*A knock.*] Come in.

THE MAYOR [*coming in from the hall*]: Good morning.

DR STOCKMANN: I'm glad to see you, Peter.

MRS STOCKMANN: Good morning; how are you?

THE MAYOR: Oh, so-so, thank you. [*To the Doctor*] Last night after office hours, I received a communication from you concerning the condition of the water at the Baths.

DR STOCKMANN: Yes; have you read it?

THE MAYOR: I have.

DR STOCKMANN: What did you think of it?

THE MAYOR [*with a glance at the others*]: Well . . .

MRS STOCKMANN: Come along, Petra. [*She and* PETRA *go out to the left.*]

THE MAYOR [*after a moment*]: Was it necessary to carry out all these inquiries behind my back?

DR STOCKMANN: Well, until I had absolute proof, I —

THE MAYOR: Are you saying that you have it now?

DR STOCKMANN: Yes — surely that has convinced you?

THE MAYOR: Is it your intention to submit this document to the Directorate of the Baths as some sort of official report?

DR STOCKMANN: Of course. Something must be done about the state of affairs — and quickly, too.

THE MAYOR: As usual, you make use of some very strong expressions in your report. You say, among other things, that what we offer to our visitors at the Baths is consistently poisonous.

DR STOCKMANN: But, Peter, what else can you call it? Just think — water that's poisonous to drink *and* to bathe in? And we give it to unfortunate invalids who come to us in good faith, and pay us an exorbitant price to be made well again!

THE MAYOR: And so you arrive at the conclusion that we must build a sewer to carry off the alleged impurities from Mølledal, and that all the water-pipes must be relaid.

DR STOCKMANN: Yes. Can you see any other way out? I can't.

THE MAYOR: I made a pretext for calling on the Town Engineer this morning, and I touched on the subject of these alterations – half-jokingly, as something that we might possibly have to consider at some time in the future.

DR STOCKMANN: Some time in the *future*?

THE MAYOR: He smiled at what he naturally imagined to be my caprice. Have you taken the trouble to consider what your proposed alterations would cost? According to the information which I have accumulated, the outlay would probably amount to several hundred thousand kroner!

DR STOCKMANN: As much as that?

THE MAYOR: Yes. And what is worse, the work would take at least two years.

DR STOCKMANN: Two years, you say? Two whole years?

THE MAYOR: At least. And what should we do with the Baths in the meanwhile? Close them? We should be forced to. . . . Unless perhaps you imagine that anyone would come here if ever the rumour got about that the water might be a menace to health.

DR STOCKMANN: But, Peter, that's exactly what it is.

THE MAYOR: And to think that all this should come now – just now, when the Baths are building up a reputation! Other towns in the neighbourhood certainly possess the conditions that could attract visitors in search of cures. Do you imagine that they would not immediately do everything in their power to divert our entire flow of visitors to themselves? Undoubtedly they would . . . and then where should we be? We should probably have to abandon the entire costly undertaking, and then you would have ruined your native town.

DR STOCKMANN: *I* . . .? Ruined . . .?

THE MAYOR: It is simply and solely thanks to the Baths

that this town has any future worthy of the name. You must know that as well as I do.

DR STOCKMANN: Then what do you think should be done?

THE MAYOR: I have not been able to convince myself, from your report, that the condition of the water at the Baths is as serious as you represent.

DR STOCKMANN: But it's even worse! Or it will be next summer when the hot weather comes.

THE MAYOR: As I say, it is my belief that you have exaggerated things considerably. A competent physician should be able to achieve some sense of proportion. He should be able either to prevent any harmful influences, or to counteract them if they should be felt to have become too obvious.

DR STOCKMANN: Well? What do you –?

THE MAYOR: The existing water supply to the Baths is, once and for all, a fact, and must obviously be considered as such. When the time comes, however, the Directorate will probably not be unwilling to consider whether it might not be feasible – provided the cost were not too exorbitant – to introduce certain improvements –

DR STOCKMANN: You don't think I'd ever be a party to such a swindle?

THE MAYOR: A swindle?

DR STOCKMANN: Yes, it'd be a swindle – a lie, a fraud, a positive crime against the public – against the whole community.

THE MAYOR: I have not – as I have already remarked – been able to convince myself that there is really any imminent danger.

DR STOCKMANN: But you must have – you can't get away from it! My report's particularly clear and accurate, I'm sure of that. And you understand it perfectly well, Peter, only you won't admit it. It was you who arranged that both the Baths and the conduits should be where they are today . . . and *that*'s what you won't acknowledge – that you've made a damnable blunder. Pooh, d'you think I can't see through you?

THE MAYOR: Even if that were true – even if I do cherish my prestige with a certain care, I do so in the interests of the town. Without my reputation for integrity, I could no longer guide and direct affairs in the way which I consider most conducive to the general good. On that account – and for various other reasons – it is a matter of the greatest concern to me that your report should not be submitted to the Directorate of the Baths. It must be withheld for the good of the community. Later on, I shall bring up the matter for discussion, and we shall deal with it as best we can – discreetly. But nothing of this dangerous business – not a single word – must become known to the public.

DR STOCKMANN: But my dear Peter, that can't be prevented now.

THE MAYOR: It must be prevented and it shall be.

DR STOCKMANN: I tell you it can't – too many people know about it already.

THE MAYOR: Know about it? Who? Not those fellows on the *People's Herald*!

DR STOCKMANN: Oh yes, they know about it. The liberal-minded, independent Press will certainly see to it that you do your duty.

THE MAYOR [*after a moment*]: You are an extremely impetuous person, Tomas. Has it not occurred to you that this may have certain repercussions on yourself?

DR STOCKMANN: Repercussions? On me?

THE MAYOR: On you and your family, yes.

DR STOCKMANN: What the devil d'you mean by that?

THE MAYOR: I consider that, all my life, I have been glad to act in a helpful, brotherly manner towards you.

DR STOCKMANN: You have, and I'm very grateful.

THE MAYOR: There is no occasion for gratitude. Indeed, to a certain extent it was necessary for me to act as I did — for my own sake. I always hoped that if I helped to improve your financial position I might be able to keep some sort of check on you.

DR STOCKMANN: What? So it was only for your own sake...?

THE MAYOR: To some extent, yes. It is painful for a man in an official position when his nearest relative goes and compromises himself time after time.

DR STOCKMANN: And you think I do that?

THE MAYOR: Yes, I'm sorry to say that you do — without ever being aware of it. You have a turbulent, aggressive, rebellious nature. And then there is your unfortunate habit of rushing into print on every possible and impossible occasion. No sooner do you get an idea than you immediately write a pamphlet or a newspaper article on the subject.

DR STOCKMANN: Well, but isn't it a citizen's duty, if he gets a new idea, to share it with the public?

THE MAYOR: The public doesn't need new ideas. What's best for the public are the good, old-established ideas that they already have.

DR STOCKMANN: And you say that openly!

THE MAYOR: Yes, for once I must speak openly to you. So far, knowing how quick you are to take offence, I've tried to avoid it, but now, Tomas, I must tell you the truth. You have no conception what harm your impetuosity does you. You complain about the authorities — yes, about the Government, even. You revile them.

insisting that you've been slighted and passed over – but what else can you expect when you're so intractable?

DR STOCKMANN: Oh, so I'm intractable as well, am I?

THE MAYOR: Yes, Tomas, you're an extremely intractable man to work with, as I know from experience. You ride roughshod over everyone. You seem to have completely forgotten that it is I whom you have to thank for your position as Medical Officer to the Baths.

DR STOCKMANN: I was entitled to it – I and no one else! I was the first to see that the town could become a prosperous watering-place – and in those days I was the only one. For years I campaigned single-handed for the idea; I wrote and wrote –

THE MAYOR: I don't deny it; but in those days the time wasn't ripe – though naturally you could hardly realize that, living, as you did, up in that out-of-the-way corner. But when the right moment arrived, then I – and others – took up the matter.

DR STOCKMANN: Yes, and a fine mess you made of my wonderful plan! Oh yes, it's quite clear now what clever fellows you've been!

THE MAYOR: To my mind, it's perfectly obvious that you're looking for another outlet for your intransigence. You wish to attack your superiors – an old habit of yours.[39] You can't bear to have anyone in authority over you; you look askance at anyone who has a higher post than yours, and you consider him a personal enemy . . . and immediately any stick's good enough to beat him with. Now, however, I've pointed out to you exactly how much is at stake for the whole town – and that includes myself, of course – and I warn you, Tomas, that I shall be absolutely inflexible about the demands that I'm about to make of you.

DR STOCKMANN: What demands?

THE MAYOR: Since you've been so indiscreet as to chatter to outsiders about this delicate matter, which should have been treated as an official secret, obviously it can't be hushed up. All kinds of rumours will get about. . . . And everyone with a grudge against us will spread those rumours – with embellishments. It will therefore be necessary for you to contradict such rumours, publicly.

DR STOCKMANN: I? How? I don't understand.

THE MAYOR: We expect that, after further investigations, you will come to the conclusion that matters are not nearly so serious or so urgent as you had imagined at first sight.

DR STOCKMANN: Oh you *do*, do you?

THE MAYOR: And what is more, it is expected that you will not only maintain, but also publicly proclaim, your confidence in the Board of Governors and in the thorough and conscientious steps which they will take to remedy any possible shortcomings.

DR STOCKMANN: Yes, but that's just what you'll never be able to do – not as long as you just go on patching and tinkering. You can take my word for that, Peter; it's my most carefully considered opinion.

THE MAYOR: As a member of the Staff, you have no right to any personal opinions.

DR STOCKMANN [*astonished*]: No right . . . ?

THE MAYOR: Not as a member of the Staff. As a private individual, naturally, it's a different matter; but as a minor official of the Baths, you have no right to express any opinion which conflicts with that of your superiors.

DR STOCKMANN: This is too much! I'm a doctor – a man of science. . . . Am I to have no right to –

THE MAYOR: The point at issue is not a purely scientific one; it is a complex question, with both technical and economic aspects.

DR STOCKMANN: As far as I'm concerned, it can be anything it damn well likes; but I mean to be free to speak my mind on any subject on earth.

THE MAYOR: As you please – so long as it does not concern the Baths. That we forbid.

DR STOCKMANN: You forbid . . . ? You? A pack of –

THE MAYOR: *I* forbid it! I, your senior director. And when I forbid anything, you must obey.

DR STOCKMANN [*controlling himself*]: Peter – if you weren't my brother . . . !

PETRA [*flinging the door open*]: Father, don't you stand for that!

MRS STOCKMANN [*following her*]: Petra! Petra!

THE MAYOR: Oh, so you've been eavesdropping!

MRS STOCKMANN: You were talking so loud, we couldn't help –

PETRA: Yes, I was listening.

THE MAYOR: On the whole, I am quite glad –

DR STOCKMANN [*going to him*]: You were telling me something about forbidding and obeying . . . ?

THE MAYOR: You obliged me to take that tone.

DR STOCKMANN: And I'm to make a public declaration, eating my own words?

THE MAYOR: We consider it imperative that you make a public statement on the lines which I have indicated.

DR STOCKMANN: And if I – don't obey?

THE MAYOR: Then we ourselves will issue a statement to reassure the public.

DR STOCKMANN: Very well, then I shall write and deny it. I stand by what I've said – I shall prove that I'm right and you're wrong. What will you do then?

THE MAYOR: In that case, I shall be unable to save you from dismissal.

DR STOCKMANN: What?

PETRA: Dismissal? Father!

MRS STOCKMANN: Dismissal?

THE MAYOR: Your dismissal from the staff of the Baths. I shall find myself obliged to propose that you receive your notice immediately, and are prevented from any further meddling in the affairs of the Baths.

DR STOCKMANN: You'd never dare do that!

THE MAYOR: It's you who are playing the daring game.

PETRA: Uncle, this is a disgraceful way to treat a man like Father.

MRS STOCKMANN: Petra, do be quiet.

THE MAYOR [*looking at Petra*]: Oh, so we volunteer our opinion already, do we? Well, it's only to be expected! [*To Mrs Stockmann*] Katrina, you appear to be the most sensible person in this house; you must use whatever influence you may have over your husband, and try to make him see what the consequences of this will be, both for his family –

DR STOCKMANN: My family is my concern and no one else's!

THE MAYOR: – as I was saying – both for his family, and for the town where he lives.

DR STOCKMANN: I'm the one who has the good of the town at heart; I want to show up defects that must come to light sooner or later. Oh yes, it'll soon be obvious that I love my native town.

THE MAYOR: You? When your blind obstinacy would destroy the town's chief source of income?

DR STOCKMANN: But the source is poisoned, man. Are you mad? We live by trafficking in filth and corruption! The whole life of our flourishing community is founded on a lie!

THE MAYOR: Imagination! If it is not something even worse! Anyone who can spread such offensive accusations against his own town must be an enemy of society.

DR STOCKMANN [advancing on him]: You dare to –

MRS STOCKMANN [throwing herself between them]: Tomas!

PETRA [seizing her father's arm]: Careful, Father!

THE MAYOR: I will not expose myself to violence. You have had your warning; just remember what is due to your family. [He goes.]

DR STOCKMANN [striding up and down]: To have to put up with that sort of treatment – in my own house! What do you say, Katrina?

MRS STOCKMANN: It's a shame, Tomas – absolutely disgraceful.

PETRA: I'd like to tell Uncle what I think of him.

DR STOCKMANN: It's my own fault; I should have stood up to them long ago. I should have shown my teeth – and used them, too. And to be called an enemy of society . . . me! I won't stand for it – upon my soul, I won't!

MRS STOCKMANN: You know, Tomas dear, your brother's very powerful. . . .

DR STOCKMANN: Yes, but I have right on my side.

MRS STOCKMANN: Right? Oh yes, you may have right; but what's the use of right if you haven't got might?

PETRA: Mother! How can you talk like that?

DR STOCKMANN: Do you think in a free country it doesn't help to have right on your side? Don't be ridiculous, Katrina. Besides, haven't I the liberal-minded, independent Press on my side, and a solid majority behind me? That's might enough, I should think.

MRS STOCKMANN: But good heavens, Tomas, you're surely not thinking of . . .

DR STOCKMANN: What am I 'not thinking of'?

MRS STOCKMANN: – of setting yourself up against your brother.

DR STOCKMANN: What the devil else do you expect me to do, except stand up for right and truth?

PETRA: Yes, that's what I was going to say.

MRS STOCKMANN: But what earthly good will it do you? If they won't, they won't.

DR STOCKMANN: Aha, Katrina, just give me time. You'll see, I'll fight this to the very end.

MRS STOCKMANN: Oh yes, and it'll end in your getting dismissed – that's what'll happen.

DR STOCKMANN: Well, at least I shall have done my duty to the people – to society . . . although they call me its enemy!

MRS STOCKMANN: But your family, Tomas – all of us here who depend on you . . . would you have done your duty to them, do you think?

PETRA: Oh, Mother, don't always put us first.

MRS STOCKMANN: It's all very well for you to talk – you can stand on your own feet if need be. But remember the boys, Tomas. And think of yourself a bit, too . . . and of me.

DR STOCKMANN: But you must be raving mad, Katrina. If I were to be such a miserable coward as to give in to Peter there, and his damned gang, d'you think I'd ever have another moment's happiness for the rest of my life?

MRS STOCKMANN: I don't know about that; but heaven preserve us from the sort of happiness that we shall have if you go on defying them. There you'll be with nothing to live on again – with no regular income. I should have thought we'd had enough of that in the old days. Remember that, Tomas, and think what it would mean.

DR STOCKMANN [clenching his fists as he struggles with

himself]: And this is what those bureaucrats can do to a plain honest man. It's terrible, Katrina!

MRS STOCKMANN: Yes, they're treating you shamefully, there's no doubt about that; but goodness knows there's plenty of injustice in the world – we just have to put up with it. Here come the boys, Tomas. Look at them. What's to become of them? No, no, you'd never have the heart to –

[*During this,* EYLIF *and* MORTEN *have come in with their schoolbooks.*]

DR STOCKMANN: The boys! [*Suddenly coming to a decision*] No! Even if the whole world collapses, I will not bend my neck to the yoke! [*He starts towards his room.*]

MRS STOCKMANN [*following him*]: Tomas! What are you going to do?

DR STOCKMANN [*at the door*]: When my boys grow up to be free men, I want to have the right to look them in the face. [*He goes.*]

MRS STOCKMANN [*bursting into tears*]: Oh, God help us and keep us all!

PETRA: Father's wonderful – he'll never give in!

[*The boys, surprised, wonder what it all means;* PETRA *signs to them not to speak.*]

ACT THREE

————————— * —————————

The Editor's office at the People's Herald.[40] *The main door is in the back wall to the left. To the right is another door with glass panels, through which the printing-room can be seen. In the right-hand wall is a third door.*

In the middle stands a large table covered with papers, journals, and books.

To the left in the foreground is a window, with a desk and a high stool in front of it. There are a couple of armchairs at the table, and a few other chairs round the walls.

The room is dingy and cheerless, the furniture old, and the armchairs shabby and torn. In the printing-room a few men can be seen at work, and in the background a hand-press is in use.

[HOVSTAD, *the Editor, is sitting at the desk writing. After a moment or two,* BILLING *comes in from the right, with Dr Stockmann's manuscript in his hand.*]

BILLING: Well, I must say . . . !

HOVSTAD [*writing*]: Have you read it through?

BILLING [*putting the* MS. *on the desk*]: I certainly have.

HOVSTAD: The Doctor's been pretty blunt, don't you think?

BILLING: Blunt? Why, but he's pulverizing, I'm hanged if he isn't! Every word comes crashing down like – what shall I say? – like a sledgehammer.

HOVSTAD: Yes, but it'll take more than one blow to demolish these fellows.

BILLING: That's true; but we'll keep on hammering at them, blow after blow, till the whole of this privileged class comes crashing down. When I was sitting in there reading this, I could almost see the Revolution coming over the horizon!

HOVSTAD [*turning round*]: Sh! Don't let Aslaksen hear you say that.

BILLING [*lowering his voice*]: Aslaksen's a chicken-hearted fellow – a coward, without an ounce of manly feeling in him. You're going to have your way this time, eh? You'll put the Doctor's article in?

HOVSTAD: Yes – always provided the Mayor doesn't surrender.

BILLING: That'd be a damn nuisance.

HOVSTAD: Well, whichever way it goes, we'll be able to turn the situation to good account. If the Mayor won't agree to the Doctor's proposal, then he'll bring all the small tradesmen down on him – the Householders' Association and the rest. And if he *does* agree to it, he'll fall out with the whole mob of big shareholders in the Baths, who've been his chief supporters up to now.

BILLING: Yes, of course; they'll certainly have to cough up a pretty penny.

HOVSTAD: Yes, you bet they will; and that'll break the ring up, you'll see. And then we'll din it into the public, in every single issue of the paper, that the Mayor's incompetent in one thing after another. We'll make it clear that all the important posts in the town – the whole Municipal control – ought to be put into the hands of the Liberals.

BILLING: You're right, I'm hanged if you aren't! I see it – yes! We're standing right on the brink, as it were, of a revolution!

[*There is a knock on the door.*]

HOVSTAD: Sh! [*Calls*] Come in!

    [DR STOCKMANN *comes through the left of the two doors at the back.*]

Ah! [*He goes to meet him.*] Here is the Doctor. Well?

DR STOCKMANN: Print ahead, Mr Hovstad!

HOVSTAD: It's come to that, has it?

BILLING: Hurrah!

DR STOCKMANN: Print ahead, I tell you. Yes, it's come to that, all right! If that's the way they want it, they shall have it. There'll be war in this town, Mr Billing.

BILLING: War to the knife, I hope. Heads will fall, Doctor!

DR STOCKMANN: This article's only the beginning. I've plans for four or five others in my head already. Have you got Aslaksen there?

BILLING [*calling into the printing-room*]: Aslaksen, come here a second, will you?

HOVSTAD: Four or five more articles, eh? On the same lines?

DR STOCKMANN: No, my dear fellow – not at all. They're about something quite different. Though they all arise from the water supply and the sewage – one thing leads to another, you know. It's like starting to pull down an old house. . . . Yes, just like that.

BILLING: You're right – you feel you can't stop till you've torn down the whole ramshackle place, I'm hanged if you can.

ASLAKSEN [*coming from the printing-room*]: Torn it down? The Doctor surely isn't thinking of tearing down the Baths?

HOVSTAD: Far from it; don't worry.

DR STOCKMANN: No, we were talking about something quite different. Well, Mr Hovstad, what do you think of my article?

HOVSTAD: I think it's an absolute masterpiece.

DR STOCKMANN: It is, isn't it? I'm delighted you should think so – delighted.

HOVSTAD: It's clear and to the point – no need to be an expert to follow it. Take my word for it, you'll have every thinking man on your side.

ASLAKSEN: The prudent ones too, I hope.

BILLING: Prudent and imprudent. I think it'll be practically the whole town.

ASLAKSEN: Ah, so we're venturing to print it?

DR STOCKMANN: I should think so, indeed!

HOVSTAD: It'll be in tomorrow morning.

DR STOCKMANN: Yes; hell and damnation, we mustn't waste a single day. Look, Mr Aslaksen, this is what I wanted to ask you: will you personally supervise the printing of it?

ASLAKSEN: Certainly I will.

DR STOCKMANN: Look after it as if it were pure gold. No printer's errors – every word's important. And perhaps, if I come back a little later, I might be able to see a proof. Oh, I can't tell you how impatient I am to have it in print, and launched –

BILLING: Yes, launched – like a thunderbolt!

DR STOCKMANN: – and submitted to the judgement of every intelligent citizen. Ah, you can't imagine what I've had to go through today. I've been threatened with one thing after another – they've tried to rob me of my most elementary human rights –

BILLING: What? Your human rights?

DR STOCKMANN: – they've tried to degrade me, to turn me into a coward, to make me put personal gain above my deepest, holiest principles.

BILLING: Disgraceful! I'm hanged if it isn't.

HOVSTAD: Ah, it's just what you'd expect from that quarter.

DR STOCKMANN: But they'll get the worst of it with me –
they'll get it in black and white! I shall make the
People's Herald my headquarters, and every single day
I'll bombard them with one explosive article after
another....

ASLAKSEN: Yes, but –

BILLING: Hurrah, it's war – war!

DR STOCKMANN: I'll beat them to the ground – I'll smash
them – I'll flatten all their defences in the eyes of right-
minded people, that's what I'll do!

ASLAKSEN: But temperately, Doctor! Attack, but with
temperance!

BILLING: No no! Don't spare the dynamite!

DR STOCKMANN [*continuing imperturbably*]: Because now,
you see, it isn't just a question of water supplies and
sewers. No, the whole community must be cleaned and
disinfected.

BILLING: Spoken like a crusader!

DR STOCKMANN: All the old fogies must be sent packing, you see – driven from all their possible hiding-places.
Such endless vistas have opened out before me today ...
I haven't got it quite clear yet, but I'll soon put that
right. What we must go out and find now, my friends,
are vigorous young standard-bearers; we must have new
leaders at all our outposts –

BILLING: Hear hear!

DR STOCKMANN: It'll all be so easy if only we stand together – the whole revolution will be launched as
smoothly as a ship off the stocks. Don't you agree?

HOVSTAD: If you ask *me*, I believe we've got every hope
of getting the local government into the right hands
now.

ASLAKSEN: And if only we proceed temperately, I can't
see how there can be any danger.

DR STOCKMANN: Who the devil cares if there's danger or not? What I'm doing now, I'm doing in the name of truth and of my own conscience.

HOVSTAD: You deserve every support, Doctor.

ASLAKSEN: Yes, it's obvious that the Doctor is a true friend to the town . . . a friend of Society – that's what he is!

BILLING: You know, Aslaksen, I'm hanged if the Doctor isn't a public benefactor!

ASLAKSEN: I expect the Householders' Association'll take that up as a slogan!

DR STOCKMANN [*moved, taking their hands*]: Thank you, my dear, faithful friends – thank you. It's good to hear you say that. My high-and-mighty brother called me something quite different! But he shall have it back, with interest. Well, I must be off now, to see a poor devil of a patient – but I'll be back, as I said. Take particular care of the manuscript, Mr Aslaksen; and whatever you do, don't cut out any of the exclamation marks . . . if anything, put in a few more. Splendid! splendid! Good-bye for the present – good-bye!

[*General good-byes as they see him to the door. He goes.*]

HOVSTAD: He can be very useful to us.

ASLAKSEN: As long as he keeps to this matter of the Baths, yes. It mightn't be prudent to follow him if he goes beyond that.

HOVSTAD: Hm . . . that all depends.

BILLING: You're too damned timid, Aslaksen.

ASLAKSEN: Timid? Yes, Mr Billing, when it's a question of those in authority *locally*, I am timid. I may say, that's something I've learned by experience. But try me in *National* politics – set me up against the Government itself, and then see if I'm timid.

BILLING: No, of course you're not; but that's just where you're inconsistent.

ASLAKSEN: I'm a conscientious man, that's what it is. You can let fly at the Government, and at least you don't do society any harm. The politicians don't mind, you see – they just stay where they are, in spite of you. But the *local* authorities – they can be turned out, and then you might get inexperienced men at the helm who could do irreparable damage to the householders and everyone else.

HOVSTAD: But men must get their experience through local politics – haven't you thought of that?

ASLAKSEN: When a man has interests of his own to protect, he can't think of everything, Mr Hovstad.

HOVSTAD: Then I hope I never have interests of my own to protect.

BILLING: Hear hear!

ASLAKSEN [*smiling*]: Hm! [*Pointing to the desk*] Councillor Stensgård sat in that Editor's chair before you.[41]

BILLING [*spitting*]: Pah! That turncoat!

HOVSTAD: I'm no deserter – and I never will be.

ASLAKSEN: A politician should never be too positive about anything in this world, Mr Hovstad. As for you, Mr Billing, I should think you'd be well advised to take a reef or two in your sails now that you're trying for the post of Secretary to the Council.

BILLING: I –!

HOVSTAD: Billing! Are you?

BILLING: Well, yes . . . but good Lord, I'm only doing it to annoy the bigwigs.

ASLAKSEN: Well, its no business of mine. But if I'm to be accused of being timid and inconsistent in my principles, there's one thing I'd like to point out: my political record is an open book; I've not changed at all – except to become more moderate, of course. My heart is still with the people . . . though I won't deny that my reason leans a little towards the authorities – the local ones, that is. [*He goes into the printing-room.*]

BILLING: Oughtn't we to try to get rid of him, Hovstad?

HOVSTAD: Do you know anyone else who'd advance the money for our paper and printing?

BILLING: It's an infernal nuisance not to have the working capital we need.

HOVSTAD [*sitting at the desk*]: Yes, if only we had that. . . .

BILLING: Suppose you approached Dr Stockmann?

HOVSTAD [*going through his papers*]: What'd be the use? He hasn't any money.

BILLING: No, but he's got a good man behind him: old Morten Kiil – the Badger, as they call him.

HOVSTAD [*writing*]: Are you quite sure *he* has anything?

BILLING: Why, of course he has; and I'm hanged if part of it doesn't go to the Stockmanns – he must provide for the children, at least.

HOVSTAD [*half turning*]: Are you counting on that?

BILLING: Counting on it? Of course I don't count on anything.

HOVSTAD: Very wise. And you certainly shouldn't count on that post with the Council, because I can assure you you won't get it.

BILLING: D'you think I don't know that perfectly well? That's the whole point – not to get it! A rebuff like that stimulates your will to fight – gives you a fresh supply of venom, as it were. And that's what you need in a dead-alive place like this, where nothing really stimulating ever happens.

HOVSTAD [*writing*]: Quite so, quite so.

BILLING: Well, they'll soon be hearing from me! Now I'm

going to write that appeal to the Householders' Association. [*He goes into the room on the right.*]

HOVSTAD [*slowly, as he sits at his desk biting his penholder*]: Hm . . .! So *that's* it, is it? [*A knock.*] Come in!
[PETRA *comes in by the left-hand door at the back.*]

HOVSTAD [*rising*]: Ah, it's you! Is there anything I can do?

PETRA: You must forgive me. . . .

HOVSTAD [*pulling out an armchair*]: Won't you sit down?

PETRA: No thank you, I can't stay.

HOVSTAD: Is it something from your father?

PETRA: No, I've come on my own account. [*Producing a book from her coat pocket*] Here's that English story.

HOVSTAD: Why have you brought it back?

PETRA: Because I won't translate it.

HOVSTAD: But you promised me faithfully –

PETRA: Yes, but I hadn't read it then. And you can't have read it either.

HOVSTAD: No, you know I don't read English; but –

PETRA: Exactly. That's why I wanted to tell you that you'll have to look for something else. [*She puts the book on the table.*] This could certainly never appear in the *Herald*.

HOVSTAD: Why not?

PETRA: Because it goes against everything you stand for.

HOVSTAD: Well, for that matter . . .

PETRA: You still don't understand. According to this, there's a supernatural power in the world that looks after all the so-called good people, so that everything turns out well for them in the end; while all the so-called bad people are punished.

HOVSTAD: Well, that's all right; it's just what the public wants.

PETRA: Will you be the one to give them that sort of stuff? You don't believe a word of it yourself – you know perfectly well that things don't happen like that in real life.

HOVSTAD: You're absolutely right; but an editor can't always do as he'd like. He often has to bow to the public taste in little things. The most important thing in life – for a newspaper, at any rate – is politics; and if I want to carry the public with me over questions of Freedom and Progress, I mustn't frighten them away. If they find a moral tale like this down in the bottom corner, then they're more likely to accept what we tell them at the top of the page – they feel somehow safer.[42]

PETRA: Oh no! You can't be so deceitful as to set traps for your readers – you're not a spider!

HOVSTAD [smiling]: I'm glad you think so well of me. As a matter of fact, it was Billing's idea, not mine.

PETRA: Mr Billing?

HOVSTAD: Yes. At any rate he was talking on those lines in here the other day. It's Billing who's so keen to have the story in; I don't know the book.

PETRA: But how can Mr Billing, with his advanced views . . .?

HOVSTAD: Well, Billing's a versatile fellow – I hear he's trying for the post of Secretary to the Council!

PETRA: I can't believe that, Mr Hovstad; how could he bring himself to do such a thing?

HOVSTAD: You must ask him that yourself.

PETRA: I should never have thought it of him.

HOVSTAD [looking more intently at her]: No? Does it surprise you so much?

PETRA: Yes. At least – perhaps not. . . . Oh, I don't really know.

HOVSTAD: We journalists aren't worth much, Miss Petra.

PETRA: Do you really mean that?

HOVSTAD: It's what I sometimes feel.

PETRA: In little everyday matters, I can understand it; but now that you've taken up a great cause. . . .

HOVSTAD: This business of your father's, you mean?

PETRA: Exactly. I should have thought that *now* you must feel you're more worth while than the rest.

HOVSTAD: Yes, today I do feel something of the sort.

PETRA: You do, don't you? It's a wonderful career that you've chosen: to pave the way for unpopular truths, and for daring new opinions. . . . Or simply to stand up bravely on the side of a man who's been wronged.

HOVSTAD: Especially when the wronged man is – well, I don't quite know how to put it. . . .

PETRA: You mean when he's so straight and honourable?

HOVSTAD [*softly*]: I meant – especially when he's your father.

PETRA [*suddenly upset*]: Oh *no*!

HOVSTAD: Yes, Petra – Miss Petra.

PETRA: So that's what really matters most to you? Not the cause; not the truth; not father's great generous spirit?

HOVSTAD: Oh, of course – all those things too.

PETRA: No thank you, Mr Hovstad, you've said quite enough already. Now I shall never trust you over anything again.

HOVSTAD: Do you really blame me so much – just because it was mostly for your sake?

PETRA: What I'm angry with you for, is that you haven't been honest with Father. You've been talking to him as if truth and the public good were the things that mattered most to you. You've been deceiving both Father and me. You're not the man you've been pretending to be, and I shall never forgive you for that. Never!

HOVSTAD: You oughtn't to speak so harshly, Miss Petra — least of all *now*.

PETRA: Why not now, especially?

HOVSTAD: Because your father can't do without my help.

PETRA [*looking him up and down*]: So you're *that* sort of a man, are you? You ought to be ashamed of yourself!

HOVSTAD: No no — this all took me by surprise. I'm not like that — you mustn't think that of me!

PETRA: I know just what to think. Good-bye.

ASLAKSEN [*slipping in hurriedly from the printing-room*]: Oh Lor', Mr Hovstad — [*Noticing Petra*] Oh . . . that's awkward!

PETRA: There's your book; you must give it to someone else. [*She starts towards the main door.*]

HOVSTAD [*following her*]: But, Miss Stockmann . . .

PETRA: Good-bye. [*She goes.*]

ASLAKSEN: Mr Hovstad —

HOVSTAD: Well well, what is it?

ASLAKSEN: The Mayor's out there in the printing-room!

HOVSTAD: The Mayor?

ASLAKSEN: Yes, he wants a word with you. He came in by the back way — he didn't want anyone to see him, you understand.

HOVSTAD: What does he want? No wait — I'll see him myself.

[*He goes and opens the door of the printing-room and, with a bow, invites the Mayor in.*]

Keep a look out, Aslaksen, and see that no one —

ASLAKSEN: Of course. [*He goes into the printing-room.*]

THE MAYOR: You didn't expect to see me here, Mr Hovstad.

HOVSTAD: I certainly didn't.

THE MAYOR [*looking round*]: It's nice here; you've managed to make yourself comfortable.

HOVSTAD: Well . . .

THE MAYOR: And here I am dropping in uninvited and taking up your time.

HOVSTAD: Oh please, Mr Mayor . . . I'm at your service. Let me take your things.[43] [*He puts the Mayor's hat and staff on a chair.*] Won't you sit down?

THE MAYOR [*sitting at the table*]: Thank you. [HOVSTAD *sits at the table too.*]
Mr Hovstad . . . something annoying – really annoying – has happened to me today.

HOVSTAD: Really? Oh well, with your duties as Mayor. . . .

THE MAYOR: This particular annoyance concerns the Medical Officer at the Baths.

HOVSTAD: Indeed? The Doctor?

THE MAYOR: He has addressed a species of Memorandum to the Board of Governors, concerning certain alleged shortcomings at the Baths.

HOVSTAD: Has he really?

THE MAYOR: Yes, didn't he tell you? I thought he said –

HOVSTAD: Ah yes, that's right . . . he did just mention –

ASLAKSEN [*coming from the printing-room*]: I'd better have that manuscript –

HOVSTAD [*annoyed*]: Er – there it is on the desk.

ASLAKSEN [*finding it*]: Oh yes.

THE MAYOR: But look . . . that's the very –

ASLAKSEN: Yes, Mr Mayor, that's the Doctor's article.

HOVSTAD: Oh, is *that* what you were talking about?

THE MAYOR: It certainly is. What do you think of it?

HOVSTAD: Well . . . I'm not an expert; I've hardly glanced at it.

THE MAYOR: Yet you're about to print it?

HOVSTAD: I can hardly refuse an article signed by –

ASLAKSEN: I have no say in the paper's policy, Mr Mayor.

THE MAYOR: Naturally not.

ASLAKSEN: I simply print what's handed to me.

THE MAYOR: That is as it should be.

ASLAKSEN [*making for the printing-room*]: So if you'll excuse me . . .

THE MAYOR: No, wait a moment, Mr Aslaksen. With your permission, Mr Hovstad. . . .

HOVSTAD: Please, Mr Mayor.

THE MAYOR: Mr Aslaksen, you are a discreet and sensible person.

ASLAKSEN: It's very kind of you to say so, sir.

THE MAYOR: A man with a good deal of influence.

ASLAKSEN: Chiefly among the poorer folk, yes.

THE MAYOR: Here, as elsewhere, the small taxpayers form the majority.

ASLAKSEN: That's very true.

THE MAYOR: And I have no doubt that you know the general trend of opinion among them, do you not?

ASLAKSEN: Yes, I think I may say that I do, sir.

THE MAYOR: Yes . . . Well – since there appears to be such a praiseworthy spirit of self-sacrifice among the town's less wealthy citizens . . .

ASLAKSEN: What's that?

HOVSTAD: Self-sacrifice?

THE MAYOR: It's a welcome sign of public spirit – an extremely welcome sign. I was about to say that I should not have expected it, but you know public feelings so much better than I do. . . .

ASLAKSEN: Yes, but –

THE MAYOR: And indeed it'll be no small sacrifice that the town will be called upon to make.

HOVSTAD: The town?

ASLAKSEN: But I don't understand. Surely it's the Baths. . . .

THE MAYOR: At a provisional estimate, the alterations that

the Medical Officer feels would be desirable would cost some two hundred thousand kroner.

ASLAKSEN: That's a lot of money, but —

THE MAYOR: Naturally it will be necessary to raise a municipal loan.

HOVSTAD [rising]: You surely don't mean that the town ...

ASLAKSEN: Would it come from the rates? Out of the pockets of the struggling shopkeepers?

THE MAYOR: Well, my dear Mr Aslaksen, where else could the funds come from?

ASLAKSEN: The gentlemen who own the Baths should see to it.

THE MAYOR: The proprietors find themselves in no position to incur any greater expense than they are already bearing.

ASLAKSEN: Are you quite certain of that, sir?

THE MAYOR: I have satisfied myself that it is so. So if these extensive alterations are thought desirable, then the town will have to pay for them.

ASLAKSEN: But goddam it — Excuse me! Mr Hovstad, this puts it in quite a different light.

HOVSTAD: It certainly does.

THE MAYOR: The worst of it is that we should have to close the Baths for at least two years.

HOVSTAD: Close them? Close them completely?

ASLAKSEN: For two years?

THE MAYOR: Oh yes, the work would take at least as long as that.

ASLAKSEN: Damn it all, we'll never stand for that, sir! How are we householders to live in the meantime?

THE MAYOR: Unfortunately it's extremely difficult to say, Mr Aslaksen. But what do you want us to do? Do you imagine that we should have a single patient here if anyone puts the idea into their heads that the waters are polluted? – that we live on a plague-spot – that the whole town . . .?

ASLAKSEN: And it's all sheer imagination?

THE MAYOR: With the best will in the world I have not been able to persuade myself otherwise.

ASLAKSEN: Then it's absolutely unforgivable of Dr Stockmann – I beg your pardon, sir, but –

THE MAYOR: Unfortunately I'm afraid that what you were saying, Mr Aslaksen, is only too true. My brother has always been impetuous. . . .

ASLAKSEN: Yet you mean to back him up over this, Mr Hovstad!

HOVSTAD: But who would have thought that –

THE MAYOR: I've prepared a short statement on the situation as it would appear from a more reasonable point of view, in which I have indicated how any minor deficiencies that might exist could be remedied within the Baths' financial means .

HOVSTAD: Have you the article with you, Mr Mayor?

THE MAYOR [*feeling in his pockets*]: Yes, I brought it with me just in case you –

ASLAKSEN [*suddenly*]: Hell and damnation, there he is!

THE MAYOR: Who? My brother?

ASLAKSEN: He's coming through the printing-room.

THE MAYOR: How annoying! I've no desire to meet him here, and I still have several matters I wish to discuss with you.

HOVSTAD [*pointing to the door on the right*]: Go in there for the moment.

THE MAYOR: But –?

HOVSTAD: You'll only find Billing there.

ASLAKSEN: Hurry – hurry, Mr Mayor. He's just coming.

THE MAYOR: Yes yes, of course . . . but do get rid of him quickly.

[*He goes out to the right, as* ASLAKSEN *opens and shuts the door for him.*]

HOVSTAD: Look as if you're busy, Aslaksen.

[*He sits and starts writing;* ASLAKSEN *goes through a pile of newspapers on a chair to the right.*]

DR STOCKMANN [*coming in from the printing-room*]: Well, here I am back again. [*He puts down his hat and stick.*]

HOVSTAD [*writing*]: Already, Doctor? Aslaksen, hurry up with what we were just talking about – we've no time to waste today.

DR STOCKMANN [*to Aslaksen*]: No proof yet, I hear?

ASLAKSEN [*without turning round*]: You couldn't expect it yet, Doctor.

DR STOCKMANN: No, of course not . . . but you can guess how impatient I am – I can hardly wait to see it in print.

HOVSTAD: Hm . . . It'll be some time yet, don't you agree, Aslaksen?

ASLAKSEN: Yes, I'm afraid it will.

DR STOCKMANN: All right, my dear friends, I'll come back. My goodness, I don't mind coming back twice. Over an important thing like this – the good of the whole town – one mustn't grudge a little trouble. [*He starts to go, but turns and comes back.*] Oh, there's still one thing I'd like to talk over with you . . .

HOVSTAD: Some other time, if you'll excuse me, Doctor.

DR STOCKMANN: It won't take a moment. . . . It's just this: when people read my article in tomorrow's paper, and realize that I've spent the whole winter quietly working for the good of the town –

HOVSTAD: But, Doctor –

DR STOCKMANN: I know what you're going to say – you

think it was only my plain duty as a citizen . . . of course I know that just as well as you. But my fellow-townsmen, you know . . . well, bless their hearts, they think so much of me –

ASLAKSEN: Yes, the townspeople have thought most highly of you, Doctor, up to now.

DR STOCKMANN: Yes, that's just why I'm afraid they . . . This is what I was going to say: when they read it – especially the poorer classes – they'll look on it as a call to take the town's affairs into their own hands from now on.

HOVSTAD [*getting up*]: Er – look, Doctor, I think you ought to know –

DR STOCKMANN: Aha! I knew there was something in the air! But I won't hear of it! If they're getting up anything like that –

HOVSTAD: Like what?

DR STOCKMANN: Well, anything at all . . . a demonstration, or a luncheon, or a subscription for a presentation, or whatever it's to be – you must promise me faithfully that you'll stop it. You too, Mr Aslaksen, do you understand?

HOVSTAD: You must forgive me, Doctor, but we might as well tell you the plain truth now as later. . . .

[MRS STOCKMANN, *in her outdoor clothes, comes in by the street door.*]

MRS STOCKMANN [*seeing the doctor*]: Ah, I thought as much!

HOVSTAD [*going towards her*]: What, your wife here too?

DR STOCKMANN: What the dickens do *you* want here, Katrina?

MRS STOCKMANN: You know perfectly well what I want.

HOVSTAD: Won't you sit down? Or would you rather –

MRS STOCKMANN: No thank you, don't trouble. . . . And

you must forgive me for coming here to fetch my husband. Remember that I'm the mother of three children.

DR STOCKMANN: Fiddlesticks! We all know that!

MRS STOCKMANN: Well, it doesn't look as if you're giving much thought to your wife and children today, or you wouldn't have gone and plunged us all into ruin.

DR STOCKMANN: You're out of your mind, Katrina! Just because a man has a wife and children, hasn't he the right to proclaim the truth? Hasn't he the right to act the good citizen? Hasn't he the right to serve the town he lives in?

MRS STOCKMANN: Yes, within reason, Tomas.

ASLAKSEN: That's what I say: temperance in all things.

MRS STOCKMANN: That's why it's very wrong of you, Mr Hovstad, to lure my husband away from house and home and make a fool of him over all this.

HOVSTAD: I'm not making a fool of anyone.

DR STOCKMANN: A fool? D'you think I let anyone make a fool of me?

MRS STOCKMANN: Yes, I do! I know you're the cleverest man in the town, Tomas, but it's so easy to make a fool of you. [To Hovstad] Just remember that if you print what he's written, he'll lose his post at the Baths.

ASLAKSEN: What?

HOVSTAD: Well, Doctor, you know –

DR STOCKMANN [laughing]: Aha – just let them try! Oh no – they wouldn't dare . . . you see, I have the solid majority behind me.

MRS STOCKMANN: That's just the trouble – having a nasty thing like that behind you.

DR STOCKMANN: Nonsense, Katrina . . . Go home and take care of your house, and leave me to take care of the community. What are you afraid of? Can't you see that

I'm perfectly happy and confident? [*He paces up and down, rubbing his hands.*] The Truth and the People together will prevail, you can be sure of that. Oh, I can see the whole of the liberal-minded middle class ranged like a conquering host – [*Stopping by a chair*] What? What the devil's this?

ASLAKSEN [*seeing it*]: Oh Lor'!

HOVSTAD [*also realizing*]: Er –

DR STOCKMANN: Here we have the pinnacle of authority! [*He carefully takes the Mayor's official hat between his fingers and holds it up.*]

MRS STOCKMANN: The Mayor's hat!

DR STOCKMANN: And here's the staff of office too! How the dickens –?

HOVSTAD: Well, the fact is –

DR STOCKMANN: Ah, I see! He's been here trying to talk you round! Aha! He's come to the wrong place! And then he caught sight of me in the printing-room. . . . [*He bursts out laughing.*] Did he run away, Mr Aslaksen?

ASLAKSEN [*quickly*]: Ye-yes . . . he ran away, Doctor.

DR STOCKMANN: Ran off and left his stick and – No, that won't do; Peter never left anything behind. But where the devil have you put him? Ah – in here, of course! Just watch this, Katrina!

ASLAKSEN: Be careful, Doctor.

[DR STOCKMANN *has put on the Mayor's hat and taken his staff; now he goes to the door and throws it open, giving a salute.* THE MAYOR *comes out, red with anger.* BILLING *follows.*]

THE MAYOR: What is the meaning of this tomfoolery?

DR STOCKMANN: Show a little respect, my good Peter; I'm in authority in this town now! [*He struts up and down.*]

MRS STOCKMANN [*almost in tears*]: Tomas, don't!

THE MAYOR [*following him*]: Give me my hat and staff!

DR STOCKMANN: You may be the Chief of Police, but I'm the Mayor! I'm master of the whole town, you know, that's what I am!

THE MAYOR: Take off the hat, I tell you. That's an official hat, remember!

DR STOCKMANN: Pooh! The lion of Public Opinion has been roused – d'you think it's going to be frightened by an official hat? You'll see – there'll be a revolution in this town tomorrow. You threatened to dismiss me, but now I dismiss you – from all your important positions! D'you think I can't? Ah, I have the triumphant forces of society on my side. Hovstad and Billing will thunder in the *People's Herald*, and Aslaksen will march forth at the head of the entire Householders' Association –

ASLAKSEN: Oh no I won't, Doctor.

DR STOCKMANN: But of course you will!

THE MAYOR: Ah! But perhaps Mr Hovstad intends to join the agitation after all?

HOVSTAD: No, Mr Mayor.

ASLAKSEN: No, Mr Hovstad isn't such a fool as to ruin himself and his paper for a mere theory.

DR STOCKMANN [*looking from one to the other*]: What does this mean?

HOVSTAD: You've put your case in a false light, Doctor, and I can't support it.

BILLING: And after what Mr Mayor was kind enough to explain to me in there, I –

DR STOCKMANN: A false light? Well, that's my responsibility. Just print my article, and I'll stand by every word of it.

HOVSTAD: I'm not printing it. I neither can nor will . . . I dare not print it!

DR STOCKMANN: You *dare* not? What nonsense! You're

the editor, I should have thought the editor controlled the paper!

ASLAKSEN: No, Doctor, it's the readers who do that.

THE MAYOR: Fortunately, yes.

ASLAKSEN: It's public opinion – the enlightened majority, the householders and the like . . . they're the ones who control the paper.

DR STOCKMANN [*restraining himself*]: And I have all these forces against me?

ASLAKSEN: You have. If your article were printed, it'd mean utter ruin for the town.

DR STOCKMANN: I see . . .

THE MAYOR: My hat and staff!

    [DR STOCKMANN *takes off the hat, and lays it and the staff on the table.*]

THE MAYOR [*taking them*]: Your civic dignity has come to an untimely end!

DR STOCKMANN: It isn't the end yet. [*To Hovstad*] Then it's quite impossible to get my article into the *Herald*?

HOVSTAD: Quite impossible . . . Out of consideration for your family, if for no other reason.

MRS STOCKMANN: Oh, you needn't concern yourself about our family, Mr Hovstad!

THE MAYOR [*bringing a paper from his pocket*]: It will be sufficient for the guidance of the public if this appears; it's an official statement. If you would kindly . . .

HOVSTAD [*taking the paper*]: Good; I'll see that it's printed.

DR STOCKMANN: But you won't print mine? Do you really imagine you can silence me and suppress the truth? It won't be as easy as you think! Mr Aslaksen, will you kindly take my manuscript and print it as a pamphlet at once – at my expense. I'll publish it myself! I'll have four hundred copies – no, five – six hundred!

ASLAKSEN: No, Doctor; even if you offered me its weight in gold, I daren't lend my press for such a thing. I daren't go against public opinion. You won't get that printed anywhere in the whole town.

DR STOCKMANN: Give it me back, then.

HOVSTAD [*handing him the* MS.]: Certainly.

DR STOCKMANN [*picking up his hat and stick*]: It shall be made known all the same. I shall read it at a public meeting – all my fellow-citizens shall hear the voice of truth!

THE MAYOR: Not a single organization in the town would lend their hall for such a purpose.

ASLAKSEN: Not a single one, I'm quite sure of that.

BILLING: No, I'm hanged if they would.

MRS STOCKMANN: But this is disgraceful! Why should everyone turn against you like this?

DR STOCKMANN [*angrily*]: I'll tell you why: it's because all the men in this town are old women – like you. They only think of their families – not of the general good.

MRS STOCKMANN [*taking his arm*]: Then I'll show them that an – an old woman can be a man for once. I'll stand by you, Tomas!

DR STOCKMANN: Good for you, Katrina! I'll make it public – on my soul I will! If I can't rent a hall, I'll hire a drummer to march through the town with me, and I'll read this at every street-corner.

THE MAYOR: You can't be as completely mad as that!

DR STOCKMANN: Oh yes I can.

ASLAKSEN: You won't get a single man in the whole town to go with you.

BILLING: No, I'm hanged if you will.

MRS STOCKMANN: Don't give in, Tomas; I'll tell the boys to go with you.

DR STOCKMANN: That's a splendid idea!

MRS STOCKMANN: Morten'll be delighted, and Eylif'll do whatever Morten does.[44]

DR STOCKMANN: Yes and Petra will come, and you, too, Katrina!

MRS STOCKMANN: No no, I won't do that. But I'll stand in the window and watch you – that's what I'll do!

DR STOCKMANN [*putting his arms round her and kissing her*]: Thank you! Now, my fine gentlemen, the fight is on! Now we'll see if your shabby manoeuvring can muzzle a patriot who wants to purge society!

[*He and his wife go out by the street door at the back.*]

THE MAYOR [*shaking his head thoughtfully*]: Now he's sent *her* mad, too!

ACT FOUR

————————— * —————————

A large old-fashioned room in Captain Horster's house. At the back, open doors lead to an ante-room.

In the left-hand wall there are three windows. In the middle of the opposite wall, a platform has been set up, and on it, a little table with two candles, a water-bottle and glass, and a bell.

The rest of the room is lit by lamps between the windows. In front, to the left, there is a candle-lit table with a chair beside it. Farther forward, to the right, is a door with a few chairs near it.

> [*There is a large gathering of townspeople of all walks of life; among them can be seen a few women and schoolboys.*[45] *More and more people gradually stream in from the back till the room is full.*]

FIRST MAN [*meeting another*]: Ah, Lamstad, you here too?

HIS FRIEND: Yes, I go to all the public meetings.

A BYSTANDER: Brought your whistle, eh?

SECOND MAN: You bet I have – haven't you?

THIRD MAN: Of course. Evensen, the skipper, says he's bringing a huge great fog-horn.

SECOND MAN: Good old Evensen! [*They laugh.*]

FOURTH MAN [*joining them*]: Look, what's all this about? What's going on here tonight?

SECOND MAN: Dr Stockmann's going to make a speech against the Mayor.

FOURTH MAN: But the Mayor's his brother!

FIRST MAN: What of it? That won't worry Dr Stockmann.

THIRD MAN: But he's in the wrong – it says so in the *Herald*.

SECOND MAN: Yes, he must be in the wrong this time – no one would lend him a hall . . . not the Householders' Association, nor the Townsmen's Club –

FIRST MAN: He couldn't even get the hall at the Baths.

SECOND MAN: Well, I should think not!

A MAN [*in another group*]: Who's the right one to back in this, eh?

ANOTHER [*with him*]: Watch Aslaksen, and do what he does.

BILLING [*making his way through the crowd with a brief-case under his arm*]: Excuse me, gentlemen . . . If you wouldn't mind letting me through. . . . I'm reporting this for the *People's Herald*. . . . Many thanks. [*He sits at the table on the left.*]

A WORKMAN: Who was that?

ANOTHER: Don't you know him? That's Billing – he writes for Aslaksen's paper.

[CAPTAIN HORSTER *brings* MRS STOCKMANN *and* PETRA *in through the door on the right.* EYLIF *and* MORTEN *follow them.*]

HORSTER: I thought the family could sit here – then you could easily slip out if anything should happen.

MRS STOCKMANN: Do you think there'll be any trouble?

HORSTER: You can never tell with a crowd like this. Just sit here quietly.

MRS STOCKMANN [*sitting*]: It was so kind of you to offer my husband this room.

HORSTER: No one else would, so . . .

PETRA [*who has also sat down*]: And it was brave of you, too, Captain Horster.

HORSTER: Oh, I don't know that there was anything particularly brave about it.

[HOVSTAD *and* ASLAKSEN *enter at the same time, but each makes his own way through the crowd.*]

ASLAKSEN [*going up to Horster*]: Hasn't the Doctor come yet?

HORSTER: He's waiting in there.

[*There is a movement in the doorway at the back.*]

HOVSTAD [*to Billing*]: There's the Mayor, look.

BILLING: Well I'm hanged! He's turned up after all!

[*The* MAYOR *makes his way quietly through the middle of the crowd, bowing graciously and taking his stand by the wall on the left. Soon afterwards,* DR STOCKMANN *comes in from the right. He is wearing a black frock-coat with a white tie. There is a little tentative applause which is answered by subdued hissing. Then there is quiet.*]

DR STOCKMANN [*in a low voice*]: How do you feel, Katrina?

MRS STOCKMANN: I'm all right. [*Dropping her voice*] Now, Tomas, don't lose your temper!

DR STOCKMANN: Oh, I know how to keep myself in hand, dear. [*He looks at his watch, climbs up on to the platform, and bows.*] It's just a quarter past, so I'll begin. [*He takes out his* MS.]

ASLAKSEN: We ought to elect a chairman first.

DR STOCKMANN: Oh, there's no need for that.

SEVERAL GENTLEMEN [*shouting*]: Yes, yes!

THE MAYOR: I'm of the opinion that someone should be elected to direct the proceedings.

DR STOCKMANN: But, Peter, I've only called this meeting to read a paper.

THE MAYOR: The Medical Officer's paper might possibly give rise to differences of opinion.

SEVERAL VOICES [*from the crowd*]: A chairman! Order, order!

HOVSTAD: The general wish of the meeting seems to be for a chairman.

DR STOCKMANN [*restraining himself*]: Very well, then, let the meeting have its way.

ASLAKSEN: Wouldn't the Mayor be willing to undertake the task?

THREE GENTLEMEN [*clapping*]: Hear hear!

THE MAYOR: For several obvious reasons I must decline. Fortunately, however, we have in our midst a man whom I think we can all accept – I refer to the President of the Householders' Association, Mr Aslaksen.

MANY VOICES: Yes yes ... Good old Aslaksen. ... Hurrah for Aslaksen!

[DR STOCKMANN *picks up his* MS. *and comes down from the platform.*]

ASLAKSEN: Since my fellow-citizens have shown their confidence in me, I cannot refuse.

[*Applause and cheers.* ASLAKSEN *mounts the platform.*]

BILLING [*writing*]: So ... 'Mr Aslaksen was elected with acclamation'...

ASLAKSEN: And now, since I am in this position, may I be allowed to say a few brief words? I am a quiet, peace-loving man, who believes in temperate discretion – and discreet temperance ... as everyone who knows me is aware.

MANY VOICES: Yes, Aslaksen ... yes, of course.

ASLAKSEN: I have learned by experience in the school of life that temperance is the virtue that serves a citizen best –

THE MAYOR: Hear hear!

ASLAKSEN: – and also that it is discretion and temperance

G.P.—9

that best serve the community. I would therefore suggest to our esteemed fellow-citizen who has called this meeting that he should endeavour to keep within temperate bounds.

A MAN BY THE DOOR: Three cheers for the Temperance Society.

A VOICE: To hell with that!

VOICES: Sh! Sh!

ASLAKSEN: No interruptions, please, gentlemen. Has anyone anything to say?

THE MAYOR: Mr Chairman!

ASLAKSEN: The Mayor has the floor.

THE MAYOR: On account of the close relationship which, as you probably know, I bear to the present Medical Officer to the Baths, I should have much preferred not to speak here this evening. However, my official position with regard to the Baths, and my concern for the all-important interests of the town, compel me to put forward a resolution. I venture to assume that there is not a single citizen here present who would consider it desirable that unreliable or exaggerated statements as to the hygienic conditions of the Baths and of the town should be spread abroad. . . .

MANY VOICES: No no! . . . Certainly not. . . . We protest . . . !

THE MAYOR: I therefore beg to propose that this meeting do not permit the Medical Officer to read or deliver his statement on the subject.

DR STOCKMANN [*bursting out*]: Not permit . . . ? What do you mean?

MRS STOCKMANN [*coughing*]: Ahem! Ahem!

DR STOCKMANN [*controlling himself*]: So . . . I'm not permitted to speak!

THE MAYOR: I have, in my statement to the *People's*

Herald, acquainted the public with the relevant facts in such a way that any right-minded citizen may easily form his own opinion. In it you will see that the Medical Officer's report – besides being a vote of no-confidence against the leading men of the town – would in fact impose on the ratepayers an unnecessary outlay of at least a hundred thousand kroner.

[*Indignation and some whistling.*]

ASLAKSEN [*ringing the bell*]: Order, gentlemen! I beg leave to second the Mayor's motion. I, too, believe that there is something behind this agitation of the Doctor's. He talks about the Baths, but what he is really working for is a revolution; he hopes to place the administration of the town in other hands. No one can doubt the honesty of the Doctor's intentions – heaven knows there can be no two opinions about that. I, too, believe in self-government by the people – so long as it doesn't fall too heavily on the ratepayers. But in this case, that would be the result . . . and for that reason – if you'll forgive me – I'm damned if I can support Dr Stockmann over this. If you ask *me*, I think you can pay too dearly even for gold!

[*Brisk applause from all sides.*]

HOVSTAD: I, too, feel called upon to explain my position. At first it seemed that Dr Stockmann's agitation was finding favour in certain quarters, and as far as I could I gave it my impartial support. Soon, however, we began to realize that we had allowed ourselves to be misled by a false statement –

DR STOCKMANN: False –!

HOVSTAD: – a somewhat inaccurate statement, then. The Mayor's report has proved that. I hope that no one present doubts my liberal outlook – the *Herald's* policy on all important political questions is well known to you all. But I have learned from men of experience and discretion that in purely local matters a newspaper should proceed with a certain caution.

ASLAKSEN: I entirely agree with the speaker.

HOVSTAD: And in the matter in question, there is not the slightest doubt that Dr Stockmann has public opinion against him. But, gentlemen, where, first and foremost, does an editor's duty lie? Surely it is to work in harmony with his readers? Has he not, in a way, been given a tacit mandate to work diligently and untiringly to further the interests of his subscribers? Or am I perhaps mistaken?

MANY VOICES: No no no . . . you're right!

HOVSTAD: It has been a painful struggle for me to break with a man in whose house I've recently been a welcome guest – a man who, until today, has enjoyed the unqualified goodwill of his fellow-citizens – a man whose only fault – or at any rate his greatest fault – is that he consults his heart rather than his head.

SEVERAL SCATTERED VOICES: That's true! Hurrah for Dr Stockmann!

HOVSTAD: But my duty to the community has forced me to break with him. There is, too, another consideration that forces me to oppose him, and if possible to turn him from this disastrous course on which he has embarked – and that is consideration for his wife and family –

DR STOCKMANN: Stick to the water supply and the drains!

HOVSTAD: – consideration for his wife and his defenceless children!

MORTEN: Is that us, Mother?

MRS STOCKMANN: Hush!

ASLAKSEN: I will now put the Mayor's proposal to the vote?

DR STOCKMANN: There's no need for that! Tonight I don't intend to talk about all the filth down at the Baths! No, you shall hear something quite different.

THE MAYOR [*to himself*]: What's he up to now?

A DRUNKEN MAN [*up by the main door*]: I'm a ratepayer
— so I have a right to my opinion. And I'm completely —
firmly — *incomprehensibly* of the opinion that —⁴⁶

SEVERAL VOICES: Quiet at the back, there!

OTHERS: He's drunk — throw him out!

DR STOCKMANN: May I speak?

ASLAKSEN: Dr Stockmann has the floor.

DR STOCKMANN: A day or two ago, I should have liked
to see anyone try — as they have tried tonight — to gag
me. I should have fought like a lion for my sacred rights
as a man. But now it doesn't matter to me . . . now I
have more important things to speak about.

[*The crowd moves up closer round him;* MORTEN KIIL
comes into view among them.]

DR STOCKMANN [*continuing*]: I've done a good deal of
thinking, these last few days — wondering about so many
things, that in the end my head was in a whirl —

THE MAYOR [*coughing*]: Hm!

DR STOCKMANN: — but in the end I got it all straight, so
that I could see the whole thing clearly. That's why I'm
standing here this evening. . . . I have a great revelation
to make to you, my friends. I want to tell you about a
discovery of much more far-reaching importance than
the trifling fact that our water supply is poisoned, and
that our curative Baths are built on infected ground.

MANY VOICES [*shouting*]: Don't talk about the Baths!
We won't have that! That's enough!

DR STOCKMANN: I've already said that what I mean to tell
you about is the great discovery that I've made these last
few days . . . the discovery that it's the very sources of
our spiritual life that are poisoned — and that our whole
community stands on ground that's infected with
lies!

ASTONISHED VOICES [*under their breaths*]: What's that he's saying?

THE MAYOR: What an accusation!

ASLAKSEN [*with his hand on the bell*]: I must call on the speaker to moderate his language.

DR STOCKMANN: I've loved my native town as deeply as any man can love the home of his childhood. I was still young when I went away, and separation, memories, and homesickness cast a kind of enchantment over the town and its people. [*Some applause and shouts of approval.*] For many years I lived in a terrible hole up north; when I came to meet some of the people who lived there, thinly scattered among the rocks, I sometimes thought that what those poor stunted creatures up there really needed wasn't a doctor like me, but a vet!

    [*Murmurs.*]

BILLING [*putting down his pen*]: Well, I'm damned if I've ever heard . . .!

HOVSTAD: That's an insult to decent country folk!

DR STOCKMANN: Just wait a minute. I don't think anyone can accuse me of forgetting about my native town up there! No, I sat there brooding like an eider-duck,[47] and what I hatched out was – the plan for these Baths here. [*Applause and protests.*] And when, at long last, fate granted me the great happiness of coming home again, it seemed to me, my friends, that there was nothing else I wanted in the whole world! At least, there was just one thing: I had an urgent, tireless, burning desire to work for the good of my native town and its people.

THE MAYOR [*gazing into space*]: Hm! A strange way of doing it!

DR STOCKMANN: So I went about here uncritically, rejoicing in my good fortune. But yesterday morning – no, it was actually two evenings ago – my eyes were suddenly opened, and the first thing I saw was the overwhelming stupidity of the authorities!

[*Uproar; shouts and laughter.* MRS STOCKMANN *coughs repeatedly.*]

THE MAYOR: Mr Chairman!

ASLAKSEN [*ringing his bell*]: By virtue of my office –!

DR STOCKMANN: It's petty to pull me up over a single word, Mr Aslaksen. All I mean is that I got on the track of the colossal muddle down at the Baths that our leading citizens are to blame for. I can't, for the life of me, stand Leading Citizens – I've seen too many of 'em in my time.[48] They're like billy-goats in a young plantation – destroying everything, and standing in the way of a free man wherever he turns. I only wish we could exterminate them like other vermin.

[*Uproar.*]

THE MAYOR: Mr Chairman – are such expressions to be allowed?

ASLAKSEN [*with his hand on the bell*]: Doctor –!

DR STOCKMANN: I can't understand how it's only now that I've come to see these gentry at their true worth, when, day in and day out, I've had such a magnificent specimen right under my nose: my brother Peter – slow-witted, pig-headed, and –

[*Uproar, laughter, and whistling.* MRS STOCKMANN *coughs.* ASLAKSEN *rings violently.*]

THE DRUNKEN MAN [*who has come back*]: Are you referring to *me*? My name's Petersen, all right, but I'm damned if –

ANGRY VOICES: Throw him out! He's drunk! Out with him! [*He is thrown out again.*]

THE MAYOR: Who was that person?

A BYSTANDER: I don't know him, Mr Mayor.

ANOTHER: He isn't a local man.

A THIRD: I think he's a timber-merchant from out at –
[*The rest is inaudible.*]

ASLAKSEN: Obviously the fellow has had too much beer.
Continue, Doctor, but more temperately, please.

DR STOCKMANN: Very well, fellow-townsmen, I'll say no
more about our leading citizens. But if anyone imagines
from what I've just been saying that it's these gentlemen
that I'm out after tonight, then he's wrong – completely
and utterly wrong. . . . You see, I cherish the comfortable
belief that those sluggards – those relics of a dying school
of thought – are very busy cutting their own throats!
They don't need any doctor's help to speed them on their
way. No, it isn't people like that who are the greatest
danger to the Community. They're not the ones who are
poisoning our spiritual life at the source, and infecting
the ground under our feet. They're not the ones who're
the most dangerous enemies of truth and freedom in our
society. . . .

SHOUTS [*from all sides*]: Who then? Who are they? Name
them!

DR STOCKMANN: Oh yes, I'm going to name them – you
can be quite sure of that. That's precisely the great discovery that I made yesterday. [*Raising his voice*] The
most dangerous enemy of truth and freedom among us
is . . . the solid majority! Yes, the damned, solid, liberal
majority – that's it! So now you know!

[*Tremendous noise in the room. Most of the audience
are shouting, stamping, or whistling. Some of the elder
men exchange covert glances and seem to be enjoying
themselves.* MRS STOCKMANN *rises in alarm.* EYLIF
and MORTEN *advance menacingly on some unruly
schoolboys.* ASLAKSEN *rings his bell and shouts for
order;* HOVSTAD *and* BILLING *are both speaking at*

once, but can't make themselves heard. At last there is quiet.]

ASLAKSEN: As chairman, I must ask the speaker to withdraw his ill-advised remarks.

DR STOCKMANN: Never, Mr Aslaksen. It's this very majority in our community that's denying me my freedom, and wants to stop me from speaking the truth.

HOVSTAD: The majority always has right on its side.

BILLING: Yes, and truth, too – I'm hanged if it hasn't!

DR STOCKMANN: The majority *never* has right on its side ... never, I tell you! That's one of the social lies that an intelligent, independent man has to fight against. Who makes up the majority of the population in a country – the wise men or the fools? I think you'll agree with me that, all the wide world over, nowadays the fools are in a quite terrifyingly overwhelming majority. And how the devil can it be right for the fools to rule over the wise men?

[*Shouts and cries.*]

Oh yes, you can shout me down, but you can't refute me. The majority is strong – unfortunately – but *right* it certainly is not! *I'm* right – I and a few others – the minority is always right!

[*Renewed uproar.*]

HOVSTAD: Aha! So since the day before yesterday, Dr Stockmann has become an aristocrat!

DR STOCKMANN: I've told you already that I don't mean to waste any time on the puny, flat-chested, short-winded crew that we're leaving in our wake. Active, pulsating life no longer concerns them. I'm thinking of the few – the very few – among us who've absorbed all the new, vigorous truths. These are the men who stand at the outposts, as it were – so far in advance that the solid majority hasn't been able to catch them up. They're fighting for truths so newly-born in the world of thought as to have only the few on their side.

HOVSTAD: Ah, so the Doctor's a revolutionary now!

DR STOCKMANN: Yes, by god, I am, Mr Hovstad. I'm starting a revolution against the lie that truth and the majority go hand in hand. What sort of truths do the majority always rally round? Why, truths so stricken with age that they're practically decrepit! But when a truth's as old as that, gentlemen, it's well on the way to becoming a lie. [*Laughter and jeers.*] All right, don't believe me if you don't want to . . . but truths certainly aren't the tenacious old Methuselahs that some people think. As a general rule, an ordinary common-or-garden truth lives – let's say – seventeen or eighteen years . . . twenty at the outside. Rarely longer. But although those elderly truths are always shockingly scrawny, it isn't till then that the majority takes them up and recommends them to society as wholesome spiritual food. There isn't much nourishment in that sort of diet, I can assure you – and I'm speaking as a doctor! All these majority-truths are like last year's salt pork – like mouldy, rancid, half-cured ham! And that's what's at the root of the moral scurvy that's rampaging through society.

ASLAKSEN: Our worthy speaker seems to be straying rather far from his subject.

THE MAYOR: I must endorse the chairman's remark.

DR STOCKMANN: You must be mad, then, Peter – I'm sticking as close to my subject as possible. Because what I want to tell you is precisely this: that the masses, the majority – this damned solid majority – is, as I tell you, precisely what is poisoning our spiritual life at the source, and infecting the ground we stand on.

HOVSTAD: And all this, because the great independent

majority of the people has the sense to accept only those truths that are well-founded and generally accepted!

DR STOCKMANN: Oh, my dear Mr Hovstad, don't talk to me about accepted truths! The truths that the masses and the majorities accept are the truths that the leaders of thought accepted in our grandfathers' day! We leaders of thought of the present day don't accept them any longer. And I don't believe that there's any truth more well-founded than this: that no community can live a healthy life on old dry bones of truth like that.

HOVSTAD: Instead of standing there and talking into the blue like this, it'd be interesting if you'd give us some examples of these old dry bones of truth that we live on.

[*Agreement from all sides.*]

DR STOCKMANN: Oh, I could rake up a whole heap of the disgusting muck . . . but for the moment I'll confine myself to just *one* accepted truth that's a rotten lie at heart . . . yet it's what both Mr Hovstad and the *People's Herald* – yes, and all the *Herald*'s readers – live by.

HOVSTAD: And what is that?

DR STOCKMANN: It's the doctrine that you've inherited from your forefathers, and that you've been thoughtlessly spreading abroad . . . the doctrine that the common herd – the masses – the mob – are the backbone of the People – that they *are* the People. That the common man, this ignorant and uneducated part of society, has the same right to sanction and condemn, to govern and advise, as the intellectually superior few.

BILLING: Well, I'm hanged if I –

HOVSTAD [*shouting simultaneously*]: Citizens – take note of that!

ANGRY VOICES: Oh? We're the People, aren't we? Is it only the big-wigs who can govern?

A WORKER: Throw him out if he talks like that!

OTHERS: Out with him!

A TOWNSMAN [*shouting*]: Blow your horn, Evensen!

[*Loud blasts on a horn, and angry uproar.*]

DR STOCKMANN [*when the noise has subsided a little*]:
Now, be reasonable! Can't you listen to the truth just
for once? Of course I don't expect you all to agree with
me straight away, but I'd certainly hoped that Mr Hovstad would admit I'm right, once he'd had a chance to
think it over a bit. Mr Hovstad claims to be a free-
thinker —

SEVERAL VOICES [*in astonished murmurs*]: A free-
thinker? What? Is the editor a free-thinker?

HOVSTAD [*furious*]: Prove that, Dr Stockmann! When
have I said so in print?

DR STOCKMANN [*thoughtfully*]: No, damn it, you're right
there — you've never had the courage. All right, I won't
put you in the pillory, Mr Hovstad — let's say *I'm* the
free-thinker, then. And now I'm going to prove to you
all — scientifically — that the *Herald*'s been quite shame-
lessly leading you by the nose when it assures you that
the ordinary people — the common herd — the mob — are
the real backbone of the country. You know, that's
nothing but a newspaper lie. The common herd is just
the raw material from which a People is made.

[*Murmurs, laughter, and disturbance throughout the
room.*]

Well, isn't that true with all the rest of living creatures?
Look at the difference between pedigree and non-pedigree
stock. Look at an ordinary barn-door fowl: how much
meat is there on a stringy carcase like that? And what
sort of eggs does she lay? Any self-respecting crow or
rook could lay one almost as big! But now take a pedigree
Spanish or Japanese hen — or a good pheasant or a turkey

– and then you'll see the difference. Or look at dogs – they're nearer to us human beings in lots of ways. First think of an ordinary mongrel – one of those filthy, ragged, plebeian curs that does nothing but run round the streets fouling the doorposts. Then put that mongrel beside a poodle with a pedigree going back through generations of famous ancestors – who's been properly reared, and brought up among soft voices and music. D'you really think the poodle's brain won't have developed quite differently from the mongrel's? You can be sure it will. It's well-bred poodle pups like that the showmen train to do the most incredible tricks – things that an ordinary mongrel could never learn, even if it stood on its head!

[*Uproar and shouts from all sides.*]

A CITIZEN [*shouting*]: Do you want to make dogs of us now?

ANOTHER: We're not animals, Doctor!

DR STOCKMANN: But bless my soul, that's exactly what you are, my friend – we're the finest animals anyone could wish for . . . though you won't find many pedigree animals even among us. Yes, there's an enormous difference between the human poodles and the human mongrels. And the amusing thing is that Mr Hovstad entirely agrees with me – as long as we're talking about four-legged animals.

HOVSTAD: Oh, as far as *they*'re concerned . . .

DR STOCKMANN: All right. But as soon as I apply the argument to two-legged animals, then Mr Hovstad stops short. He daren't think for himself any longer, or follow the idea to its logical conclusion. No, he turns the whole principle upside down, and proclaims in the *Herald* that the barn-door fowl and the mongrel in the alley are just the finest specimens in the menagerie! But that's always the way, so long as the common man *will* stick in the muck, and won't work his way up to intellectual distinction.

HOVSTAD: I make no claim to any kind of distinction. I come of simple, humble stock, and I'm proud to have my roots deep down among the common folk whom he's insulting!

MANY VOICES: Hurrah for Hovstad! Hurrah – hurrah!

DR STOCKMANN: The sort of common people I'm talking about aren't only found among the lower classes – they're crawling in swarms all round us – right up to the very pinnacle of society. Just look at our nice smart Mayor – my brother's as common a man as ever went on two legs. . . .

[*Laughter and hissing.*]

THE MAYOR: I must protest against such personal remarks.

DR STOCKMANN [*imperturbably*]: – and that's not because, like me, he's descended from a rascally old pirate from Pomerania or thereabouts – because that's where we –

THE MAYOR: A preposterous legend! I deny it!

DR STOCKMANN: – he's common because he thinks the thoughts his bosses think, and holds the opinions they hold. Men who do that are spiritually common; and that, you see, is why my distinguished brother Peter is so sadly lacking in distinction at heart . . . and, consequently, lacking in broad-mindedness.

THE MAYOR: Mr Chairman!

HOVSTAD: So it's the bosses who are the liberals in this country? That's quite a new idea.

[*Laughter among the crowd.*]

DR STOCKMANN: Yes, that's another part of my new discovery – and it's linked with the idea that broad-mindedness is almost exactly the same thing as morality. That's why I say that it's absolutely unpardonable of the *Herald* to go on, day in and day out, propounding the heresy that it's the masses, the mob, the solid majority, who have the monopoly of broad-mindedness and morality . . . and that vice and corruption and all kinds of intellectual uncleanness are things that seep out of culture – just as all that filth seeps down to the Baths from the tannery up at Mølledal. [*Noise and interruptions.* DR STOCKMANN, *undisturbed and smiling, continues eagerly*:] And yet this same *Herald* can preach that the masses and the mobs ought to be raised to higher stations in life. But, in the devil's name, if this doctrine of the *Herald*'s holds good, then elevating the masses would amount precisely to toppling them straight into depravity! It's a lucky thing that this notion that culture corrupts is only an old wives' tale. No, it's stupidity, poverty, and ugly surroundings that do the devil's work. In a house that isn't swept and aired every day – my wife Katrina maintains that it ought to be scrubbed, too, but that's a moot point – well, in that sort of house, I tell you, after two or three years people lose the power to think or behave decently. Lack of oxygen weakens the conscience . . . and it looks as if there's a terrible shortage of oxygen in all sorts of houses here in this town, when the solid majority can be unscrupulous enough to want to found the town's prosperity on a quagmire of lies and fraud!

THE MAYOR: You cannot fling a gross accusation like that against a whole community!

A GENTLEMAN: I move that the chairman rule the speaker out of order.

ANGRY VOICES: Yes! That's right! He's out of order!

DR STOCKMANN [*flaring up*]: Then I'll shout the truth at every street corner! I'll write to papers in other towns. The whole country shall know how things stand here.

HOVSTAD: It almost looks as if the Doctor's aim is to ruin the town.

DR STOCKMANN: Yes! I love my native town so much that I'd rather ruin it than see it flourish on a lie.

ASLAKSEN: That's plain speaking! [*Noise and whistling.* MRS STOCKMANN *coughs in vain — the Doctor no longer hears her.*]

HOVSTAD [*shouting through the noise*]: A man who wants to ruin a whole community must be the citizens' enemy.

DR STOCKMANN: What does it matter if a lying community is ruined? Let it be razed to the ground, I say! All those who live by lies should be wiped out like vermin. It'll end in the whole country being infected. You'll bring things to such a pass that the whole country will deserve to be destroyed. And if ever it should come to that, then with all my heart I say: Let it all be destroyed — let all the people perish!

A MAN [*in the crowd*]: He talks like a proper enemy of the public!

BILLING: That's the Voice of the People, I'm hanged if it isn't!

THE WHOLE CROWD [*shouting*]: Yes yes! He's a public enemy! He hates his country — he hates the whole people!

ASLAKSEN: Both as a citizen of this town, and as a human being, I'm deeply shocked at what I've been forced to listen to here. Dr Stockmann has unmasked himself in a way I should never have dreamed of. I must reluctantly subscribe to the sentiments just expressed by these worthy citizens, and in my opinion we ought to express those sentiments in a resolution. I propose the following: This meeting declares that it considers the Medical Officer of the Baths, Dr Tomas Stockmann, to be a public enemy.

[*Thunderous applause and cheers. A crowd surrounds the Doctor, hissing him.* MRS STOCKMANN *and* PETRA *have risen;* MORTEN *and* EYLIF *are fighting with their schoolfellows who have been joining in the hissing, and several people try to pull them apart.*]

DR STOCKMANN [*to those who are hissing*]: Fools that you are! I tell you –

ASLAKSEN [*ringing his bell*]: Dr Stockmann is out of order. A formal vote must be taken. However, out of regard for personal feelings, it shall be done by secret ballot. Mr Billing, have you any blank paper?

BILLING: Here's some blue and some white.

ASLAKSEN [*stepping down*]: Excellent. That'll save time. Cut it into strips – yes, like that. [*To the meeting*] White for Aye, blue for Nay. I will go round and collect the votes myself.

[THE MAYOR *leaves the room.* ASLAKSEN *and a few other townspeople go round with the strips of paper in hats.*]

A GENTLEMAN [*to Hovstad*]: What's come over the Doctor, d'you think? What's it all about?

HOVSTAD: Well, you know how he always rushed things.

ANOTHER MAN [*to Billing*]: Look, you go to his house a lot, have you ever noticed if the fellow drinks?

BILLING: I'm hanged if I know what to say. There's always toddy on the table when anyone calls.

A THIRD MAN: No, I think he's off his head sometimes.

FIRST MAN: Ah, I wonder if there's any madness in the family.

BILLING: Could very well be.

FOURTH MAN: No, it's sheer spite; he wants to get his own back about something or other.

BILLING: He was certainly talking about a rise in salary the other day – but he didn't get it.

ALL THE MEN [*together*]: Ah, that explains it.

THE DRUNKEN MAN [*among the crowd*]: I want a blue one! And I want a white one, too!

VOICES: That's that drunken man again — throw him out!

KIIL [*coming up to the Doctor*]: Well, Stockmann, now you see where your monkey-tricks have got you!

DR STOCKMANN: I've done my duty.

KIIL: What was it you said about the Mølledal tanneries?

DR STOCKMANN: You heard what I said — that's where all the filth comes from.

KIIL: From my tannery too?

DR STOCKMANN: I'm sorry to say yours is the worst of the lot.

KIIL: Are you putting *that* in the papers?

DR STOCKMANN: I'm not keeping anything back.

KIIL: You may find that expensive, Stockmann.[49] [*He goes.*]

A FAT MAN [*going up to Captain Horster, without bowing to the ladies*]: Well, Captain, so you lend your house to public enemies?

HORSTER: Surely I can do what I like with my own property, sir?

THE FAT MAN: Then you can have no objection if I do the same with mine.

HORSTER: What do you mean, sir?

THE FAT MAN: You'll be hearing from me in the morning. [*He turns and goes.*]

PETRA: Captain Horster — wasn't that the owner of your ship?

HORSTER: Yes, that was Mr Vik.

ASLAKSEN [*with the ballot papers in his hand, he climbs the platform and rings the bell*]: Gentlemen, I must now announce the result of the ballot. All the voters except one —

A YOUNG MAN: That'll be that drunk fellow!

ASLAKSEN: With the exception of one intoxicated person, this gathering of townspeople unanimously declares the Medical Officer of the Baths to be a public enemy.

[*Cheers and applause.*]

Three cheers for our ancient and honourable town! [*After the cheers*] Three cheers for our able and efficient Mayor, who has so loyally set family interests aside.

[*Cheers.*]

The meeting is adjourned. [*He gets down.*]

BILLING: Three cheers for the chairman!

THE ENTIRE CROWD: Hurrah for Aslaksen!

DR STOCKMANN: My hat and coat, Petra. Captain, have you room for some passengers to the New World?

HORSTER: For you and your family, Doctor, we'll make room.

DR STOCKMANN [*as* PETRA *helps him on with his coat*]: Good. Come, Katrina – come boys. [*He takes his wife's arm.*]

MRS STOCKMANN: Tomas dear, let's go out by the back way.

DR STOCKMANN: No back ways, Katrina. [*Raising his voice*] You shall hear from your Public Enemy before he shakes the dust of this place off his feet! I'm not as forbearing as a certain person was. . . . I don't say 'I forgive you, for you know not what you do.'

ASLAKSEN [*shouting*]: Dr Stockmann! That's a blasphemous comparison!

BILLING: Well I'll be – That a decent man should have to hear such a thing!

A ROUGH VOICE: And he threatened us, too!

ANGRY VOICES: Let's smash his windows! Chuck him in the fjord!

A MAN IN THE CROWD: Blow your horn, Evensen! Toot-toot!

[*Horn-blowing, whistling, and wild shouting. The* DOCTOR, *with his family, goes to the door,* HORSTER *clearing a passage for them.*]

ALL THE CROWD [*yelling after them as they go*]: Public Enemy! Public Enemy! Public Enemy!

BILLING [*collecting his notes*]: Well, I'm hanged if I'd care to drink toddy with the Stockmanns tonight!

[*The crowd streams for the exit. The shouting goes on outside, and from the street are heard cries of 'Public Enemy! Public Enemy!'*]

ACT FIVE

————————— * —————————

Dr Stockmann's study. Round the walls are bookcases and cabinets filled with specimens. At the back is a door leading to the hall; and in front, to the left, a door to the living-room. In the wall to the right are two windows with all the panes broken. In the middle of the room is the Doctor's desk, covered with books and papers.
The room is in disorder. It is morning.

> [DR STOCKMANN, *in dressing-gown, slippers, and skull-cap, is bending down to rake under one of the cabinets with an umbrella. Eventually he pulls out a stone.*]

DR STOCKMANN [*calling through the open door to the living-room*]: I've found another, Katrina!

MRS STOCKMANN [*from the living-room*]: Oh, I expect you'll find plenty more.

DR STOCKMANN [*adding the stone to a pile of others on the table*]: I'm going to keep these stones as sacred relics. Eylif and Morten must look at them every day, and when they grow up they'll inherit them from me. [*Raking under a bookcase*] Hasn't – now what the devil's her name? [50] – hasn't the girl gone for the glazier yet?

MRS STOCKMANN [*entering*]: Yes, but he said he didn't know if he could come today.

DR STOCKMANN: You'll see – he daren't come!

MRS STOCKMANN: Yes, that's what Randina thought – he daren't come because of the neighbours. [*Calling into the living-room*] What is it, Randina? Oh, all right. [*She goes, and comes straight back.*] It's a letter for you, Tomas.

DR STOCKMANN: Let's see. [*He opens it and reads.*] Aha!

MRS STOCKMANN: Who's it from?

DR STOCKMANN: From the landlord . . . giving us notice.

MRS STOCKMANN: Really? But he's such a nice man.

DR STOCKMANN [*looking at the letter*]: He daren't do anything else, he says. He doesn't like it, but he just daren't do anything else . . . on account of his fellow-citizens . . . out of regard to public opinion . . . not a free agent . . . daren't risk offending certain influential people. . . .

MRS STOCKMANN: There, you see, Tomas!

DR STOCKMANN: Oh yes, I see all right. They're cowards in this town – all the lot of them. None of them dares do anything because of the rest. [*Throwing the letter on to the table*] But it's all the same to us, Katrina; we're off to the New World, and then . . .

MRS STOCKMANN: Yes, but Tomas, have you really thought it over – this idea of going away?

DR STOCKMANN: You wouldn't want me to stay here – where they've pilloried me as a Public Enemy, branded me, smashed my windows. . . . And look here, Katrina – they've torn a hole in my black trousers!

MRS STOCKMANN: Oh Tomas – and they were your best ones!

DR STOCKMANN: Yes, you should never wear your best trousers when you go out to fight for truth and freedom. Though, you know, I don't mind so much about the trousers – you can always catch them together for me . . . but that the mob – the rabble – should go for me as if they were my equals . . . that's what I'm damned if I can stand!

MRS STOCKMANN: Yes, they've treated you very badly

here, Tomas. But do we have to leave the country altogether, just because of them?

DR STOCKMANN: Don't you think we'd find the rabble just as insolent in other towns? Of course we should. They're all as like as two peas! Well, to blazes with the curs – let them yap. But that's not the worst of it . . . the worst thing is that, all over the country, every man is the slave of his party. Though, if it comes to that, I don't suppose it'll be much better out West, either – the solid majority and the enlightened public opinion, and all that damned nonsense flourish out there too. But, you see, things are on a bigger scale there. They may kill you, but they don't torture you . . . they don't take a free spirit and put thumbscrews on it the way they do here at home. And, if need be, you can keep out of it altogether. [*Pacing up and down*] If only I knew where there was a primeval forest or a small South Sea island going cheap. . . .

MRS STOCKMANN: Yes, but what about the boys, Tomas.

DR STOCKMANN [*coming to a halt*]: What an extraordinary woman you are, Katrina! Would you prefer the boys to grow up in a society like ours? You saw for yourself last night that half the population is raving mad, and if the other half haven't lost their senses, it's because they're such blockheads that they haven't any wits to lose!

MRS STOCKMANN: But, Tomas dear, you do say such unwise things.

DR STOCKMANN: Oh? But everything I say is true, isn't it? It's they who turn all my ideas upside down – it's they who mix up right and wrong into one complete hotchpotch – it's they who label as lies all the things that I know are the truth! But the craziest thing of all is the way that grown men – liberal men – go about in droves, persuading themselves and everybody else that they have independent minds. Did you ever hear anything like it, Katrina?

MRS STOCKMANN: Yes, it's quite mad, of course, but –

[PETRA *comes in from the living-room.*]

Back from the school already?

PETRA: Yes, I've been dismissed.

MRS STOCKMANN: Dismissed?

DR STOCKMANN: You too?

PETRA: Mrs Busk gave me notice, but I thought I'd better go straight away.

DR STOCKMANN: You were quite right.

MRS STOCKMANN: I'd never have thought Mrs Busk would do that.

PETRA: Oh, Mrs Busk isn't so bad, Mother. I could see she didn't like doing it . . . but, as she said, she daren't do anything else – so I'm dismissed.

DR STOCKMANN [*laughing and rubbing his hands*]: So she's another one who 'daren't do anything else' – this is splendid!

MRS STOCKMANN: Well, after that dreadful scene last night . . .

PETRA: It wasn't just *that*. Listen to this, Father.

DR STOCKMANN: Well?

PETRA: Mrs Busk showed me no fewer than three letters she'd had this morning.

DR STOCKMANN: Anonymous, of course?

PETRA: Yes.

DR STOCKMANN: There, Katrina, they daren't sign their names.

PETRA: And two of them said that a certain gentleman, who often came to this house, had been saying in the Club last night that I had extremely advanced opinions on several subjects.

DR STOCKMANN: You didn't deny it, of course?

PETRA: No, you know I wouldn't. Mrs Busk has some pretty advanced opinions herself when we're alone together, but now that this has come out, she daren't keep me on.

MRS STOCKMANN: And to think how often she's been to this house! There, Tomas, you see what you get for your hospitality!

DR STOCKMANN: We're not living in this filthy hole any longer. Pack up as soon as you can, Katrina, and let's get away – the sooner the better.

MRS STOCKMANN: Listen – I think that's someone out in the hall. Go and see, Petra.

PETRA [*opening the door*]: Oh, it's you, Captain Horster – do come in.

HORSTER [*from outside*]: Good morning. I thought I'd just look in and see how you were.

DR STOCKMANN [*shaking his hand*]: Thank you – that's very kind of you.

MRS STOCKMANN: And thank you for helping us last night, Captain Horster.

PETRA: But how did you get back home?

HORSTER: Oh, I managed. I'm pretty strong, you know – and those people are all bark and no bite.

DR STOCKMANN: Yes, isn't it amazing what cowardly swine they are? Here, I want to show you something. Look, here are the stones they've thrown through the windows. Just look at them – I'm damned if there are more than two decent-sized chunks in the whole pile! The rest are no bigger than pebbles – just bits of gravel. Yet there they stood, shouting and swearing to kill me . . . but when it came to *doing* anything – real action – ah no, you don't get much of that in this town!

HORSTER: This time, that was just as well for you, Doctor.

DR STOCKMANN: It certainly was. But it's infuriating, all the same, because, you see, if it should ever come to a serious national struggle, then public opinion would be all in favour of taking to its heels, and the solid majority would make for cover like a flock of sheep. That's what's such a depressing thought, Captain Horster – it really worries me . . . Oh, to hell with it – it's stupid to worry. They call me a public enemy – I'll *be* the public's enemy!

MRS STOCKMANN: That's something you'll never be, Tomas.

DR STOCKMANN: I shouldn't bank on that, Katrina. A bad name can be just like a foreign body in the lung, and that damned phrase – I can't get it out of my mind. It's sticking in my gizzard, biting and gnawing like acid – and no amount of magnesia will cure it.

PETRA: Pooh. You ought to laugh at them, Father.

HORSTER: They'll change their minds one day, Doctor.

MRS STOCKMANN: Yes, Tomas – as sure as you're standing there.

DR STOCKMANN: Ah, when it's too late, perhaps. Well, if they want it that way, they can have it. They can go on wallowing in their pigsty till they're sorry they drove a patriot into exile. When do you sail, Captain Horster?

HORSTER: Well – that's what I came to talk to you about. . . .

DR STOCKMANN: What? Is there something wrong with the ship?

HORSTER: No. But the fact is, I'm not going with her.

PETRA: Surely *you* haven't been dismissed?

HORSTER [*smiling*]: I have.

PETRA: You too?

MRS STOCKMANN: There, you see, Tomas.

DR STOCKMANN: And all in the cause of truth. Oh, if I'd thought that anything like *that* –

HORSTER: Don't worry about it; I shall get a job with another company, somewhere else.

DR STOCKMANN: So much for Mr Vik . . . a rich man – not dependent on anyone. . . . It's a damned shame.

HORSTER: Oh, he's quite a reasonable man – apart from this. He says himself he'd have liked to keep me on, if only he dared.

DR STOCKMANN: But he didn't dare – obviously.

HORSTER: Well, as he said, it's not so simple, when you belong to a Party.

DR STOCKMANN: Our fine friend never spoke a truer word! A Party's like a sausage-machine – it grinds all the brains together into a single mash – till you get nothing but a pile of blockheads and fatheads.

MRS STOCKMANN: Oh, Tomas, no!

PETRA [*to Horster*]: If only you hadn't seen us home, perhaps it wouldn't have come to this.

HORSTER: I don't regret it.

PETRA [*giving him her hand*]: Thank you.

HORSTER [*to the Doctor*]: What I wanted to say was that if you really mean to go away, I've thought of something else.

DR STOCKMANN: Splendid – as long as we can get away quickly.

MRS STOCKMANN: Sh! Wasn't that a knock at the door?

PETRA: It'll be Uncle.

DR STOCKMANN: Aha! [*Calling*] Come in.

MRS STOCKMANN: Tomas dear, promise me –

[*The* MAYOR *comes in from the hall.*]

THE MAYOR [*in the doorway*]: Oh, you're engaged. Then I'd better . . .

DR STOCKMANN: No no, come in.

THE MAYOR: But I wanted to talk to you privately.

MRS STOCKMANN: We'll go into the living-room for a bit.

HORSTER: And I'll come back later.

DR STOCKMANN: No, go in with them, Captain Horster; I want to hear more about –

HORSTER: All right, I'll wait.

> [*He follows* MRS STOCKMANN *and* PETRA *into the living-room. The* MAYOR *looks at the windows, but says nothing.*]

DR STOCKMANN: Perhaps you find it a bit draughty here today. Put your hat on.

THE MAYOR: Thank you – if I may. [*He does so.*] I think I must have caught a cold last night. I was shivering all the time.

DR STOCKMANN: Oh? I found it rather warm.

THE MAYOR: I'm sorry that it was not in my power to prevent the excesses of last night.

DR STOCKMANN: Have you anything else in particular to say to me?

THE MAYOR [*taking out a large envelope*]: I have this document for you – from the Directors of the Baths.

DR STOCKMANN: Am I dismissed?

THE MAYOR: Yes, from today. [*Putting the envelope on the table*] We are very sorry, but frankly, in view of public opinion, we dared not do otherwise.

DR STOCKMANN: 'Dared not'? I've heard those words already today.

THE MAYOR: I trust you fully realize your position; you cannot count on any future practice whatever in this town.

DR STOCKMANN: To hell with the practice. But what makes you so sure?

THE MAYOR: The Householders' Association has drawn up a manifesto which they are circulating from door to door, urging all reputable citizens to refuse to employ you. I can assure you that there is not a single head of a family who will venture to withhold his signature. In plain words, no one would dare.

DR STOCKMANN: No, I don't doubt that. But what of it?

THE MAYOR: If I might give you some advice, I'd suggest that you leave the town for a while.

DR STOCKMANN: Yes, I had considered leaving the town.

THE MAYOR: Then, when you've had some six months to think matters over, if after mature consideration you could bring yourself to acknowledge your error with a few words of apology. . . .

DR STOCKMANN: I might get my job back, you think?

THE MAYOR: Perhaps . . . It's by no means impossible.

DR STOCKMANN: But what about public opinion? You wouldn't dare – in view of public opinion.

THE MAYOR: Opinion is an extremely fickle thing . . . and, to speak frankly, it is of the greatest importance to us to have some such admission from you in writing.

DR STOCKMANN: Yes, I can see why you come snivelling round for that, but, damn it all, have you forgotten what I've already said about that sort of sharp practice?

THE MAYOR: At that time, your position was much more favourable; you then had reason to suppose that you had the whole town at your back.

DR STOCKMANN: Yes, and now I feel I have the whole town *on* my back. [*Flaring up*] But no – not if I had the devil and his dam on my back! Never, I tell you, never!

THE MAYOR: A family man has no right to behave as you are doing. You have no right, Tomas.

DR STOCKMANN: No right? There's only one thing in the world that a free man has no right to do, and do you know what that is?

THE MAYOR: No.

DR STOCKMANN: No, of course you don't. Well, I'll tell you. A free man has no right to get himself mixed up in filth like a hooligan; he has no right to get to the stage where he feels like spitting in his own face.

THE MAYOR: That all sounds extremely plausible, and if there were no other reason for your obstinacy . . . But then, of course, there *is*.

DR STOCKMANN: What do you mean by that?

THE MAYOR: You know perfectly well. But as your brother, and a man of the world, let me warn you not to build too much on prospects and expectations that may very easily come to nothing.

DR STOCKMANN: What on earth are you driving at?

THE MAYOR: Do you really expect me to believe that you are ignorant of the terms of the bequests that Morten Kiil, the tanner, has laid down in his will?

DR STOCKMANN: I know that what little he has goes to a home for old and needy workers. What has that to do with me?

THE MAYOR: In the first place, what he has is by no means 'little'. Morten Kiil is a passably wealthy man.

DR STOCKMANN: I had no idea. . . .

THE MAYOR: Indeed? Hm. And you also had no notion that a not inconsiderable part of his fortune is to go to your children, with a life interest to you and your wife? Has he never told you that?

DR STOCKMANN: No, I'm blessed if he has. On the contrary, he's never stopped grumbling about the preposterously high taxes he has to pay. But are you quite sure of this, Peter?

THE MAYOR: I have it from a thoroughly reliable source.

DR STOCKMANN: Then, good heavens, that means that Katrina's provided for, and the children too! I must tell her – [*Calls*] Katrina! Katrina!

THE MAYOR [*restraining him*]: Hush, don't say anything yet.

MRS STOCKMANN [*opening the door*]: What's the matter?

DR STOCKMANN: Nothing, dear. Go back again.

[MRS STOCKMANN *goes*. DR STOCKMANN *paces the room*.]

Provided for! Just think – all of them provided for. And for life, too! It's a wonderful feeling to know that one's provided for!

THE MAYOR: Yes, but that is precisely what you are *not*. Morten Kiil can alter his will at any moment he pleases.

DR STOCKMANN: But he won't, my dear Peter. The old Badger's absolutely delighted that I've had a go at you and your clever friends.

THE MAYOR [*with a start, giving him a searching look*]: Ah, that throws a different light on things.

DR STOCKMANN: What things?

THE MAYOR: So this whole affair has been a concerted plan. . . . These violent and reckless attacks that you have levelled – in the name of truth – against the leading citizens in this town . . .

DR STOCKMANN: Well, what about them?

THE MAYOR: They were nothing more than an agreed consideration for that vindictive old man's legacy.

DR STOCKMANN: Peter – you really are the most revolting lout I've ever come across in my whole life!

THE MAYOR: Everything is over between us! Your dismissal is irrevocable – because now we have a weapon against you. [*He goes.*]

DR STOCKMANN: Tscha! [*Calls*] Katrina, I want this floor scrubbed down after him. Get her to bring a pail – that girl – what the devil's her name? – the girl who always has a smut on her nose.

MRS STOCKMANN [*at the living-room door*]: Hush, Tomas, hush!

PETRA [*also at the door*]: Father, here's grandfather – he wants to know if he can speak to you alone.

DR STOCKMANN: Yes, of course he can. Come in.

[MORTEN KIIL *comes in; the* DOCTOR *shuts the door after him.*]

Well, what is it? Do sit down.

KIIL: I won't sit down. [*Looks round.*] Well, your house looks pretty this morning, Tomas.

DR STOCKMANN: Yes, doesn't it?

KIIL: Very pretty – nice and airy, too. You've got lots of that oxygen stuff that you were talking about last night. You must have a fine clear conscience today, I should think.

DR STOCKMANN: Yes, I have.

KIIL: So I imagine. [*Patting his chest*] D'you know what I've got here?

DR STOCKMANN: A clear conscience too, I hope.

KIIL: Pah! Something better than that. [*He takes out a thick wallet, opening it to reveal a bundle of papers.*]

DR STOCKMANN [*looking at him in amazement*]: Shares in the Baths?

KIIL: They weren't hard to come by today.

DR STOCKMANN: You've gone and bought –

KIIL: As many as I could afford.

DR STOCKMANN: But my dear man, with things at the Baths in such a state –

KIIL: If you'd only behave like a sensible fellow, you'd soon put the Baths to rights again.

DR STOCKMANN: Well, you can see for yourself I'm doing all I can, but – people in this town are mad!

KIIL: You were saying yesterday that the worst of the

filth came from my tannery. If that's true, then my grand-father and my father before me and I myself must have been poisoning this town for years, like three destroying angels. D'you think I'm going to sit down under a re-proach like that?

DR STOCKMANN: I'm afraid there's nothing you can do about it.

KIIL: I'm not having that; I set some store by my good name. They call me the Badger, so I hear, and a badger's a kind of pig, isn't it? and never in this world am I giving them the right to call me that. I'll live and die with a clean slate.

DR STOCKMANN: And how will you manage that?

KIIL: You shall clear me, Tomas.

DR STOCKMANN: I?

KIIL: D'you know where the money to buy these shares came from? No, of course you don't. Well, I'll tell you. It was the money that was coming to Katrina and Petra and the boys from me. You see, I've managed to put a little by after all.

DR STOCKMANN [flaring up]: And you've gone and taken Katrina's money for a thing like this?

KIIL: Yes, all the money's invested in the Baths now. And now I want to see if you're really so stark staring raving mad after all. If you go on making out that animals and such-like filth come from my tannery, then it'll be just the same as if you were tearing off great strips of Katrina's skin – and Petra's and the boys'. And no decent father would do that unless he was a madman.

DR STOCKMANN [pacing up and down]: But I am a mad-man. I am a madman!

KIIL: Not so raving ramping mad when it comes to your wife and children.

DR STOCKMANN [stopping in front of him]: Why

couldn't you have talked to me first, before you went and bought all that rubbish?

KIIL: What can't be cured, must be endured.

DR STOCKMANN [*pacing restlessly about*]: If only I weren't so sure about it . . . but I'm absolutely certain I'm right.

KIIL [*weighing the wallet in his hand*]: If you stick to your lunacy, these won't be worth much. [*He puts the wallet in his pocket.*]

DR STOCKMANN: Damn it, surely science can find some antidote . . . or a disinfectant –

KIIL: You mean something to kill off the animals?

DR STOCKMANN: Yes, or to make them harmless.

KIIL: Couldn't you try a little rat-poison?

DR STOCKMANN: Don't be silly. But everybody keeps saying it's just my imagination. . . . All right, let them have it their own way – why *shouldn't* it just be imagination? Didn't they label me a public enemy – the ignorant narrow-minded mongrels? And what's more, they were on the point of tearing the clothes off my back.

KIIL: And they've smashed all your windows for you, too.

DR STOCKMANN: Yes . . . and then there's the question of one's duty to one's family. I must talk to Katrina about it – she's better at these things than I am.

KIIL: That's right – just you take a sensible woman's advice.

DR STOCKMANN [*turning on him*]: I never thought you could be so tiresome – risking Katrina's money, and putting me on the rack like this. Now I come to look at you, you might be the devil himself!

KIIL: Then I'd better go. But I want to hear from you – yes or no – by two o'clock. If it's no, the shares go to charity – this very day, too.

DR STOCKMANN: And what will Katrina get?

KIIL: Not a sniff of it!

> [*The hall door opens, showing* HOVSTAD *and* ASLAK-
> SEN *outside.*]

Hullo – look at those two!

DR STOCKMANN [*staring at them*]: What's this? Do you dare to come to my house?

HOVSTAD: Certainly we do.

ASLAKSEN: You see, there's something we want to talk over with you.

KIIL [*under his breath*]: Yes or no – by two o'clock.

ASLAKSEN [*catching Hovstad's eye*]: Aha!

> [MORTEN KIIL *goes.*]

DR STOCKMANN: Well, what do you want? Keep it short.

HOVSTAD: I quite see that you must be angry with us about our attitude at last night's meeting –

DR STOCKMANN: Attitude, you call it? A fine sort of attitude! *I* call it spineless, damn it – like a lot of old women.

HOVSTAD: Call it that if you like – but what else could we do?

DR STOCKMANN: You mean what else *dared* you do.

HOVSTAD: Yes, if you like.

ASLAKSEN: But why didn't you just drop a hint before-hand? The merest word to Mr Hovstad or me?

DR STOCKMANN: A hint? What about?

ASLAKSEN: About what was behind it all.

DR STOCKMANN: I simply don't know what you're talking about.

ASLAKSEN [*with a confiding nod*]: Ah, but you do, Dr Stockmann.

HOVSTAD: There's no point in making a mystery of it any longer.

DR STOCKMANN [*looking from one to the other*]: Now what in the devil's name . . .?

ASLAKSEN: May I ask if your father-in-law isn't going round the town buying up all the shares in the Baths?

DR STOCKMANN: Yes, he's certainly been buying the shares today, but —

ASLAKSEN: You'd have been wiser to get someone else to do it — someone not related to you.

HOVSTAD: And then you shouldn't have acted under your own name — no one need have known that the attack on the Baths came from you. You ought to have let me advise you, Dr Stockmann.

[DR STOCKMANN *stares straight ahead as he begins to see daylight; then, as though thunderstruck, he says:*]

DR STOCKMANN: Is it possible? Do things like that really happen?

ASLAKSEN [*smiling*]: It certainly looks like it; but they ought to be managed with more tact, you know.

HOVSTAD: And there should have been more people in it — the liability's always lighter when there're others to share it.

DR STOCKMANN [*calmly*]: Come to the point, gentlemen — what is it you want?

ASLAKSEN: Mr Hovstad could best . . .

HOVSTAD: No, you tell him, Aslaksen.

ASLAKSEN: Well, it's like this . . . now that we know how things really stand, we feel that we might venture to put the *People's Herald* at your disposal.

DR STOCKMANN: So you do dare, now, eh? But what about public opinion? Aren't you afraid of raising a storm against us?

HOVSTAD: We must manage to ride out the storm.

ASLAKSEN: And you must be ready to change course quickly, Doctor, as soon as your attack has done its work.

DR STOCKMANN: As soon as my father-in-law and I have snapped up all the shares cheap, you mean?

HOVSTAD: Presumably it's mainly on scientific grounds that you want to take over the management of the Baths?

DR STOCKMANN: Obviously it was on scientific grounds that I got the old Badger to come in with me over this. Then we patch up the pipes a bit, and do a little digging down on the shore – and it doesn't cost the town a penny. That'll do the trick, eh?

HOVSTAD: I think so – if you have the *Herald* behind you.

ASLAKSEN: In a free society, Doctor, the Press is a power.

DR STOCKMANN: Yes indeed, and so is public opinion; I suppose, Mr Aslaksen, you'll answer for the Householders' Association?

ASLAKSEN: Both the Householders' Association and the Temperance Society, you can rely on that.

DR STOCKMANN: But, gentlemen – I hardly like to mention it, but ... what return do *you* ...?

HOVSTAD: As you'll realize, we'd much rather have given you our support quite freely . . . but the *Herald*'s in rather a shaky condition – it's not doing as well as it should, and I shouldn't like to have to close it down just now, when there's so much political work that needs doing.

DR STOCKMANN: Obviously that would be very hard for a public benefactor like you. [*Flaring up*] But I'm a public enemy, I am! [*Rushing about the room*] Where's my stick? Where the devil's my stick?

HOVSTAD: What *do* you mean?

ASLAKSEN: Surely you wouldn't . . .

DR STOCKMANN [*coming to a halt*]: And suppose I don't give you a single penny out of all my shares? Don't forget we rich men don't like parting with our money!

HOVSTAD: And don't *you* forget that this business with the shares can be presented in two ways!

DR STOCKMANN: Yes, and you're the man to do it! If I don't rescue the *Herald*, you'll certainly show the affair in a bad light. You'll hunt me down, won't you? hound me, try to get me by the throat, like a dog with a hare.

HOVSTAD: That's a law of nature – every animal wants to live.

ASLAKSEN: And get its food where it can find it, eh?

DR STOCKMANN: Then you can go and look for yours in the gutter. [*Charging round the room*] Because now, by God, we're going to see who's the strongest animal of us three. [*He finds his umbrella and brandishes it.*] Now for it!

HOVSTAD: You wouldn't assault us!

ASLAKSEN: Careful with that umbrella!

DR STOCKMANN: Out of the window with you, Mr Hovstad!

HOVSTAD [*at the hall door*]: Have you gone mad?

DR STOCKMANN: Out of the window, Mr Aslaksen! Go on – jump . . . you might as well get it over!

ASLAKSEN [*running round the desk*]: Temperately, Doctor! I'm not strong – I can't stand much. . . . [*Calling*] Help! Help!

[MRS STOCKMANN, PETRA, *and* HORSTER *come in from the living-room.*]

MRS STOCKMANN: Good heavens, Tomas, what's happening?

DR STOCKMANN [*brandishing the umbrella*]: Jump, I tell you – into the gutter!

HOVSTAD: Unprovoked assault! I call you to witness, Captain Horster. [*He scuttles out into the hall.*]

ASLAKSEN [*hesitating*]: If only I knew my way about. . . . [*He slips into the living-room.*]

MRS STOCKMANN [*holding the Doctor back*]: Tomas –
control yourself!

DR STOCKMANN [*throwing away the umbrella*]: I'm
blessed if they haven't got away after all!

MRS STOCKMANN: What did they want with you?

DR STOCKMANN: I'll tell you later; I've got other things
to think about now. [*He goes to the table and writes on
a visiting-card.*] Look, Katrina, what have I written there?

MRS STOCKMANN: Three big 'No's'. What does that
mean?

DR STOCKMANN: I'll tell you that later, too. Petra [*giving
her the card*], get Smutty-nose to run to the Badger's with
that – as quickly as she can. Hurry, now.

[PETRA *goes out to the hall with the card.*]
Well, if all my callers today haven't come straight from
the devil, I don't know where they *did* come from! But
now I'm going to sharpen my pen against them like a
dagger. I'll dip it in gall and venom – I'll fling my inkpot
right in their faces!

MRS STOCKMANN: Yes, but Tomas – we're going away.

[PETRA *comes back.*]

DR STOCKMANN: Well?

PETRA: She's taken it.

DR STOCKMANN: Good. Going away, you say? No, I'm
damned if we do – we're staying where we are, Katrina.

PETRA: Staying?

MRS STOCKMANN: In this town?

DR STOCKMANN: Yes, *here*. This is the battlefield – here's
where the fight is, and here's where I shall triumph. As
soon as I've got my trousers patched up, I'm going out to
look for a house – we must have a roof over our heads
for the winter.

HORSTER: You can have that with me.

DR STOCKMANN: Can I really?

HORSTER: Yes, easily. There's plenty of room, and I'm hardly ever at home.

MRS STOCKMANN: Oh, that *is* kind of you, Captain Horster.

PETRA: Thank you.

DR STOCKMANN [*grasping his hand*]: Thank you – thank you. Now *that's* off my mind, I can get to work in earnest this very day. Oh, there's no end of things that need looking into, Katrina. Luckily I shall have plenty of time to spare now, because, you know, I've been dismissed from the Baths.

MRS STOCKMANN [*sighing*]: Yes, I was expecting that.

DR STOCKMANN: And they want to take away my practice, too. All right, let them. I shan't lose the poorer people, anyway – the ones that don't pay – and good heavens, they're the ones who need me most. But by God, they're going to listen to me. I shall 'preach to them in season and out of season', as it says somewhere.[51]

MRS STOCKMANN: But Tomas dear, surely you've seen that preaching doesn't do much good?

DR STOCKMANN: That's utter nonsense, Katrina. Do you want me to be routed in the field by public opinion and the solid majority, and all the rest of that devil's work? No thank you, my dear. You see, what I want to do is quite simple and straightforward: I just want to knock it into these mongrels' heads that the liberals are the craftiest enemies a free man has – that party programmes simply wring the necks of any promising young truth – that expediency turns justice and morality upside down, till life here just isn't worth living. Now, Captain Horster, don't you think I ought to be able to make people understand that?

HORSTER: Probably – I don't know very much about that sort of thing.

DR STOCKMANN: Well, look here, I'll explain. It's the party leaders who must be wiped out; because, you see, a party leader's like a wolf – a ravening wolf who needs to eat up a certain number of smaller creatures every year if he's to survive. Just look at Hovstad and Aslaksen – how many small animals *they* polish off, or mangle and maim till they're not fit to be anything but householders and subscribers to the *People's Herald*. [*He sits on the edge of the table.*] Come here, Katrina – look what a lovely sunny day it is. And what wonderful, fresh spring air I'm breathing in.

MRS STOCKMANN: Yes . . . if only we could live on sunshine and spring air, Tomas!

DR STOCKMANN: Well, you'll have to pinch and scrape a bit on your side of the house, and we'll manage all right. That's the least of my worries. No, the worst of it is that I can't think of anyone with enough integrity and independence to take on my work after me.

PETRA: Oh, don't worry about that, Father, you've plenty of time ahead of you. Hullo, here are the boys back already.

[EYLIF *and* MORTEN *come in from the living-room.*]

MRS STOCKMANN: Have you got a holiday today?

MORTEN: No, but we were fighting with the others during the break.

EYLIF: That isn't true – it was the others who were fighting with us.

MORTEN: Yes, so Mr Rørlund said we'd better stay at home for a day or two.

DR STOCKMANN [*snapping his fingers and jumping down from the table*]: I've got it! Yes, my goodness, I've got it! You'll never set foot in that school again.

BOYS: No more school?

MRS STOCKMANN: But Tomas . . .

DR STOCKMANN: Never, I tell you – I'll teach you myself
. . . that's to say, you won't learn a single blessed fact –

MORTEN: Hooray!

DR STOCKMANN: – but I'll turn you into decent, independent men . . . and you shall help me, Petra.

PETRA: Yes, you can count on me, Father.

DR STOCKMANN: And we'll hold our classes in the room
where they called me a public enemy. But we must have
more pupils – I need at least a dozen boys for a start.

MRS STOCKMANN: You won't get them in this town.

DR STOCKMANN: We shall see! [*To the boys*] Do you
know any street-urchins – real guttersnipes?

MORTEN: Yes, Father, I know lots.

DR STOCKMANN: Splendid – just you bring me a few. For
once in a way, I'm going to try an experiment on some
mongrels . . . there may be some excellent material
among them.

MORTEN: But what shall we do when we're decent, independent men, Father?

DR STOCKMANN: Drive all the wolves out to the Far West,
boys!

[EYLIF *looks a bit doubtful, but* MORTEN *jumps about
shouting* 'Hooray!']

MRS STOCKMANN: Just as long as the wolves don't drive
you out, Tomas.

DR STOCKMANN: You're off your head, Katrina! Drive
me? Why, I'm the strongest man in the place.

MRS STOCKMANN: You the strongest? Now?

DR STOCKMANN: Yes, I'll go as far as to say that now I'm
the strongest man in the whole world!

MORTEN: *Are* you?

DR STOCKMANN [*dropping his voice*]: Sh! You mustn't
say anything about it yet, but I've made a great discovery!

MRS STOCKMANN: What – again?

DR STOCKMANN: I certainly have! [*Gathering them round him, and speaking confidentially*] You see, the fact is that the strongest man in the world is the man who stands most alone.

MRS STOCKMANN [*smiling and shaking her head*]: Oh, Tomas!

PETRA [*enthusiastically, grasping his hands*]: Father!

WHEN WE DEAD WAKE

A Dramatic Epilogue

in Three Acts

CHARACTERS

———— * ————

PROFESSOR ARNOLD RUBEK, a sculptor[52]
MAIA RUBEK, his wife
THE MANAGER, at the Spa
SQUIRE ULFHEIM[53]
A Lady Traveller
A Nun
Waiters, visitors, and children[54]

The first act takes place at a watering-place on the coast; the second and third acts at a health resort in the mountains, and on a peak near by

ACT ONE

——————— * ———————

Outside a hotel at a spa, the main building of which is partly seen on the right. It is an open, park-like place, with springs, clumps of shrubs, and large old trees. To the left is a small pavilion, nearly covered with ivy and virginia creeper; outside it are a table and a chair. In the background there is a view out over the fjord to the sea, with promontories and small islands in the distance. It is a sunny summer morning, hot and still.

[PROFESSOR RUBEK *and* MÀIA, *his wife, are sitting in basket chairs by a laid table on the lawn outside the hotel. They have had breakfast and are now drinking champagne and seltzer. They both have newspapers. The Professor is a distinguished-looking elderly man; he is in light summer clothes except for a black velvet jacket. His wife, Maia, is quite young, with a lively face and gay, mocking eyes, yet with a suggestion of weariness. She is fashionably dressed in travelling clothes.* MAIA *sits for a moment as if she were waiting for the Professor to say something; then she lowers her newspaper and sighs.*]

MAIA: Oh dear!
PROFESSOR RUBEK [*looking up from his newspaper*]: Well, Maia? What's the matter?
MAIA: It's so quiet here . . . just listen!
PROFESSOR RUBEK [*with an indulgent smile*]: And can you hear it?

MAIA: What?

PROFESSOR RUBEK: The quietness!

MAIA: I certainly can.

PROFESSOR RUBEK: Well, *mein Kind*, you may be right; perhaps one really *can* hear quietness.

MAIA: Heaven knows you can, when it's as overpowering as it is here, and when –

PROFESSOR RUBEK: Here at the Spa, you mean?

MAIA: I mean everywhere back here at home. Of course in the towns there was a certain amount of noise and bustle, but even there I felt that the noise and bustle had something dead about them.

PROFESSOR RUBEK [*looking at her searchingly*]: Aren't you glad to be home again, Maia?[55]

MAIA: Are *you*?

PROFESSOR RUBEK [*evasively*]: I?

MAIA: Yes, you; after all, you've travelled a very great deal farther than I have. Are *you* really happy now that you're home again?

PROFESSOR RUBEK: No . . . to tell you the truth, I don't think I am – not entirely happy.

MAIA [*gaily*]: There you are! I *knew* you weren't.

PROFESSOR RUBEK: Perhaps I've lived abroad too long; I've become so far removed from this – this life back here at home.

MAIA [*eagerly, pulling her chair nearer to his*]: There, you see, Rubek! Let's get away again . . . just as quickly as we can!

PROFESSOR RUBEK [*rather impatiently*]: Well, my dear Maia, that's exactly what we intend to do. You know it is.

MAIA: But why can't we go at once? Think how nice and comfortable we could be down there in our lovely new house.

PROFESSOR RUBEK [*smilingly indulgently*]: You should say 'in our lovely new *home*'.

MAIA [*dryly*]: I prefer 'house', let's leave it at that.

PROFESSOR RUBEK [*with a long look at her*]: You really are an extraordinary little person.

MAIA: Am I so extraordinary?

PROFESSOR RUBEK: *I* think so.

MAIA: But why? Simply because I don't want to hang about aimlessly up here?

PROFESSOR RUBEK: Now which of us was it who was so desperately anxious that we should come up north this summer?

MAIA: Oh yes, it was I all right.

PROFESSOR RUBEK: It certainly wasn't I.

MAIA: But good heavens, who would have thought that everything here at home could have changed so dreadfully? And in such a short time! When you think that it isn't much more than four years since I went away –

PROFESSOR RUBEK: – since you got married, yes.

MAIA: Married? What has that to do with it?

PROFESSOR RUBEK [*continuing*]: – since you became 'Frau Professor',[56] the mistress of a charming home – or perhaps I should say 'a highly desirable house'. And a villa on Lake Taunitz, surrounded by the best of everything. Because it really is charming, Maia, you must admit; and with plenty of room too, so that we aren't always falling over each other.

MAIA [*casually*]: Oh no, there's plenty of room – all we could want!

PROFESSOR RUBEK: And remember, too, that you've been moving in much more distinguished society – living in a more spacious world than ever you were used to at your own home.

MAIA [*looking at him*]: Oh? So you think it's I who've changed?

PROFESSOR RUBEK: Yes Maia, I do.

MAIA: Only me? Not the people back here?

PROFESSOR RUBEK: Oh yes, they've changed too – a little. And it hasn't made them any more likeable; that I must admit.

MAIA: Yes, you must certainly admit that.

PROFESSOR RUBEK [*a new thought*]: When I look round me at the way people live here, do you know what it makes me think of?

MAIA: No – what?

PROFESSOR RUBEK: It reminds me of the night we spent in the train on our way up here.

MAIA: Why, you sat in the compartment and slept the whole way.

PROFESSOR RUBEK: Not quite. I noticed how quiet it was at all the little stations we stopped at. I could hear the quietness, just like you, Maia.

MAIA: Like me? Could you?

PROFESSOR RUBEK: That was how I knew that we'd crossed the border, and that we were really home again. Because the train stopped at every little station, although absolutely nothing happened.

MAIA: Why did it stop like that, if there was nothing there?

PROFESSOR RUBEK: I don't know. No one got off and no one got on, but the train stood there, silently, for what seemed like hours. And at every station I heard two railwaymen walking along the platform – one of them carrying a lantern – and they mumbled quietly to each other in the night, without expression or meaning.

MAIA: Yes, you're right; there are always two men talking. . . .

PROFESSOR RUBEK: – about nothing at all. [*More*

brightly] But just wait till tomorrow: then the great comfortable steamer will put into the harbour, and we'll get on board and sail northward all round the coast – right up into the Arctic.

MAIA: But then you won't see anything of the country or the people, and that was what you particularly wanted.

PROFESSOR RUBEK [*curtly and ungraciously*]: I've seen more than enough.

MAIA: You think a sea voyage will suit you better?

PROFESSOR RUBEK: Well, it's always a change.

MAIA: Oh well, if it'll do you any good. . . .

PROFESSOR RUBEK: Do *me* good? Me? There's nothing the matter with me.

MAIA [*getting up and going to him*]: There *is*, Rubek – surely you must realize it yourself.

PROFESSOR RUBEK: By my dear Maia, what could there be?

MAIA [*behind him, leaning over the back of his chair*]: You tell me. You've taken to wandering about restlessly; you can't settle anywhere, either at home or abroad. And lately you've begun to dislike your fellow-men.

PROFESSOR RUBEK [*rather bitterly*]: Oh? So *you've* noticed that?

MAIA: No one who knows you could help noticing it. But worst of all, I think, is that you've lost all pleasure in your work.

PROFESSOR RUBEK: Have I indeed?

MAIA: Remember how you used to work – without a break from morning till night.

PROFESSOR RUBEK [*gloomily*]: Used to, yes.

MAIA: But once you'd put the finishing touches to your great masterpiece . . .

PROFESSOR RUBEK [*nodding thoughtfully*]: 'Resurrection Day' –

MAIA: Yes – which has been shown all over the world and has made you so famous –

PROFESSOR RUBEK: Perhaps that's what's wrong, Maia.

MAIA: What?

PROFESSOR RUBEK: When I'd finished my masterpiece – [*with a vehement gesture of his hand*] because 'Resurrection Day' *is* a masterpiece . . . or *was* at first. No, it still is. It must be a masterpiece, it must, it *must*!

MAIA [*looking at him in surprise*]: But Rubek, the whole world knows that.

PROFESSOR RUBEK: The whole world knows nothing – and understands nothing!

MAIA: It may guess – something at any rate.

PROFESSOR RUBEK: Something that doesn't exist, yes. Something that never even entered my head! Oh yes, they can go into ecstasies over that! [*Muttering to himself*] What's the *use* of working oneself to death for the masses – the mob – for 'the whole world'?

MAIA: Then do you think it's better – do you think it's more worthy of you – just to go on turning out a portrait-bust every now and again?[57]

PROFESSOR RUBEK [*with a forbearing smile*]: What I turn out aren't just portraits, Maia.

MAIA: Then heaven knows what else they are. For these last two or three years – ever since you got your great group finished and out of the house –

PROFESSOR RUBEK: All the same, I can assure you they're not simply portrait-busts.

MAIA: What else are they then?

PROFESSOR RUBEK: There's something subtle and equivocal lurking below the surface of all those portraits . . . a secret something that the mob can't see.

MAIA: Oh?

PROFESSOR RUBEK: Only I can see it – and how it makes

me laugh! On the surface, there's the 'striking likeness', as they call it, that they all stand and gape with wonder at. [*Lowering his voice*] But deep down underneath, there's the pompous self-righteous face of a horse, the obstinate muzzle of a mule, the lop-eared shallow-pated head of a dog, a greasy hog's snout . . . and sometimes the gross, brutal mask of a bull!

MAIA [*indifferently*]: All the dear old farmyard, in fact.

PROFESSOR RUBEK: Just the dear old farmyard, Maia.[58] All the animals that man has perverted for his own ends, and who, in their turn, have perverted man. [*He empties his champagne glass and smiles.*] And it's these equivocal works of art that our worthy celebrities come and commission from me – and pay for in good faith, and pay through the nose, too. Almost their 'weight in gold', as they say.

MAIA [*filling his glass*]: Shame on you, Rubek! Have a drink and cheer up.

PROFESSOR RUBEK [*passing a hand across his forehead once or twice, and leaning back in his chair*]: I am happy, Maia – really happy. In a way. [*After a moment*] You see, there's a certain happiness in knowing that one is completely free and independent . . . and in having everything one could possibly wish for – outwardly, at any rate. Don't you agree, Maia?

MAIA: Oh yes, that's all very well as far as it goes. [*Looking at him*] But do you remember what you promised me the day that we came to an agreement on . . . on a rather difficult subject? –

PROFESSOR RUBEK [*nodding*]: – an agreement that you and I should marry. Yes, it *was* rather difficult for you, Maia.

MAIA [*going on imperturbably*]: – and that I should travel with you, and live abroad for the rest of my life – and that I should enjoy myself. Do you remember what you promised me then?

PROFESSOR RUBEK [*shaking his head*]: No, not exactly. Well, what did I promise?

MAIA: You said that you would take me up a high mountain with you, and show me all the glory of the world.[59]

PROFESSOR RUBEK [*surprised*]: Did I really promise that to *you*, too?

MAIA [*looking at him*]: Me 'too'? Who else?

PROFESSOR RUBEK [*casually*]: No no, I only meant 'did I promise to show you ...'

MAIA: 'All the glory of the world.' Yes that was what you said. And all that glory was to be yours and mine, you said.

PROFESSOR RUBEK: It was only a figure of speech that I used to use in those days.

MAIA: Only a figure of speech?

PROFESSOR RUBEK: Yes, something from my school-days; the sort of thing I used to say to the children next door when I wanted them to come out and play with me in the woods or on the mountains.

MAIA [*looking him full in the face*]: I suppose you only wanted to get *me* out to play, too?

PROFESSOR RUBEK [*passing it off as a joke*]: Well, it's been quite an amusing game, hasn't it, Maia?

MAIA [*coldly*]: I didn't go away with you just for a game.

PROFESSOR RUBEK: No, no, of course you didn't.

MAIA: And you never took me up any high mountain, nor showed me –

PROFESSOR RUBEK [*annoyed*]: – all the glory of the world? No, I didn't. You see, little Maia, I'd better tell you, you weren't really cut out to be a mountaineer.

MAIA [*trying to control herself*]: You once seemed to think I was.

PROFESSOR RUBEK: Four or five years ago, yes. [*Stretching in his chair*] But four or five years is a very long time, Maia.

MAIA [*giving him a bitter look*]: Has it seemed so long to you, Rubek?

PROFESSOR RUBEK: I'm beginning to find it rather long now – [*yawning*] from time to time.

MAIA [*going back to her chair*]: Then I won't bore you any longer.

[*She sits down, picks up her paper, and turns the pages. They are both silent for a while.*]

PROFESSOR RUBEK [*leaning on his elbows across the table and giving her a quizzical look*]: Is the Frau Professor offended? [60]

MAIA [*coldly, without looking up*]: No, not in the least.

[*Visitors to the Spa, mostly ladies, start to come, singly and in groups, through the park from right to left. Waiters carry refreshments out from the hotel to behind the pavilion. The MANAGER, carrring his gloves and a stick, comes from his round of the park.*[61] *As he meets the visitors, he greets them cordially, exchanging a word or two with some of them.*]

MANAGER [*coming down to Professor Rubek's table and politely raising his hat*]: May I wish you a very good morning, Madam? Good morning, Professor.

PROFESSOR RUBEK: Good morning, Manager, good morning.

MANAGER [*turning to Maia*]: Might I ask, Madam, if you had a good night?

MAIA: Excellent, thank you – *I* did, at any rate; I always sleep like a log.

MANAGER: I'm delighted to hear it – one's first night in a strange place can be rather restless. And you, Professor?

PROFESSOR RUBEK: Oh, I never sleep very well; especially lately.

MANAGER [*with a sympathetic look*]: I'm sorry to hear that. But a few weeks here at the Hydro will soon put that right.

PROFESSOR RUBEK [*looking up at him*]: Tell me, is there one of your patients who's in the habit of taking the treatment during the night?

MANAGER [*surprised*]: During the night? No, I haven't heard of one.

PROFESSOR RUBEK: You haven't?

MANAGER: No, I don't know of anyone here who's ill enough to require that.

PROFESSOR RUBEK: Well then, is there anyone in the habit of walking about the grounds at night?

MANAGER [*smiling, and shaking his head*]: No, Professor, that would be against the rules.

MAIA [*becoming impatient*]: There you are, Rubek! What did I tell you this morning – you dreamed it.

PROFESSOR RUBEK [*dryly*]: Oh? Did I? Thank you. [*He turns to the Manager.*] The fact is, I got up during the night because I couldn't sleep, and I thought I'd see what the weather was like. . . .

MANAGER [*interested*]: Yes, Professor; and then –?

PROFESSOR RUBEK: I looked out of the window, and I saw a white figure down there among the trees.

MAIA [*with a smile at the Manager*]: And the Professor insists that the figure was wearing a bathrobe.

PROFESSOR RUBEK: – or something like it, I said. I couldn't see very clearly, but it was certainly something white.

MANAGER: How extraordinary. Was it a gentleman or a lady?

PROFESSOR RUBEK: It certainly seemed to me to be a

lady. But behind it came another figure – quite dark –
like a shadow....

MANAGER [*with a start*]: A dark one? In black, perhaps?

PROFESSOR RUBEK: Yes, as far as I could make
out.

MANAGER [*beginning to see daylight*]: And behind the
white figure? Close behind her?

PROFESSOR RUBEK: Yes, only a little way behind.

MANAGER: Ah, then I think I can explain, Professor.

PROFESSOR RUBEK: Well, what was it?

MAIA [*simultaneously*]: You mean the Professor really
wasn't dreaming?

MANAGER [*suddenly dropping his voice and pointing back
to the right*]: Ssh – if you wouldn't mind. Look over
there. If you'd speak quietly for a moment....

[*A slender* LADY, *dressed in fine creamy white cashmere, comes from behind the corner of the hotel: she
is followed by a* NUN *dressed in black with a silver
cross on a chain at her breast.*[62] *She goes through the
park to the left, towards the pavilion in the foreground.
Her face is pale and drawn, as if it were frozen: her
eyelids are lowered, and her eyes seem without sight.
Her dress hangs down to her feet in long straight close-
fitting folds.*[63] *A large shawl of white crêpe covers
her head, arms, and the upper part of her body. She
keeps her arms folded over her breast. She carries herself stiffly, and her walk is staid and measured. The*
NUN'S *bearing is also measured, and rather that of a
servant. She keeps her sharp brown eyes continually
on the lady. Waiters, with napkins over their arms,
come to the door of the hotel and watch the two
strangers curiously, but they take no notice and, without looking round, go into the pavilion.*]

PROFESSOR RUBEK [*who has risen slowly and involuntarily from his chair, and is staring at the closed door of the pavilion*]: Who was that lady?

MANAGER: She's a visitor who has taken that little pavilion.

PROFESSOR RUBEK: A foreigner?

MANAGER: I imagine so. At any rate, they both came here from abroad. About a week ago. They've not been here before.

PROFESSOR RUBEK [*looking at him with certainty*]: It was she whom I saw in the grounds last night.

MANAGER: It must have been; I thought so from the first.

PROFESSOR RUBEK: What is the lady's name?

MANAGER: She has registered as 'Madame de Satoff and Companion'. That's all we know.

PROFESSOR RUBEK [*thoughtfully*]: Satoff . . . Satoff?

MAIA [*mockingly*]: Well, Rubek – do you know anyone of that name?

PROFESSOR RUBEK [*shaking his head*]: No, I don't. Satoff . . . it sounds Russian; or Slav, at any rate. [*To the Manager*] What language does she speak?

MANAGER: When the two ladies are talking together, they use a language that I can't identify; but, apart from that, she speaks perfect Norwegian.

PROFESSOR RUBEK [*with a sharp exclamation*]: Norwegian? You're sure you're not mistaken?

MANAGER: No, I could hardly be mistaken about that.

PROFESSOR RUBEK [*tensely, looking at him*]: You've actually heard her yourself?

MANAGER: Oh yes, in fact I've talked with her – several times. Only a word or two – she's very reserved, but –

PROFESSOR RUBEK: But it was Norwegian?

MANAGER: Perfect Norwegian – with possibly a trace of North-country accent.

PROFESSOR RUBEK [*in a low voice, staring straight ahead in surprise*]: That too!

MAIA [*rather disturbed and annoyed*]: Perhaps the lady has been one of your models at some time, Rubek. Try to remember.

PROFESSOR RUBEK [*with a sharp look at her*]: My 'models'?

MAIA [*with a provoking smile*]: In your younger days, I mean. You must have had innumerable models – years ago, of course.

PROFESSOR RUBEK [*matching her tone*]: Oh no, my dear little Maia; as a matter of fact, I've had only one single model. Only one, for everything that I've ever done.

MANAGER [*who has turned away, and stands looking out to the left*]: If you'd excuse me, I'll leave you now. There's a man over there whom I particularly don't wish to meet – especially in the presence of a lady.

PROFESSOR RUBEK [*looking in the same direction*]: That man in the shooting jacket? Who is he?

MANAGER: He's Squire Ulfheim, from –

PROFESSOR RUBEK: Oh, Squire Ulfheim.

MANAGER: The 'bear-slayer' as they call him.

PROFESSOR RUBEK: I know him.

MANAGER: Yes, who doesn't?

PROFESSOR RUBEK: Only very slightly, though. Has he come here for treatment – at last?

MANAGER: Not yet – oddly enough. He merely passes through once a year, on his way up to his hunting-ground. If you'd excuse me. . . . [*He tries to escape into the hotel.*]

ULFHEIM [*off*]: Wait a minute! What the devil . . .? Stop, I say! Why do you always run away from me?

MANAGER [*stopping*]: I was certainly not running, Mr Ulfheim!

[SQUIRE ULFHEIM *enters from the left, followed by a* SERVANT *leading a couple of hunting-dogs.* ULFHEIM *wears a shooting jacket, high boots, and a felt hat with a feather in it. He is a long, lean, sinewy person, with unkempt hair and beard, and a loud voice.*[64] *It is hard to judge his age from his appearance, but he is no longer young.*]

ULFHEIM [*pouncing on the Manager*]: Is *this* the way you receive visitors, eh? Scuttling away with your tail between your legs, as if the devil were after you!

MANAGER [*calmly, ignoring this*]: Did you come by the steamer, sir?

ULFHEIM [*growling*]: Haven't had the honour of seeing any steamer. [*With his arms akimbo*] Don't you know *I* sail my own cutter? [*To the servant*] Look after your fellow-creatures, Lars; mind you keep 'em ravenous, though. Fresh bones, but not too much flesh on 'em, eh? And see that what there *is* is raw and reeking and bloody! And get something in your own belly while you're about it! [*Aiming a kick at him*] Go on – get to hell with you!

[*The* SERVANT *takes the dogs out behind the corner of the hotel.*]

MANAGER: Wouldn't you like to go into the dining-room, sir, in the meanwhile?

ULFHEIM: In among all those half-dead flies and half-dead people? *Very* many thanks, Mr Manager, but no!

MANAGER: Well, just as you please.

ULFHEIM: No, get the housekeeper to pack my usual hamper. Plenty of food, and lots of brandy. You can tell her that either I or Lars'll come and raise hell unless she –

MANAGER [*interrupting*]: We've learned to expect that. [*Turning*] Can I give the waiter any order for you Professor? Or for Mrs Rubek?

PROFESSOR RUBEK: No thank you, not for me.

MAIA: Nor for me thank you.

[*The* MANAGER *goes into the hotel.*]

ULFHEIM [*glaring at them for a moment, then lifting his hat*]: Hell and damnation! So this country bumpkin's got himself in among the nobs?

PROFESSOR RUBEK [*looking up*]: I beg your pardon?

ULFHEIM [*quieter and more politely*]: Haven't I the honour of addressing the great sculptor Professor Rubek in person?

PROFESSOR RUBEK [*nodding*]: We *have* met once or twice socially – the last winter that I was in this country.

ULFHEIM: That was many years ago, though. In *those* days you weren't nearly as famous as you've become now. In those days, even a filthy bear-hunter could venture to approach you.

PROFESSOR RUBEK [*smiling*]: I don't bite, even now.

MAIA [*watching Ulfheim with interest*]: Are you really and truly a bear-hunter?

ULFHEIM [*sitting down at the next table, nearer to the hotel*]: Bears for choice, ma'am, but I make do with any sort of game that comes my way–eagles, wolves, women, elk, reindeer – so long as it's fresh and lively and full-blooded. [*He drinks from his pocket-flask.*]

MAIA [*looking at him intently*]: But you hunt bears for choice?

ULFHEIM: For choice, yes. With them you can always use the knife, at a pinch. [*With a slight smile*] You know, madam, your husband and I both work with hard materials. I expect he wrestles with his blocks of marble, and I wrestle with the tense quivering sinews of my bears. And we both get the better of our material in the end – we subdue it and master it. We don't give up till we've conquered it, however much it resists us.

PROFESSOR RUBEK [*thoughtfully*]: There's a great deal
of truth in what you say.

ULFHEIM: Yes, because I'm sure the stone has something
to fight for, too. It's dead, and it'll resist with might and
main rather than let itself be hammered into life. Just
like a bear when someone comes and prods it out of its
lair.

MAIA: Are you going up to the forests to hunt now?

ULFHEIM: I'm going right up into the high mountains. I
suppose you've never been up in the high mountains,
have you, ma'am?

MAIA: No, never.

ULFHEIM: Hell and damnation, then make a point of
coming up there this summer. I'll gladly take you up
with me – both you and the Professor.

MAIA: Thank you – but Rubek's planned a sea trip this
summer.

PROFESSOR RUBEK: Up the coast and in and out of the
islands.

ULFHEIM: Ugh! Why the devil d'you want to go into
those damned unhealthy gutters? Think of it! Flounder-
ing about in rain-water – I'll even call it drain water!

MAIA: There, Rubek, you hear that?

ULFHEIM: No, you'd much better come up to the mountains with me. *There* it's free from people – it's clean. You
can't imagine what that means to me. But a little lady
like you –

> [*He breaks off. The* NUN *comes out of the pavilion and
> goes into the hotel. Ulfheim follows her with his eyes.*]

Just look at *her*, will you! That black crow ... who's to
be buried now?

PROFESSOR RUBEK: No one that I know of.

ULFHEIM: Well, there's someone, in some corner or other,
waiting to kick the bucket. I wish all sickly, weedy

people'd have the decency to go and get themselves buried . . . and the sooner the better!

MAIA: Haven't you ever been ill, Mr Ulfheim?

ULFHEIM: Never, or I shouldn't be here. But some of my best friends have, poor devils.

MAIA: Well, didn't you do anything for your best friends?

ULFHEIM: Of course. I shot them.

PROFESSOR RUBEK [*staring*]: Shot them?

MAIA [*pushing her chair back*]: Shot them dead?

ULFHEIM [*nodding*]: I never miss, ma'am.

MAIA: But you can't shoot people like that!

ULFHEIM: Who's talking about people?

MAIA: You said your best friends.

ULFHEIM: My best friends . . . that means my hounds.

MAIA: Hounds? Your best friends?

ULFHEIM: Who better? My honest, trusty, loyal companions in the field. When one of 'em gets sick and wretched . . . bang! And there's my friend sent packing — over the river.

[*The* NUN *comes out of the hotel with a tray with milk and bread on it, which she leaves on the table outside the pavilion before she goes in.*]

ULFHEIM [*with a scornful laugh*]: Look at that! Is that the sort of food to give a human being? Milk-and-water and soft soggy bread. Ah, you ought to see my friends feeding! Would you like to?

MAIA [*with a smile at the Professor as she gets up*]: Yes, very much.

ULFHEIM [*also rising*]: Good for you, ma'am! You come along with me, then. Great thick marrow bones . . . they swallow them whole — cough them up then gulp them down again. It's a grand sight to watch 'em. Come along and I'll show you; and we'll talk a bit more about this trip to the mountains.

[*He goes out round the corner of the hotel.* MAIA *follows him. Almost immediately the* STRANGE LADY *comes out of the pavilion and seats herself at her table. She picks up the glass of milk, and is about to drink, when she stops and looks at Rubek with vacant expressionless eyes.* RUBEK *remains seated at his table, staring fixedly and earnestly at her. At last he rises, goes a step or two towards her, then stops.*]

PROFESSOR RUBEK [*in a low voice*]: I remember you perfectly, Irena.

THE LADY [*tonelessly, putting down her glass*]: You've guessed who I am, then, Arnold?

PROFESSOR RUBEK [*without answering*]: And I see you remember me, too.

THE LADY: Ah, with *you* it's quite different.

PROFESSOR RUBEK: With me? Why?

THE LADY: Well – *you* are still alive.

PROFESSOR RUBEK [*not understanding*]: Alive?

THE LADY [*after a moment*]: Who was the other woman? The one you had with you – at that table there?

PROFESSOR RUBEK [*rather unwillingly*]: She? That was – my wife.

THE LADY [*nodding slowly*]: I see. That's good, Arnold. Then she's someone who doesn't concern me.

PROFESSOR RUBEK [*uncertainly*]: No – of course not.

THE LADY: – someone you've come by since my lifetime.

PROFESSOR RUBEK [*suddenly staring at her*]: Since your . . .? What does that mean, Irena?

IRENA [65] [*ignoring this*]: And the child? The child is well; our child that survived me, and achieved fame and honour.

PROFESSOR RUBEK [*smiling, as though at some distant memory*]: Our child? Yes, that's what we used to call it – in the old days.

IRENA: In my lifetime, yes.

PROFESSOR RUBEK [*trying to strike a lighter note*]: Yes, Irena, I can assure you that 'our child' has become famous all over the world. I suppose you read about it.

IRENA [*nodding*]: And it has made its father famous, too – just as you always dreamed.

PROFESSOR RUBEK [*more gently – moved*]: It's to you that I owe it all, Irena – everything. Thank you.

IRENA [*after sitting thoughtfully for a moment*]: If only I'd done as I had a right to, Arnold . . .

PROFESSOR RUBEK: Well . . .?

IRENA: I should have killed that child.

PROFESSOR RUBEK: Killed it, you say?

IRENA [*in a whisper*]: Killed it – before I left you. I should have crushed it – pounded it to dust.

PROFESSOR RUBEK [*with a reproachful shake of his head*]: You could never have done that, Irena; you wouldn't have had the heart.

IRENA: No, in those days I hadn't that sort of heart.

PROFESSOR RUBEK: But since then? Afterwards?

IRENA: Since then I've killed it more times than I can say. Day and night I've killed it – in torment, in hatred, and in revenge.

PROFESSOR RUBEK [*going up to the table and asking softly*]: Irena . . . tell me now – after all these years – why did you leave me then? You vanished so completely – I could find no trace of you.

IRENA [*shaking her head slowly*]: Oh Arnold, why should I tell you now – now that I've passed over.

PROFESSOR RUBEK: Was there someone else, whom you'd come to love?

IRENA: There was someone who had no need of my love – no more need of my life.

PROFESSOR RUBEK [*avoiding this*]: Ah . . . don't let us go on talking about the past.

IRENA: No . . . let us not talk about what is beyond the grave – because now, all *that* is beyond the grave for me.

PROFESSOR RUBEK: Where have you been, Irena? I searched and searched, but you seemed to have vanished completely.

IRENA: I went into the darkness – while the child stood transfigured in the light.

PROFESSOR RUBEK: Did you travel far?

IRENA: Yes – I travelled in many lands.

PROFESSOR RUBEK [*looking at her with compassion*]: And what did you find to do, Irena?

IRENA [*meeting his eyes*]: Wait – let me think. . . . Yes, I remember – I've posed in music-halls, naked on a turn-table, as a living statue. I made a lot of money that way – which is more than I could do with you, because you never had any. Then I've been with men whose heads I could turn. And that, too, was more than I could do with you, Arnold; you had yourself far too well in hand.

PROFESSOR RUBEK [*quickly changing the subject*]: And you've been married, too?

IRENA: Yes, I married one of them.

PROFESSOR RUBEK: Who is your husband?

IRENA: He was a South American – a distinguished diplomat. [*Staring straight to the front with a stony smile*] I managed to drive *him* right out of his mind . . . mad – incurably, irreparably mad. You can take it from me, it was great sport while it lasted. How I could have laughed inside myself – if I'd had *anything* inside myself.

PROFESSOR RUBEK: And where is he now?

IRENA: Oh, in some churchyard or other; with a fine hand-some monument over him – and a bullet rattling in his skull.

PROFESSOR RUBEK: He killed himself?

IRENA: Yes, he was good enough to save me the trouble.

PROFESSOR RUBEK: But – aren't you sorry for him, Irena?

IRENA [*uncomprehending*]: Sorry? For whom?

PROFESSOR RUBEK: For Herr von Satoff, of course.[66]

IRENA: His name wasn't Satoff.

PROFESSOR RUBEK: Not?

IRENA: My second husband's name is Satoff. He's a Russian.

PROFESSOR RUBEK: And where is he?

IRENA: Far away in the Caucasus – among all his gold-mines.

PROFESSOR RUBEK: Does he live *there*?

IRENA [*shrugging her shoulders*]: Lives? If you can call it living. Actually I've killed him.

PROFESSOR RUBEK [*with a start*]: You've *killed* . . .?

IRENA: Killed him with a fine sharp dagger that I always have with me in bed.[67]

PROFESSOR RUBEK [*vehemently*]: Irena – I don't believe you!

IRENA [*smiling gently*]: It's perfectly true, Arnold.

PROFESSOR RUBEK [*looking at her with pity*]: And did you never have a child?

IRENA: Yes, I've had many children.

PROFESSOR RUBEK: And where are they now?

IRENA: I killed them.

PROFESSOR RUBEK [*severely*]: Now you're lying to me again.

IRENA: I killed them, I tell you. I murdered them, ruthlessly, as soon as ever they were born . . . oh, before they were born – long before. One after the other.

PROFESSOR RUBEK [*sadly and earnestly*]: There's some hidden meaning behind everything you say.

IRENA: How can I help it? Every word I say to you is whispered in my ear.

PROFESSOR RUBEK: I think I'm the only one who can guess that meaning.

IRENA: You *should* be the only one.

PROFESSOR RUBEK [*resting his hands on the table and looking intently at her*]: Some of the strings of your being have broken.

IRENA [*softly*]: Surely that always happens when a young warm-blooded woman dies.

PROFESSOR RUBEK: Oh, Irena, these are only delusions – shake them off. You're alive, do you hear? Alive! Alive!

IRENA [*rising slowly from her chair, her voice trembling*]: For many years I was dead. They came and bound me – they laced my arms together behind my back, and lowered me into a tomb, with iron bars over the opening, and padded walls . . . so that no one on the earth overhead should hear the shrieks from the tomb. But now, I'm beginning to rise – a little – from the dead. [*She sits again.*]

PROFESSOR RUBEK [*after a moment*]: And you feel that *I* am to blame?

IRENA: Yes.

PROFESSOR RUBEK: That I'm guilty of your death, as you call it?

IRENA: Guilty because I *had* to die. [*Changing to a casual note*] Why don't you sit down, Arnold?

PROFESSOR RUBEK: May I?

IRENA: Yes. Don't be afraid of catching a chill – I don't think I'm quite turned to ice yet.

PROFESSOR RUBEK [*moving a chair and sitting at the table*]: There, Irena. Now you and I are sitting together just as we used to do in the old days.

IRENA: A little apart from each other – just as we used to in the old days.

PROFESSOR RUBEK [*moving nearer*]: It had to be like that then.

IRENA: Had it?

PROFESSOR RUBEK [*firmly*]: Yes, there *had* to be a gap between us.

IRENA: Did there *really*, Arnold?

PROFESSOR RUBEK [*continuing*]: Do you remember what you answered when I asked you if you'd go with me out into the world?

IRENA: I held up three fingers to heaven, and swore to follow you to the world's end, and to the end of life. And that I would serve you in all things –

PROFESSOR RUBEK: – as a model for my work –

IRENA: – in frank and utter nakedness.

PROFESSOR RUBEK [*moved*]: And how well you served me, Irena – so gladly, so freely and ungrudgingly.

IRENA: Yes, with all the pulsing blood of my youth, I served you.

PROFESSOR RUBEK [*nodding, with a look of gratitude*]: You have every right to say that.

IRENA: I fell down at your feet and served you, Arnold. [*Clenching her fist at him*] But you . . .! You . . .!

PROFESSOR RUBEK [*defensively*]: I never did you any wrong . . . never, Irena.

IRENA: You did. You wronged me to the depths of my being.

PROFESSOR [*drawing back*]: I?

IRENA: Yes, you! I showed myself, wholly and without reserve, for you to gaze at . . . [*softly*] and never once did you touch me!

PROFESSOR RUBEK: Irena, didn't you realize that, time and again, I was almost driven mad by your beauty?

IRENA .[*continuing, undisturbed*]: And yet, if you *had* touched me, I think I should have killed you then and there. I carried a sharp needle on me – hidden in my hair. [*Stroking her forehead thoughtfully*] Yes, but . . . no, after all – after all, that you should –

PROFESSOR RUBEK [*with an expressive look*]: I was an artist, Irena.

IRENA [*darkly*]: That's just it . . . that's just it.

PROFESSOR RUBEK: An artist first and foremost. And I was sick with longing to create the great work of my life. [*Lost in recollection*] It was to be called 'Resurrection Day', expressed in the form of a young woman waking from the sleep of death –

IRENA: Our child, yes.

PROFESSOR RUBEK [*continuing*]: – this waking woman was to be the noblest, purest, most flawless in the world. Then I found *you*. You were so exactly what I needed. And you consented so willingly – so gladly – to give up your home and your family and to come with me.

IRENA: To go with you was the resurrection of my child-hood.

PROFESSOR RUBEK: That was just why I could use you – you and no one else. To me you became something holy – not to be touched except in reverent thought. I was still young in those days, Irena. I was filled with the conviction that if I touched you, or desired you sensually, my vision would be so desecrated that I should never be able to achieve what I was striving after. And I still think there was some truth in that.

IRENA [*nods with a touch of scorn*]: The work of art first, and flesh and blood second!

PROFESSOR RUBEK: Condemn me if you like, but in those days my great task dominated me completely – filled me with exultant joy.

IRENA: And you achieved your aim, Arnold.

PROFESSOR RUBEK: Thanks to you – and I bless you for it – I achieved my aim. I wanted to portray the perfect woman as I felt she must awake on Resurrection Day; not marvelling at something new and unknown and unguessed-at, but filled with a holy joy at finding herself unchanged . . . she, a mortal woman, in the higher, freer, happier sphere, after the long dreamless sleep of death. [*More softly*] And so I created her . . . created her in your image, Irena.

IRENA [*laying her hands flat on the table and leaning back in her chair*]: And then you were done with me.

PROFESSOR RUBEK [*reproachfully*]: Irena!

IRENA: You had no more need of me –

PROFESSOR RUBEK: How can you say that?

IRENA: – and you began to look round for other ideals.

PROFESSOR RUBEK: I never found one – not after you.

IRENA: And no other models, Arnold?

PROFESSOR RUBEK: You were not a model to me – you were the source of my inspiration.

IRENA [*after a moment's silence*]: What poems have you written since? [68] In marble, I mean. Since the day I left you?

PROFESSOR RUBEK: I have made no poems since your day . . . only trivial modellings.

IRENA: And that woman whom you're living with now –?

PROFESSOR RUBEK [*interrupting violently*]: Don't speak of her now. It's like a knife in my heart.

IRENA: Where are you thinking of going with her?

PROFESSOR RUBEK [*dully and wearily*]: Oh, on a tedious cruise along the north coast.

IRENA [*looking at him, smiling almost imperceptibly, whispers*]: No, go up into the high mountains . . . as high as you can go. Higher – higher, Arnold, always higher.

PROFESSOR RUBEK [*eager and expectant*]: Are you going up there?

IRENA: Dare you meet me again?

PROFESSOR RUBEK [*uncertainly, struggling with himself*]: If we *could* – if we only could!

IRENA: Why shouldn't we – if we choose? [*With a beseeching look, clasping her hands*] Come, Arnold, come! Oh, come to me up there!

[MAIA *enters, flushed with happiness, from round the corner of the hotel; she makes straight for the table where she and Rubek had been sitting.*]

MAIA [*from the corner, without looking*]: Well, Rubek, you can say what you like, I – [*She stops as she sees Irena.*] Oh, I'm sorry, I see you've found a new friend!

PROFESSOR RUBEK [*shortly*]: I've found an *old* friend. [*Rising*] Did you want me for something?

MAIA: I only wanted to say that you can do as you like, but I'm not going with you on that wretched steamer.

PROFESSOR RUBEK: Why not?

MAIA: Because I want to go up to the mountains and the forests – that's what I want. [*Wheedling*] Oh, you *must* let me, Rubek; I'll be so nice to you afterwards – so very nice.

PROFESSOR RUBEK: Who's been putting these ideas into your head?

MAIA: Why, *he* has, that awful bear-slayer! Oh, you can't imagine all the wonderful things he has to say about the mountains and the life up there. Dreadful, terribly brutal stories he makes up – I'm almost sure he makes them up – but they're wonderfully fascinating all the same. Oh, won't you let me go with him – only to see if he's telling the truth, that's all. *May* I, Rubek?

PROFESSOR RUBEK: Yes, of course you may, as far as I'm concerned; go up into the mountains as far as you like – and for as long as you like. Perhaps I may be going up that way myself.

MAIA [*quickly*]: No no, you needn't do that. Not on my account.

PROFESSOR RUBEK: I *want* to go to the mountains; I've already decided on it.

MAIA: Oh, thank you – thank you! May I go straight and tell the bear-slayer?

PROFESSOR RUBEK: Tell the bear-slayer whatever you like.

MAIA: Oh, thank you, thank you, thank you! [*She tries to take his hand, but he will not let her.*] Oh, you're so nice and kind today, Rubek! [*She runs into the hotel.*]

[*As she goes, the door of the pavilion is softly and silently pushed ajar. The* NUN *stands inside the doorway, watching them intently. They do not see her.*]

PROFESSOR RUBEK [*his mind made up, turning to Irena*]: Shall we meet up there, then?

IRENA [*slowly rising*]: Yes, we shall certainly meet. I've tried so long to find you.

PROFESSOR RUBEK: When did you begin to look for me, Irena?

IRENA [*with a touch of bitter humour*]: From the moment that I realized I'd given you something I couldn't do without, Arnold – something one should never part with.

PROFESSOR RUBEK [*bowing his head*]: Yes, that is only too true; you gave me three – no, four – years of your youth.

IRENA: I gave you much more than that. What a spend-thrift I was in those days!

PROFESSOR RUBEK: Yes, you were generous, Irena; you gave me all your naked loveliness –

IRENA: – to gaze on –

PROFESSOR RUBEK: – and to glorify.

IRENA: Yes, for your own glorification – and the child's.

PROFESSOR RUBEK: For yours too, Irena.

IRENA: But you've forgotten the richest gift of all.

PROFESSOR RUBEK: The richest –? What was that?

IRENA: I gave you my soul – young and living. And since then I've been empty – soulless. [*Looking fixedly at him*] That was why I died, Arnold.

> [*The* NUN *opens the door fully, and makes way for her. She goes into the pavilion.*]

PROFESSOR RUBEK [*stands staring after her . . . then he whispers*]: Irena!

ACT TWO

————————*————————

At a mountain health-resort.[69] The landscape stretches as a vast treeless plateau towards a long mountain lake. On the farther side of the lake a range of mountain peaks rises, with bluish snow in its cleft. In the left foreground, a brook divides into several streams as it ripples over a steep wall of rock, and then flows on smoothly across the plateau to the right. Its course is marked with bushes, plants, and boulders. In the right foreground is a little hill with a stone seat on it. It is a summer evening, just before sunset.

In the distance, across the brook, a group of small children sing and dance and play on the plateau. Some wear town clothes, and others peasant costume. Their happy laughter is heard faintly under the dialogue.

[PROFESSOR RUBEK is sitting on the seat, with a shawl over his shoulders, looking down at the children as they play.

Presently, MAIA enters from the left, through some bushes on the plateau; she looks round, shading her eyes with her hands. She is wearing a flat travelling-cap, and a short kilted skirt reaching only half-way down to her ankles, and long, heavy, laced boots. She carries a tall staff.]

MAIA [at last seeing Rubek and calling]: Hallo!
[She comes across the plateau, jumps over the brook with the help of her staff, and climbs up the little hill.]

MAIA [*panting*]: Oh, I've been looking everywhere for you, Rubek.

PROFESSOR RUBEK [*asking, with an uninterested nod*]: Have you come up from the Hydro?

MAIA: Yes, in the end I even tried that fly-trap!

PROFESSOR RUBEK [*giving her a quick look*]: You weren't at luncheon, I noticed.

MAIA: No, we lunched out of doors.

PROFESSOR RUBEK: We? Who?

MAIA: I and that awful bear-slayer, of course.

PROFESSOR RUBEK: Oh, him!

MAIA: Yes, and we're going out again first thing in the morning.

PROFESSOR RUBEK: After bears?

MAIA: Yes, off to kill the brutes.

PROFESSOR RUBEK: Have you found any tracks?

MAIA [*haughtily*]: You'd hardly find bears up here on the open moorland, would you?

PROFESSOR RUBEK: Where, then?

MAIA: Right down there in the foothills, where the forest's thickest. Places where ordinary townsfolk could never penetrate.

PROFESSOR RUBEK: And you two are going there in the morning?

MAIA [*throwing herself down in the heather*]: We plan to, yes. We might even start this evening – if you don't mind, that is.

PROFESSOR RUBEK: I? Far be it from me to . . .

MAIA [*quickly*]: Lars goes with us, of course – with the dogs.

PROFESSOR RUBEK: I'm not really interested in Mr Lars and his dogs. [*Changing the subject*] Wouldn't you rather sit properly on the seat?

MAIA [*drowsily*]: No thank you; the heather's so lovely and soft to lie on.

PROFESSOR RUBEK: Obviously you're tired.

MAIA [*yawning*]: I rather think I soon shall be.

PROFESSOR RUBEK: That always comes afterwards – when the excitement's over.

MAIA [*sleepily*]: Yes . . . I'll just lie here and shut my eyes. [*Pause.*] [*With sudden irritation*] Ugh, Rubek, how can you bear to sit here and listen to those children yelling . . . and to watch their horseplay too?

PROFESSOR RUBEK: Every now and then, in spite of their clumsiness, there's something harmonious in their movements – almost like music. It amuses me to sit and watch for those occasional moments.

MAIA [*with a rather scornful laugh*]: Oh yes, you're always the artist, aren't you?

PROFESSOR RUBEK: I hope I always shall be.

MAIA [*turning on her side, so that she has her back to him*]: There's no trace of the artist in *him*.

PROFESSOR RUBEK [*interested*]: Who? Who isn't an artist?

MAIA [*sleepily again*]: Why, *him*, of course.

PROFESSOR RUBEK: You mean the bear-shooter?

MAIA: Yes . . . nothing of the artist about *him* – not a thing.

PROFESSOR RUBEK [*smiling*]: No, I'm quite sure you're right there.

MAIA [*impetuously, but without moving*]: And how ugly he is! [*Pulling up a tuft of heather and then throwing it away*] Ugly – ugly! Ugh!

PROFESSOR RUBEK: Is that why you're so glad to be going off into the wilds with him?

MAIA [*curtly*]: I don't know. [*Turning towards him*] You're ugly too, Rubek.

PROFESSOR RUBEK: Have you only just noticed that?

MAIA: No, I saw it long ago.

PROFESSOR RUBEK [*shrugging his shoulders*]: One grows older . . . one grows older, Mrs Rubek.

MAIA: I don't mean that sort of ugliness at all. But nowadays there's such a tired look in your eyes – a look of defeat . . . on the rare occasions when you bother to glance at me!

PROFESSOR RUBEK: So you've noticed that, have you?

MAIA [*nodding*]: Little by little, an evil look has come into your eyes. It's almost as if you were hatching some dark plot against me.

PROFESSOR RUBEK: Oh? [*Friendly but earnestly*] Come here and sit beside me, Maia, and then we can talk.

MAIA [*half rising*]: Will you let me sit on your knee, then – as I used to in the old days?

PROFESSOR RUBEK: No, you mustn't do that – people can see us from the hotel. [*Moving a little*] But you can sit here beside me on the seat.

MAIA: No thank you; I'd rather lie here where I am. I can hear quite well from here. [*With an inquiring look*] Well . . . what was it you wanted to talk about?

PROFESSOR RUBEK [*hesitating at first*]: What do you think was my real reason for agreeing that we should come on this holiday trip?

MAIA: Well . . . among other things, you announced that it would do *me* so much good. But . . .

PROFESSOR RUBEK: But?

MAIA: But now I don't believe for a moment that that was the real reason.

PROFESSOR RUBEK: Well, what do you think now?

MAIA: I think it was because of that washed-out woman.

PROFESSOR RUBEK: Madame von Satoff?

MAIA: Yes, she's always at our heels; and then last night she turns up here, too.

PROFESSOR RUBEK: But what in the world . . .?

MAIA: Well, I'm sure you knew her – very well indeed – long before you met me.

PROFESSOR RUBEK: And I'd forgotten her, too – long before I met you.

MAIA [*sitting up*]: Can you forget so easily? Can you, Rubek?

PROFESSOR RUBEK [*curtly*]: Very easily indeed. [*Adding harshly*] When I *want* to forget.

MAIA: Even a woman who's been your model?

PROFESSOR RUBEK [*discouragingly*]: When I don't need her any longer, yes.

MAIA: A woman who has stripped herself naked for you?

PROFESSOR RUBEK: That means nothing. Not to us artists. [*On a different note*] Besides, how – if I might venture to ask – was I to guess that she was here in this country?

MAIA: Oh, you might have seen her name in one of the newspapers, in a list of visitors.

PROFESSOR RUBEK: Yes, but I hadn't the least idea what her name is now. I'd never heard of any Herr von Satoff.

MAIA [*pretending to be bored*]: Oh Lord, then I suppose there was some other reason why you finally wanted to come here.

PROFESSOR RUBEK [*sincerely*]: Yes, Maia – there *was* another reason ... quite a different one. And that's what you and I will have to discuss sometime.

MAIA [*stifling a fit of laughter*]: Heavens, how serious you look!

PROFESSOR RUBEK [*watching her suspiciously*]: Yes, perhaps I'm rather more serious than I need be.

MAIA: What do you mean?

PROFESSOR RUBEK: And *that's* just as well – for both our sakes.

MAIA: You're beginning to make me curious, Rubek.

PROFESSOR RUBEK: Only curious? Not at all uneasy?

MAIA [shaking her head]: Not in the least.

PROFESSOR RUBEK: Good. Then listen to me. Down at the Spa the other day, you said that you thought I'd become rather unstable recently. . . .

MAIA: Yes, and so you certainly have.

PROFESSOR RUBEK: And what do you think can have caused that?

MAIA: How should I know? [Impulsively] Perhaps you've got tired of my continual company.

PROFESSOR RUBEK: Continual? Why don't you say 'eternal'?

MAIA: My daily company, then. For four or five whole years now, you and I – two solitary people – have lived down there and hardly spent an hour apart from each other. Just we two – quite alone!

PROFESSOR RUBEK [interested]: Well? What of it?

MAIA [rather depressed]: You're not a very sociable man, Rubek – you prefer to go your own way, and to think for yourself; and of course I can't talk to you properly about your interests – about art and all that sort of thing. . . . [With an impatient gesture] And Lord knows I don't particularly want to!

PROFESSOR RUBEK: I see; so that's why we sit by the fire most of the time and chatter about your interests.

MAIA: Good heavens, I've no interests to chatter about.

PROFESSOR RUBEK: Well, perhaps they're not very important, but at any rate it passes the time for us as well as anything else, Maia.

MAIA: Yes, you're right . . . time passes. And your time's running out, Rubek! I suppose that's what makes you so uneasy.

PROFESSOR RUBEK [with a vehement nod]: And so restless. [*He twists on the seat as if in torment.*] No, I shan't be able to endure this wretched life much longer.

MAIA [*she rises, and stands for a moment looking at him*]: If you want to be quit of me, you've only to say so.

PROFESSOR RUBEK: What a way to talk! 'Be quit' of you!

MAIA: Yes, if you want to get rid of me, just say so, straight out – and I'll go at once.

PROFESSOR RUBEK [*with an almost imperceptible smile*]: Is that meant to be a threat, Maia?

MAIA: It certainly wouldn't be a threat to you.

PROFESSOR RUBEK [*rising*]: No, you're quite right there. [*After a moment*] You and I can't possibly go on living together like this.

MAIA: Well then . . .?

PROFESSOR RUBEK: There's nothing 'well' about it. [*Speaking with emphasis*] Because you and I can't go on living together *alone*, it doesn't necessarily follow that we must part.

MAIA [*smiling scornfully*]: Simply go our own ways for a little, you mean?

PROFESSOR RUBEK [*shaking his head*]: Even that isn't necessary.

MAIA: Well . . .? Out with it! What do you want to do with me?

PROFESSOR RUBEK [*tentatively*]: I do feel strongly – painfully even – that what I need now is to have someone about me who is – truly near to me. . . .

MAIA [*interrupting anxiously*]: Aren't I, Rubek?

PROFESSOR RUBEK [*repulsing her*]: Not in the way I mean. I must have someone who can complete me – fulfil me . . . be one with me in all my aspirations.

MAIA [*slowly*]: Yes, in those important things, I certainly can't be much help to you.

PROFESSOR RUBEK: No, Maia, they're certainly not your strong point.

MAIA [*vehemently*]: And Lord knows I don't want them to be, either!

PROFESSOR RUBEK: I know that only too well. I didn't marry you with the idea that you'd be any help in my life's work.

MAIA [*watching him*]: I can see by your face that you're thinking of someone else.

PROFESSOR RUBEK: Oh? I'd never realized that you were a thought-reader. So you can see *that*?

MAIA: Yes, I can. Oh, I know you inside out, Rubek!

PROFESSOR RUBEK: Then perhaps you can also see whom I'm thinking of?

MAIA: I certainly can.

PROFESSOR RUBEK: Well? Perhaps you'll be good enough –

MAIA: You're thinking of that – that model you once used for – [*Suddenly switching her train of thought*] You know, don't you, that people down in the hotel think she's mad?

PROFESSOR RUBEK: Oh? And what do people down in the hotel think about you and your bear-hunter, then?

MAIA: That has nothing to do with it. [*Returning to her earlier subject*] But it *was* that washed-out woman you were thinking of.

PROFESSOR RUBEK [*cheerfully*]: Exactly – of her. When I didn't need her any longer, and when she, in her turn, went away from me – vanished, without a trace –

MAIA: Then, I suppose, you accepted me as a sort of second-best?

PROFESSOR RUBEK [*more recklessly*]: Yes, my dear Maia, something of the sort, to tell you the truth. I'd lived there, lonely and brooding, for a year and more; I'd put the finishing touches – the very last strokes – to my great work. 'Resurrection Day' had gone all over the world, and had brought me fame – and everything else the heart could desire. [*More warmly*] But I didn't love my own work any longer. All the garlands and the incense only sickened me, and drove me out in despair to hide myself deep in the woods. [*Looking at her*] You're a thought-reader, can you guess what occurred to me then?

MAIA [*uninterestedly*]: Yes, you took to making portrait-busts of society people.

PROFESSOR RUBEK [*nodding*]: All commissioned, yes! With animals' faces behind the mask. I threw *them* in gratis, for good measure, you understand. [*Smiling*] But that's not quite what I meant.

MAIA: Then what?

PROFESSOR RUBEK [*serious again*]: Simply this: that all the talk about an artist's vocation and an artist's mission and so on began to strike me as empty and hollow . . . as fundamentally meaningless.

MAIA: Well, what do you want instead?

PROFESSOR RUBEK: Life, Maia.

MAIA: Life?

PROFESSOR RUBEK: Yes, isn't life in sunshine and beauty altogether more worth while than to go on till the end of one's days in some damp clammy hole, tiring oneself to death wrestling with lumps of clay and blocks of stone?

MAIA [*with a little sigh*]: Yes, I've certainly always thought so.

PROFESSOR RUBEK: And I've become rich enough to live in luxury and idleness in the blazing sunshine. I was able to build myself a villa on Lake Taunitz, and a big town house in the capital, and all the rest of it.

MAIA [*catching his tone*]: And then, to crown it all, you could afford to acquire me, too. And you promised that I should share all your worldly goods.

PROFESSOR RUBEK [*turning it into a joke*]: Didn't I promise to take you with me up a high mountain and show you all the glory of the world?

MAIA: Perhaps you *have* taken me up quite a high mountain, Rubek – but you haven't shown me all the glory of the world.

PROFESSOR RUBEK [*with an irritable laugh*]: You're insatiable, Maia – really insatiable! [*In a violent outburst*] But do you know what's the most appalling thing of all? Can you guess?

MAIA [*quietly defying him*]: Yes, it must be that you have got yourself tied to me – for life!

PROFESSOR RUBEK: I shouldn't have put it quite as heartlessly.

MAIA: That wouldn't make your meaning any less heartless.

PROFESSOR RUBEK: You haven't the least idea how an artist's mind works.

MAIA: Good heavens, I haven't any idea how my own mind works.

PROFESSOR RUBEK [*continuing imperturbably*]: I live at such a pace, Maia – we artists *do*. For example, I've lived through a whole lifetime in the few years that you and I have known each other. I've come to realize that it isn't in me to find happiness in idle pleasure. Life doesn't go like that for me and my kind. I must keep on working – creating work after work – till the day I die. [*Managing to say it*] *That* is why I can't go on with you any longer, Maia; not with just you.

MAIA [*calmly*]: Does that mean, in plain words, that you've got tired of me?

PROFESSOR RUBEK [*violently*]: Yes, that's what it means. I've grown tired of this life with you – unbearably tired and slack and irritable. Now you know. [*Controlling himself*] Oh, I know perfectly well that that's an ugly, cruel way to talk to you, and I freely admit that you're not to blame for it. It is simply and solely that *I* have suffered a new upheaval – an awakening to what my life really means.

MAIA [*involuntarily clasping her hands*]: Then why on earth don't we separate?

PROFESSOR RUBEK [*looking at her in surprise*]: Would you be willing?

MAIA [*shrugging her shoulders*]: Oh yes . . . if there's nothing else for it, then –

PROFESSOR RUBEK [*eagerly*]: But there *is* something else . . . there's an alternative.

MAIA [*shaking a finger at him*]: You're thinking of that washed-out woman again!

PROFESSOR RUBEK: Yes, to tell you the truth, I think of her continually – ever since I met her again. [*Coming a step nearer to her*] And now I want to tell you something, Maia.

MAIA: Well?

PROFESSOR RUBEK [*tapping himself on the chest*]: Inside here, you see, I have a little casket with a secret lock, and in that casket lies all my vision as an artist, but when she disappeared without a trace, the lock snapped shut. She had the key, and she took that with her. You, my dear Maia, had no key . . . and so all that is in the casket is lost to me. And time is passing – and there's no way for me to reach the treasure.

MAIA [*struggling with a subtle smile*]: Then get her to unlock it for you again.

PROFESSOR RUBEK [*not understanding*]: Maia –?

MAIA: After all, she's here. And it's clearly because of the casket that she's come.

PROFESSOR RUBEK: I've not said a word to her about it.

MAIA [*with an innocent look*]: My dear Rubek! Is it really worth making all this fuss and commotion over such a simple thing?

PROFESSOR RUBEK: Do you think it so very simple?

MAIA: I certainly do. Just attach yourself to whomever you need most. [*Nodding at him*] I shall always manage to find a place for myself.

PROFESSOR RUBEK: Where do you mean?

MAIA [*casually evasive*]: Well – if necessary, I could always go to the villa. But it won't be necessary; in our huge town house, surely with a little give and take there'd be room for three.

PROFESSOR RUBEK [*uncertainly*]: And do you think that would work in the long run?

MAIA [*lightly*]: Well, good heavens, if it won't, it won't; it's no good talking about it.

PROFESSOR RUBEK: But if it doesn't work, Maia? What do we do then?

MAIA [*serenely*]: Then we simply get out of each other's way . . . completely. I shall always find something new for myself somewhere in the world. Something free . . . free! You have nothing to worry about *there*, Professor Rubek! [*Suddenly pointing off to the right*] Look! There she is!

PROFESSOR RUBEK [*turning*]: Where?

MAIA: Down there in the fields. Striding along like a marble statue. She's coming this way.

PROFESSOR RUBEK [*rising and watching her, shading his eyes with his hand*]: Doesn't she look like the embodiment of resurrection? [*To himself*] And to think that I could replace *her* – send her to outer darkness – make her into . . . fool that I was!

MAIA: What does *that* mean?

PROFESSOR RUBEK [*evasively*]: Not a thing! Nothing that you could understand.

[IRENA *approaches across the plateau from the right. The children at their play have already caught sight of her, and run to meet her. Soon she is surrounded by a whole flock of them, some happy and trusting, others shy and uneasy. She talks quietly to them, and signifies that they must go down to the Hydro, while she rests a little by the stream. The children run off down the slope to the left.* IRENA *goes over to the rock face, and lets the waterfall trickle over her hands to cool them.*]

MAIA [*low*]: Go down by yourself and talk to her, Rubek.

PROFESSOR RUBEK: And where will *you* go, meanwhile?

MAIA [*giving him a significant look*]: From now on, I shall go my own way. [*She goes down the hillock, leaping the brook with her staff. She halts beside Irena.*]

Professor Rubek is up there waiting for you, madam.

IRENA: What does he want?

MAIA: He wants you to help him open a casket that has snapped shut.

IRENA: Can I help him with it?

MAIA: He says you are the only one who can.

IRENA: Then I must try.

MAIA: Yes, madam, you definitely must. [*She goes down the path to the Hydro.*]

[*After a moment,* PROFESSOR RUBEK *comes down towards Irena, yet keeps the brook between them.*]

IRENA [*after a pause*]: The other woman said that you were waiting for me.

PROFESSOR RUBEK: I've been waiting for you for years – though I didn't know it.[70]

IRENA: I couldn't come to you, Arnold. I was lying asleep down there – a long, deep sleep, filled with dreams.

PROFESSOR RUBEK: But now you're awake, Irena.

IRENA [*shaking her head*]: A deep sleep still weighs on my eyes.

PROFESSOR RUBEK: You will see – day will come . . . and it will be light for both of us.

IRENA: Never believe that.

PROFESSOR RUBEK [*urgently*]: I do believe it! I know it now that I've found you again –

IRENA: Risen from the grave.

PROFESSOR RUBEK: Transfigured!

IRENA: Only risen, Arnold, not tranfigured.

[PROFESSOR RUBEK *picks his way over to her, by the stepping-stones below the waterfall.*]

PROFESSOR RUBEK: Where have you been all day, Irena?

IRENA [*pointing*]: Far away, over there on that great dead plain.

PROFESSOR RUBEK [*changing the subject*]: You haven't your – your friend with you today, I see.

IRENA [*smiling*]: My friend's keeping a close watch on me, all the same.

PROFESSOR RUBEK: Can she?

IRENA [*glancing furtively round*]: Believe me, she can – wherever I go; she never lets me out of her sight. [*Whispering*] Until, one fine sunny morning, I shall kill her.

PROFESSOR RUBEK: Would you do that?

IRENA: Very, very gladly – if only I could get the chance.

PROFESSOR RUBEK: Why do you want to?

IRENA: Because she practises witchcraft. [*Mysteriously*] Do you know, Arnold, she has transformed herself into my shadow?

PROFESSOR RUBEK [*trying to calm her*]: Well, well, we must all have a shadow.

IRENA: I am my own shadow. [*Vehemently*] Don't you understand that?

PROFESSOR RUBEK [*sadly*]: Yes, Irena, I understand.
[*He sits on a stone by the brook, while she stands behind him, leaning against the rock face.*]

IRENA [*after a moment*]: Why do you sit there and turn your eyes away?

PROFESSOR RUBEK [*softly, shaking his head*]: I dare not. I dare not look at you.

IRENA: Why daren't you look at me any more?

PROFESSOR RUBEK: *You* have a shadow that haunts you, and *I* have my heavy conscience.

IRENA [*with a happy cry of release*]: At last!

PROFESSOR RUBEK [*springing up*]: Irena! What is it?

IRENA [*fending him off*]: Gently, gently! [*Drawing a deep breath, as if relieved of a burden*] There! Now they've let me go – for the moment. Now we can sit and talk as we used to – when I was alive.

PROFESSOR RUBEK: Oh, if only we *could* talk as we used to.

IRENA: Sit down again, where you were before; and I'll sit here beside you.
[*He sits again, and she sits on another stone near him; after a short silence:*]
Now I've come back to you, Arnold, from the uttermost lands.

PROFESSOR RUBEK: Yes . . . you have – from an endless journey.

IRENA: Home to my master – my lord.

PROFESSOR RUBEK: To our home – to our own home, Irena.

IRENA: Have you hoped for me every single day?

PROFESSOR RUBEK: How could I dare to hope for you?

IRENA [*with a sidelong glance*]: No, you wouldn't dare. You didn't understand.

PROFESSOR RUBEK: Was it really not for someone else's sake that you left me so suddenly?

IRENA: Might it not have been for your own sake, Arnold?

PROFESSOR RUBEK [*looking at her uncertainly*]: But I don't understand . . .

IRENA: When I'd served you with my soul and my body – when the statue stood there finished – our child, as you called it – then I laid at your feet the greatest sacrifice of all – I obliterated myself for ever.

PROFESSOR RUBEK [*bowing his head*]: And laid waste my whole life.

IRENA [*suddenly flaring up*]: That was exactly what I wanted! You were never to create anything again, after you had created our only child.

PROFESSOR RUBEK: It was jealousy, then?

IRENA [*coldly*]: I think rather it was hatred.

PROFESSOR RUBEK: Hatred? Hatred of me?

IRENA [*vehemently again*]: Yes, of you. Of the artist who so lightly and carelessly took a warm, living body – a young human life – and wrenched the soul out of it . . , because you needed it to create a work of art.

PROFESSOR RUBEK: How can you say that? You who dedicated yourself to my work so ardently, with such a deep holy joy. That work for which we met each morning as if for an act of worship.

IRENA [*coldly again*]: There's something I want to tell you, Arnold.

PROFESSOR RUBEK: Well?

IRENA: I never loved your art, before I met you. Or after, either.

PROFESSOR RUBEK: But the artist, Irena?

IRENA: I hate the artist.

PROFESSOR RUBEK: The artist in me, as well?

IRENA: In you most of all. When I stripped myself completely and stood there for you, I hated you, Arnold.

PROFESSOR RUBEK [*vehemently*]: You did not, Irena; that's not true.

IRENA: I hated you because you could stand there so unmoved —

PROFESSOR RUBEK [*laughs*]: Unmoved? Do you believe that?

IRENA: — so unbearably self-controlled, then! And because you were an artist and only an artist; not a man. [*Changing to a note of warmth and tenderness*] But that statue in the wet living clay — *that* was what I loved, as it grew out of the raw shapeless mass into a vivid human creature. *That* was our creation — our child. Yours and mine.

PROFESSOR RUBEK [*sadly*]: Yes, both in spirit and in truth.

IRENA: Do you know, Arnold, that it is for the sake of this child of ours that I have undergone this long pilgrimage?

PROFESSOR RUBEK [*suddenly alert*]: For that marble statue?

IRENA: Call it what you like — I call it our child.

PROFESSOR RUBEK [*uneasily*]: And now you want to see it finished? In the marble that you always thought so cold? [*Eagerly*] Perhaps you don't know that it's installed in a great museum far away across the world.

IRENA: I have heard some such story.

PROFESSOR RUBEK: And you always had a horror of museums; you used to call them sepulchres.

IRENA: I want to make a pilgrimage to the place where my soul, and my child's soul, lie buried.

PROFESSOR RUBEK [*worried and uneasy*]: You must never see that statue again, Irena, do you hear? I implore you never, never to see it again.

IRENA: Do you think it would kill me a second time?

PROFESSOR RUBEK [*clenching his hands*]: Oh, I don't know *what* I think! But how could I have known that you would become so obsessed with that statue – when you left me before it was even finished.

IRENA: It *was* finished. That's why I could go away, and leave you alone.

PROFESSOR RUBEK [*sitting with his elbows on his knees, rocking his head from side to side, with his hands over his eyes*]: It was not what it finally became.

IRENA [*quietly, but quick as lightning, she half-draws a thin sharp knife from her breast,*[71] *and asks in a hoarse whisper*]: Arnold – have you done some harm to our child?

PROFESSOR RUBEK [*evasively*]: Harm? How can I be sure what *you* will call it?

IRENA [*breathlessly*]: Tell me at once what you've done to the child.

PROFESSOR RUBEK: I'll tell you if you will sit and listen quietly to what I say.

IRENA [*hiding the knife*]: I'll listen as quietly as a mother can, when she –

PROFESSOR RUBEK [*interrupting*]: And you're not to look at me while I tell you.

IRENA [*moving to a stone at his back*]: I'll sit here behind you. Now tell me.

PROFESSOR RUBEK [*taking his hands from his eyes and looking straight to the front*]: When I found you, I knew at once how I should use you for my masterpiece.

IRENA: 'Resurrection Day' you called it – I called it our child.

PROFESSOR RUBEK: I was young then, and knew nothing of life. Resurrection, I thought, would be most beautifully – most exquisitely – personified as a young woman, untouched by the world, waking to light and glory, with nothing ugly or impure to shed.

IRENA [*quickly*]: Yes . . . and that is how I stand there now in our work?

PROFESSOR RUBEK [*hesitating*]: Not . . . exactly, Irena.

IRENA: Not exactly? Don't I stand there just as I stood for you?

PROFESSOR RUBEK [*not answering*]: In the years that followed, I came to know something of the world, Irena. Resurrection Day began to mean something larger, and something – something more complex. The little round pedestal where your figure stood so straight and solitary – no longer had room on it for all that I now wanted to show –

IRENA [*starting to reach for her knife, but stopping*]: What else did you show? Tell me.

PROFESSOR RUBEK: I showed what I saw with my own eyes in the world around me. I *had* to show it, Irena, I couldn't help myself. I enlarged the pedestal, made it broader and wider, and on it I placed a corner of the curved and splitting earth, and out of the fissures in the ground there now swarm human figures with secret animal faces – men and women, just as I knew them in life.

IRENA [*breathless with suspense*]: But in the middle of the throng stands the young woman rejoicing in the light. Do I not, Arnold?

PROFESSOR RUBEK [*evasively*]: Not quite in the middle. Unfortunately I had to move the figure back a little. For the sake of the composition as a whole, you understand, otherwise it would have stood out too much.

IRENA: But my face is still transfigured with joy at seeing the light?

PROFESSOR RUBEK: Yes, Irena, it is . . . in a way. A little subdued, perhaps, as my new conception demanded.

IRENA [*rising silently*]: That portrait expresses life as you now see it, Arnold?

PROFESSOR RUBEK: Yes, it does.

IRENA: And in that portrayal you have moved me back, a little subdued, to a place in the background of a group? [*She draws her knife.*]

PROFESSOR RUBEK: Not the background. The worst you could say is that your figure isn't quite in the foreground – that more or less describes it.

IRENA [*in a hoarse whisper*]: Now you've pronounced your own doom. [*About to strike.*]

PROFESSOR RUBEK [*turning to look up at her*]: My doom?

IRENA [*quickly hiding the knife, and speaking as if choked with feeling*]: My whole soul . . . you and I . . . We – we and our child – were in that single figure.

PROFESSOR RUBEK [*eagerly tearing off his hat and wiping the sweat from his forehead*]: Yes, but you must let me tell you where I placed myself in the group. In front, by a stream – *here*, as it were – sits a man so laden with guilt that he cannot quite free himself from the earth's crust. I call him remorse for a wasted life. He sits and dips his fingers in the running brook to wash them clean, and he is racked and tormented by the knowledge that he will never succeed – never in all eternity will he be free to live the resurrected life. He must stay for ever in his own hell.

IRENA [*in a hard cold voice*]: Poet!

PROFESSOR RUBEK: Why poet?

IRENA: Because you are weak and torpid and full of self-forgiveness for your lifetime of sins both of thought and deed. You have killed my soul – and then for penance you model yourself in remorse and shame . . . [*smiling*] and you think *that* settles the account.

PROFESSOR RUBEK [*defiantly*]: I am an artist, Irena; and I'm not ashamed of such weaknesses as may cling to me. You see, I was *born* an artist, and whatever happens I can never be anything but an artist.

IRENA [*gently and softly, but with a secret evil smile*]: You are a poet, Arnold. [*Stroking his hair gently*] And a dear great over-grown baby not to be able to see it.

PROFESSOR RUBEK [*annoyed*]: Why do you keep calling me a poet?

IRENA [*with a sinister look*]: Because there's something conciliatory about the word, my friend – something that excuses all misdeeds and cloaks all weaknesses. [*With a sudden change of expression*] But *I* was a human being, in those days. I had a life to lead too, and a human destiny to fulfil. And I let it all go, you see – gave it up to become servant to you. That was self-murder – a mortal sin against myself – [*half-whispering*] a sin that I can never atone for. [*She sits near him beside the stream, keeping her eyes on him, though he does not notice it. Almost as if without thinking, she picks a few flowers from the shrubs around them. When she speaks, she seems under control.*] I *should* have brought children into the world, many children – real children, not the kind that are hidden away in tombs. That should have been my vocation; I should never have served you, you poet!

PROFESSOR RUBEK [*lost in his memories*]: Yet those

were wonderful days, Irena – wonderfully beautiful, now that I look back on them.

IRENA [*looking at him with a gentle expression*]: Can you remember a little word that you used, when you were finished . . . finished with me and with our child? [*With a nod*] You remember that little word, Arnold?

PROFESSOR RUBEK [*with an inquiring look*]: Did I use some little word that you remember still?

IRENA: You did. Don't you remember it any more?

PROFESSOR RUBEK [*shaking his head*]: No, I certainly don't – not at the moment, at any rate.

IRENA: You took my hands and pressed them fervently, and I stood there breathless with expectation. Then you said: 'Irena, I thank you with all my heart; This,' you said, 'has been a very happy episode for me.'

PROFESSOR RUBEK [*with a doubtful look*]: Did I say 'episode'? [72] It's not a word that I generally use.

IRENA: You said 'episode'.   -

PROFESSOR RUBEK [*with attempted cheerfulness*]: Well – after all, it *was* an episode.

IRENA [*curtly*]: After that word, I left you.

PROFESSOR RUBEK: You take everything far too seriously, Irena.

IRENA [*passing a hand over her forehead*]: Perhaps you're right. Let's forget weighty, serious things. . . . [*Picking the petals from a rock-rose and sprinkling them on the stream*] Look, Arnold, those are our birds swimming there.

PROFESSOR RUBEK: What sort of birds are they?

IRENA: They're flamingos, of course; can't you see? They're rose-red.

PROFESSOR RUBEK: Flamingos don't swim, they only wade.

IRENA: Then they're not flamingos, they're sea-gulls.

PROFESSOR RUBEK: Yes, they could be gulls with red beaks. [*He picks broad green leaves and throws them in.*] Now I'm sending my ships after them!

IRENA: But there mustn't be any hunters on board!

PROFESSOR RUBEK: No, there'll be no hunters. [*Smiling at her*] Do you remember how we used to sit like this in the summer outside the little cottage on Lake Taunitz?

IRENA [*nodding*]: On Saturday evenings, after we'd finished our week's work.

PROFESSOR RUBEK: We used to take the train out there, and stay over Sunday. . . .

IRENA [*with a wicked glint of hate in her eye*]: An episode, Arnold!

PROFESSOR RUBEK [*as if he hadn't heard*]: You used to send birds swimming in the brook there, too. It was water lilies you used –

IRENA: That were white swans.

PROFESSOR RUBEK: I meant swans, of course. And I remember tying a great broad leaf to one of the swans – a dockleaf, it must have been.

IRENA: – and it became Lohengrin's boat – drawn by the swan.

PROFESSOR RUBEK: How you loved that game, Irena.

IRENA: We played it over and over again.

PROFESSOR RUBEK: Every single Saturday, I think – all through the summer.

IRENA: You said I was the swan that drew your boat.

PROFESSOR RUBEK: Did I? Yes, I may well have done. [*Lost in the game*] Just look how the sea-gulls are swimming down the river.

IRENA [*laughing*]: And all your ships have run aground!

PROFESSOR RUBEK [*putting more leaves in the water*]: Oh, I've plenty more ships in reserve. [*He follows them with his eyes, and throws in more. After a little, he speaks.*] Irena . . . I've bought that little cottage on Lake Taunitz.

IRENA: Have you? You always said you'd buy it when you could afford it.

PROFESSOR RUBEK: One day I found I could easily afford it, so I bought it.

IRENA [*with a sidelong look at him*]: Do you live out there now – in our old house?

PROFESSOR RUBEK: Oh no, I had it pulled down long ago. I've built myself a fine big comfortable villa on the site, with a park round it. It's where we – [*stopping and correcting himself*] – where I usually stay in the summer.

IRENA [*controlling herself*]: So you and – that other woman live out there now?

PROFESSOR RUBEK [*rather defiantly*]: Yes, when my wife and I aren't travelling, as we are this year.

IRENA: It was lovely – lovely, living on Lake Taunitz.

PROFESSOR RUBEK [*as if looking back into himself*]: And yet, Irena –

IRENA [*taking up his thought*]: And yet you and I let all that lovely life slip away.

PROFESSOR RUBEK [*softly and urgently*]: Is it too late to put right now?

[IRENA *sits silent for a while, without answering; then she points out over the plain.*]

IRENA: Look, Arnold, the sun's going down behind the mountains. Just look how those last rays glow on the tufts of heather.

PROFESSOR RUBEK [*following her gaze*]: It's a long time since I've seen the sun set in the mountains.

IRENA: Or the sunrise?

PROFESSOR RUBEK: I don't think I've ever seen the sun rise.

IRENA [*smiling as if lost in memory*]: *I* once saw a wonderfully beautiful sunrise.

PROFESSOR RUBEK: Did you? Where was that?

IRENA: High up on a mountain top – a dizzy height. You enticed me up there, and promised me that I should see all the glory of the world if only I – [*She stops abruptly.*]

PROFESSOR RUBEK: Well? If only you –?

IRENA: I did as you told me – followed you to the heights. And there I fell on my knees, and worshipped you . . . and served you. [*She is silent for a moment, then she goes on softly*] Then I saw the sunrise.

PROFESSOR RUBEK [*changing the subject*]: Wouldn't you like to come down and live with us at the villa?

IRENA [*looking at him with a scornful smile*]: With you – and the other woman?

PROFESSOR RUBEK [*urgently*]: With *me* – as in the days when we worked together. Open all that is locked up in me. Couldn't you bring yourself to do that, Irena?

IRENA [*shaking her head*]: I haven't the key to you any longer, Arnold.

PROFESSOR RUBEK: You have the key, and no one but you. [*Imploring*] Help me – so that I can begin to live again!

IRENA [*unrelenting, as before*]: Empty dreams – dead, idle dreams. There's no resurrection of a partnership like ours.

PROFESSOR RUBEK [*curtly breaking off*]: Then let us go on playing.

IRENA: Yes, playing – playing . . . only playing.

[*They sit and strew leaves and petals on the stream and let them float away.*

Up the hill in the background to the left come SQUIRE ULFHEIM *and* MAIA *in hunting clothes. After them* comes the SERVANT with the leash of dogs which he takes out to the right.]

PROFESSOR RUBEK [*catching sight of them*]: Look, there's little Maia, going out with her bear-hunter.[73]

IRENA: Your lady, yes.

PROFESSOR RUBEK: Or his.

MAIA [*looking round as she crosses the plateau, she sees the two by the stream and calls*]: Good night Professor – dream about me, I'm off on an adventure!

PROFESSOR RUBEK [*calling back*]: What's the goal of your adventure?

MAIA [*coming nearer*]: I'm going to *live* – for a change.

PROFESSOR RUBEK [*mockingly*]: Ah, so you want that, too, Maia, my dear?

MAIA: Yes, I do. And I've written a song about it – it goes like this: [*Singing triumphantly*]

> I am free, I am free, I am free!
> No longer in prison I'll be,
> I am free as a bird, I am free!

Yes, I believe I've woken up now – at last!

PROFESSOR RUBEK: It almost looks like it.

MAIA [*taking a deep breath*]: Oh, how gloriously light I feel now that I'm awake!

PROFESSOR RUBEK: Good night, Maia – and good luck.

ULFHEIM [*breaking in with a shout*]: Hey, stop it! To hell with good wishes – you'll bring the trolls on us! Can't you see we're going out shooting?

PROFESSOR RUBEK: What trophy will you bring me home, Maia?

MAIA: You shall have a bird of prey to model. I'll wing one for you.

PROFESSOR RUBEK [*with a bitter mocking laugh*]: Yes,

winging things – quite thoughtlessly – that's always been your way.

MAIA [*tossing her head*]: Well, just let me look after myself from now on, and then . . . [*With a nod and a mischievous laugh*] Good-bye – and a nice peaceful summer night on the hillside.[74]

PROFESSOR RUBEK [*jovially*]: Thank you – and all the bad luck in the world to you both – and to your hunting.

ULFHEIM [*roaring with laughter*]: Ah, that's the sort of wish I like!

MAIA [*laughing*]: Thank you, Professor, thank you!
[*They have both crossed what can be seen of the plateau, and they go out through the bushes on the right.*]

PROFESSOR RUBEK [*after a short pause*]: A summer night on the hillside – yes, *that* would have been life!

IRENA [*suddenly, with a wild look in her eyes*]: Would you like a summer night on the hillside – with me?

PROFESSOR RUBEK [*opening his arms*]: Yes . . . yes. Come!

IRENA: My dearest master – my lord!

PROFESSOR RUBEK: Oh, Irena!

IRENA [*hoarsely, smiling as she gropes in her breast*]: It will be only an episode. . . . [*Suddenly, whispering*] Sh! Don't look round, Arnold!

PROFESSOR RUBEK [*also speaking quietly*]: What is it?

IRENA: A face – staring at me.

PROFESSOR RUBEK [*turning involuntarily*]: Where? [*With a start*] Ah!
[*The* NUN'S *head has come partly into view among the bushes on the slope to the left; her eyes are fixed on Irena.*]

IRENA [*rising and speaking softly*]: We must part, then. No, don't get up. I tell you, you're not to come with me.

[*Bending over him and whispering*] Till we meet again tonight – on the hillside.

PROFESSOR RUBEK: You will come, Irena?

IRENA: I'll come – I promise. Wait for me here.

PROFESSOR RUBEK [*repeats dreamily*]: A summer night on the hillside. With you! With you! [*Their eyes meet*] Oh, Irena – that might have been our life. That's what we have thrown away, you and I.

IRENA: We see the irreparable only when – [*She breaks off.*]

PROFESSOR RUBEK [*with an inquiring look*]: When –?

IRENA: When we dead wake.

PROFESSOR RUBEK [*shaking his head sadly*]: What do we really see then?

IRENA: We see that we have never lived.

[*She crosses to the hill and climbs down. The* NUN *stands aside for her and then follows.* PROFESSOR RUBEK *sits on motionless by the brook.*]

MAIA [*is heard singing joyously up in the mountains*]:

> I am free, I am free, I am free!
> No longer in prison I'll be,
> I am free as a bird, I am free!

ACT THREE

———————— * ————————

A wild jagged mountain-side, with sheer precipices falling away at the back. Snow-covered peaks rise to the right, and lose themselves in high drifting mist. To the left, on a scree, stands an old half-ruined hut. It is early morning; dawn is breaking, but the sun has not yet risen.

[MAIA, *flushed and annoyed, comes down the scree to the left:* ULFHEIM *follows, half angry, half laughing, holding her tightly by the sleeve.*]

MAIA [*trying to free herself*]: Let me go – let me go, I tell you!

ULFHEIM: Now now! You're as vicious as a ferret – you'll be biting me in a minute!

MAIA [*hitting his hand*]: Let me go, I said! And be quiet.

ULFHEIM: I'm damned if I will!

MAIA: All right, then I won't go another step with you, do you hear? Not a single step.

ULFHEIM: Aha! How will you get away from me, here on the bare mountainside?

MAIA: I'll jump down that chasm if need be!

ULFHEIM: And smash yourself into mincemeat for the dogs – all dripping with blood? [*Letting her go*] All right, now, jump down the chasm if you want to. It's a frightful drop, with only one narrow path down, and that's pretty well impassable.

MAIA [*brushing her skirt with her hand, and glaring angrily at him*]: You're a fine one to go hunting with!

ULFHEIM: Let's say 'to go out for a bit of sport with'.

MAIA: So you call this sport, do you?

ULFHEIM: Yes, with your kind permission; it's the kind of sport I like best.

MAIA [*with a toss of her head*]: Well, really! [*After a moment, with a searching look*] Why did you let the hounds loose up there?

ULFHEIM [*with a wink and a grin*]: So that *they* could do a little hunting on their own, too, of course.

MAIA: That's an absolute lie; you weren't thinking of them when you unleashed them.

ULFHEIM [*still smiling*]: Very well, why did I? Tell me.

MAIA: You let them go to get Lars out of the way. You said he was to go after them and fetch them back. And in the meantime . . . Oh yes, it was a charming trick of yours!

ULFHEIM: And in the meantime?

MAIA [*curtly, breaking off*]: Never mind.

ULFHEIM [*confidentially*]: Lars won't find them; you can bet your life on that. He won't be back with them before his time.

MAIA [*with an angry look*]: No, I'm sure he won't.

ULFHEIM [*taking hold of her arm*]: You see, Lars knows my – my sporting habits.

MAIA [*avoiding him, and measuring him with her eyes*]: Do you know what you look like, Squire Ulfheim?

ULFHEIM: Probably like myself, I should think.

MAIA: Yes, you're perfectly right there – because you're the living image of a satyr.

ULFHEIM: A satyr?

MAIA: Exactly – a satyr.

ULFHEIM: A satyr? Isn't that a kind of monster – some sort of wood-demon?

MAIA: Yes, just like you. A thing with a goat's beard and legs like a billy goat. Yes, and a satyr has horns too.

ULFHEIM: Oho – has *he* horns too?

MAIA: A pair of ugly horns, just like you!

ULFHEIM: Can you see the poor little horns that *I* have?

MAIA: Yes, I think I see them quite plainly.

ULFHEIM [*taking the dog's leash from his pocket*]: Then I'd better tie you up!

MAIA: Have you gone quite mad? Tie me up?

ULFHEIM: If I'm a demon, you must expect me to act like one, mustn't you? So you can see my horns, can you?

MAIA [*soothingly*]: Now, now! Please try to behave like a gentleman, Squire Ulfheim. [*Breaking off*] Besides, what's become of the hunting-lodge you talked such a lot about? It ought to be somewhere near here, according to you.

ULFHEIM [*pointing to the hut with a flourish*]: There it is – before your very eyes!

MAIA [*glaring*]: That old pigsty?

ULFHEIM [*laughing in his beard*]: It's housed more than one king's daughter, anyway!

MAIA: Was that when that brute of a man in your story came to the king's daughter in the shape of a bear?

ULFHEIM: Yes, my dear sporting friend, this is the very place. [*With an inviting wave of his hand*] If you'd be pleased to enter . . .!

MAIA: Ugh! I wouldn't set foot in it! Ugh!

ULFHEIM: Oh, a couple can spend a very pleasant summer night sleeping in there – a whole summer, if it comes to that.

MAIA: Thank you, they'd need to have more taste for that sort of thing than I have. [*Impatiently*] And now I've had enough of you and your hunting-trip. I'm going down to the hotel, before everyone's awake.

ULFHEIM: And how do you propose to get down?

MAIA: That's your affair. There must be a way down somewhere or other, I'm quite sure.

ULFHEIM [*pointing to the back*]: Bless you, yes; there's a sort of way – right down that precipice there.

MAIA: Well then, if you'll be good enough . . .

ULFHEIM: But just you see if you dare go that way.

MAIA [*doubtfully*]: Do you think I daren't?

ULFHEIM: Never in this world! Not unless I help you.

MAIA [*uneasy*]: Then come and help me. What else are you here for?

ULFHEIM: Would you rather I took you on my back –?

MAIA: Don't be absurd!

ULFHEIM: – or held you in my arms?

MAIA: Don't start that nonsense again!

ULFHEIM [*mastering his anger*]: I once took a young girl – lifted her out of the mud of the street – and carried her in my arms. I carried her next to my heart, and I would have carried her all my life, so that she dashed not her foot against a stone. For her shoes were worn very thin when I found her. . . .

MAIA: And yet you picked her up and carried her in your arms?

ULFHEIM: Took her out of the gutter and carried her as high and as carefully as I could. [*With a rumbling laugh*] And do you know what thanks I got for it?

MAIA: No – what?

ULFHEIM [*looking at her with a smile and a nod*]: The horns! Those horns that you can see so clearly. There's an amusing story for you, eh, Madame Bear-killer? [75]

MAIA: Quite amusing. But I know another one that's even funnier.

ULFHEIM: What's that?

MAIA: Here it is: There was once a silly little girl; she had a father and mother, but rather a poor home. Then, into all this poverty, there came a mighty lord, and he took the little girl in his arms – just as you did – and travelled far far away with her.

ULFHEIM: Did she want to be with him so much?

MAIA: Yes, you see she was very silly.

ULFHEIM: And I daresay he was a fine splendid figure of a man?

MAIA: Oh no, there wasn't anything particularly fine about him. But he managed to persuade her that she should go with him up the highest mountain, where everything would be light and sunshine.

ULFHEIM: So he was a mountaineer, this fellow, was he?

MAIA: Yes, he was . . . in his way.

ULFHEIM: So he took the wench up with him . . .?

MAIA [*with a toss of her head*]: Oh yes, took her up with him properly, I can tell you! No, he tricked her into a cold clammy cage – as it seemed to her. There was neither sunlight nor fresh air, but only gilded walls with great stone spectres all round them.

ULFHEIM: Damn it, that served her right!

MAIA: Oh yes, but it's quite an amusing story all the same, don't you think?

ULFHEIM [*with a long look at her*]: Listen to me, my fellow-hunter . . .

MAIA: Well, what is it now?

ULFHEIM: Oughtn't you and I to tack our poor rags together?

MAIA: Is your lordship setting up as a rag-merchant?

ULFHEIM: Yes, I think he is. Mightn't we two try to patch the tatters together here and there, so as to make some sort of a human life out of them?

MAIA: But what happens when the wretched shreds are quite worn out?

ULFHEIM [*flinging his arms out*]: Then we shall stand there, brave and free – ourselves as we really are!

MAIA [*laughing*]: You with your goat's legs, yes!

ULFHEIM: And you with your – but never mind.

MAIA: Yes, let *us* go – come on!

ULFHEIM: Wait a minute. Where to, friend?

MAIA: Down to the hotel, of course.

ULFHEIM: And after that?

MAIA: Then we'll bid each other a polite farewell and say 'Thank you for your company!'

ULFHEIM: *Can* we part, you and I? Do you think we can?

MAIA: Yes, as far as I know, you didn't manage to tie me up.

ULFHEIM: I have a castle to offer you –

MAIA [*pointing to the hut*]: One like that?

ULFHEIM: It isn't quite in ruins yet.

MAIA: And all the glory of the world, perhaps?

ULFHEIM: A castle, I said –

MAIA: Thanks, I've had enough of castles.

ULFHEIM: – with miles of fine hunting country round it.

MAIA: Are there works of art in it too?

ULFHEIM [*slowly*]: No I can't say there are works of art, but –

MAIA [*relieved*]: Well, that's one good thing!

ULFHEIM: Will you come with me then? For as far and as long as I want?

MAIA: There's a tame eagle who keeps watch over me.

ULFHEIM [*wildly*]: We'll send a bullet through its wing, Maia!

MAIA [*looking at him for a moment, then speaking resolutely*]: Come on then, carry me down to the depths!

ULFHEIM [*putting his arm round her waist*]: It's high time
– the mist is coming down.

MAIA: Is the way down very dangerous?

ULFHEIM: The mountain mist is *more* dangerous.
[*She shakes herself free and goes to the edge of the
precipice and looks down, but quickly starts back.*]

ULFHEIM [*going to her, laughing*]: What, does it make
you a bit giddy?

MAIA [*faintly*]: Yes, but it's not that. Go and look over.
Those two coming up. . . .

ULFHEIM [*going and bending over the edge*]: It's only
your eagle – and his strange lady.

MAIA: Can't we get past – without them seeing us?

ULFHEIM: Impossible. The track's far too narrow, and
there's no other way down.

MAIA [*bracing herself*]: Very well; then let's face them
here.

ULFHEIM: Spoken like a real bear-slayer, my friend!
[PROFESSOR RUBEK *and* IRENA *come into sight over
the edge of the chasm in the background. He has his
plaid over his shoulder, she has a fur cloak thrown
loosely over her white dress, and a swan's-down hood
on her head.*]

PROFESSOR RUBEK [*while still only half seen over the
edge*]: Why, Maia! So you and I meet again.

MAIA [*with assumed confidence*]: At your service. Won't
you come up?
[PROFESSOR RUBEK *climbs right up, then puts out a
hand to Irena, who also comes up to the top.*]

PROFESSOR RUBEK [*coldly, to Maia*]: So you've spent all
night on the mountain, too – just as we did.

MAIA: Yes, I've been hunting. You gave me permission.

ULFHEIM [*pointing over the chasm*]: Have you come up
by that track?

PROFESSOR RUBEK: You saw that we did.

ULFHEIM: And the strange lady, too?

PROFESSOR RUBEK: So it seems. [*With a glance at Maia*] From now on, the strange lady and I mean to take the same road.[76]

ULFHEIM: Don't you know that you were risking your lives coming that way?

PROFESSOR RUBEK: We tried it, at any rate. It didn't seem too difficult at first.

ULFHEIM: No, nothing seems difficult at first; but then you come to a tight corner where you can't go forward or back. And there you stick – 'tree'd', we sportsmen call it.

PROFESSOR RUBEK [*looking at him with a smile*]: Is that meant as good advice, Squire?

ULFHEIM: God forbid that *I* should advise anyone! [*Urgently, pointing up toward the peaks*] But don't you see that the storm is almost on us? Listen to those gusts of wind!

PROFESSOR RUBEK [*listening*]: They sound like the prelude to the resurrection day.

ULFHEIM: They're squalls blowing from the peaks, man! Just look how the clouds are billowing down – soon they'll be all round us like a winding-sheet!

IRENA [*with a shudder*]: I know that sheet!

MAIA [*pulling at Ulfheim*]: Let us try to get down.

ULFHEIM [*to Rubek*]: I can't help more than one. Take shelter in the hut for the time being. When the storm's over, I'll send a party up to fetch you both down.

IRENA [*in terror*]: To fetch us down? No! No!

ULFHEIM [*brusquely*]: Yes, by force if necessary – it's a matter of life or death up here. So now you know! [*To Maia*] Come on, now. Trust yourself to me.

MAIA [*clinging to him*]: If I get down with a whole skin, I shall sing for joy!

ULFHEIM [*calling to the others as he begins the descent*]: Wait in the hut, then, till they bring ropes to fetch you down.

[ULFHEIM, *with* MAIA *in his arms, clambers quickly but carefully down the precipice.*]

IRENA [*staring for a while at Rubek with terror in her eyes*]: Did you hear that, Arnold? They're coming up here to fetch me! A crowd of men will come –

PROFESSOR RUBEK: Gently – gently, Irena.

IRENA [*in mounting horror*]: And *she*'ll come, too, the woman in black – she'll come with them. She must have missed me hours ago. And she'll seize me, Arnold, and put me in the strait-jacket. She has it with her in her trunk, I've seen it with my own eyes!

PROFESSOR RUBEK: No one shall be allowed to touch you.

IRENA [*with a distraught smile*]: Oh no – *I* have a way to stop that.

PROFESSOR RUBEK: What do you mean?

IRENA [*drawing the knife*]: This!

PROFESSOR RUBEK [*reaching for it*]: You've a knife!

IRENA: Always – Always! Day and night. Even in bed.

PROFESSOR RUBEK: Give me that knife, Irena.

IRENA [*hiding it*]: You shan't have it; I may well need it myself!

PROFESSOR RUBEK: What can you want with it up here?

IRENA [*looking straight at him*]: I meant it for *you*, Arnold.

PROFESSOR RUBEK: For me?

IRENA: Last night, when we were sitting by Lake Taunitz –

PROFESSOR RUBEK: Lake Taunitz?

IRENA: Outside the cottage – playing with swans and water lilies . . .

PROFESSOR RUBEK: Go on – go on.

IRENA: – and I heard you say, as ice-cold as death, that I was no more than an episode in your life –

PROFESSOR RUBEK: It was you who said that, Irena, not I.

IRENA [*continuing*]: – I'd drawn the knife then – because I wanted to thrust it into your back.

PROFESSOR RUBEK [*darkly*]: Why didn't you?

IRENA: Because I suddenly realized – with horror – that you were dead already . . . long ago.

PROFESSOR RUBEK: Dead?

IRENA: Dead. Dead as I am. We sat there by Lake Taunitz, two cold corpses, and we played together.

PROFESSOR RUBEK: I shouldn't call that death. But you don't understand me.

IRENA: Then where is the burning desire for me that you fought and struggled against when I stood willingly before you as the woman rising from the dead?

PROFESSOR RUBEK: Our love is *not* dead, Irena!

IRENA: The love that belongs to our earthly life – our lovely miraculous earthly life – our mysterious earthly life – *that* is dead in both of us.

PROFESSOR RUBEK [*passionately*]: I tell you, that very love is burning and seething in me as hotly as ever it did.

IRENA: But I? Have you forgotten who I am now?

PROFESSOR RUBEK: You can be who or what you will, for all I care. To me, you are the woman that I dreamed you were.

IRENA: I've stood on the turntable – naked – and made a show of myself to many hundreds of men since you.

PROFESSOR RUBEK: It was I who drove you to the turntable. How blind I was then – when I set the dead clay image above the joy of living – and of loving!

IRENA [*dropping her head*]: Too late – too late.

PROFESSOR RUBEK: Nothing that has happened since has debased you by a hairsbreath in my eyes.

IRENA [*with head held high*]: Nor in my own!

PROFESSOR RUBEK: Well, then – we are free, and there is still time for us to live our lives, Irena.

IRENA [*looking at him sadly*]: The longing for life died in me, Arnold. I'm risen now, and I seek for you: And now that I've found you, I see that both you and life are dead – as I have been.

PROFESSOR RUBEK: Oh, but you're wrong! In us and around us, life pulses and flowers as strongly as ever.

IRENA [*smiling and shaking her head*]: The woman you showed rising from the dead can see life itself lying on the bier.

PROFESSOR RUBEK [*embracing her violently*]: Then let us two dead things live life for once to the full – before we go down to our graves again.

IRENA [*with a great cry*]: Arnold!

PROFESSOR RUBEK: But not here in the half-light! Not here, with this hideous wet shroud swirling round us.

IRENA [*in a transport of passion*]: No no! Up in the light – in all its shimmering glory! Up to the promised heights!

PROFESSOR RUBEK: Up there we will hold our marriage feast, Irena, my beloved!

IRENA [*proudly*]: The sun may look on us freely, Arnold.

PROFESSOR RUBEK: All the powers of light may look on us freely – and all the powers of darkness too. [*Gripping her hand*] Will you follow me, my ransomed bride?

IRENA [*as if transfigured*]: I follow you freely and gladly, my master and my lord.

PROFESSOR RUBEK [*taking her with him*]: We must first pass through the mists, Irena – and then . . .

IRENA: Yes, through all the mists, and then right up to the topmost peak gleaming in the sunrise!

[*The clouds of mist completely blot out the view.* PROFESSOR RUBEK *and* IRENA, *hand in hand, climb up to the right over the expanse of snow, and quickly disappear into the lower clouds. Fierce gusts of wind whistle and chase through the air.*

The NUN *comes across the scree from the left. She stops, and peers about her silently and tensely.*]

MAIA [*heard singing triumphantly far down in the depths below*]:

> I am free, I am free, I am free!
> No longer the prison I'll see!
> I am free as a bird, I am free!

[*Suddenly there is a roar like thunder from high in the snows. The avalanche slides down at a terrific pace.* PROFESSOR RUBEK *and* IRENA *are dimly seen as they hurtle down in the mass of snow and are buried under it.*]

THE NUN [*with a scream, stretches out her arms to them as they fall and cries*]: Irena!

[*She stands silent for a moment, then makes the sign of the cross in the air before her, and says:*]

Pax vobiscum!

[MAIA'S *triumphant song still floats up from lower down the mountain.*]

NOTES

———————— * ————————

Ghosts

Ghosts was written during the autumn of 1881 and was published in December of the same year. It was not performed in the theatre till May 1882, when a Danish touring company produced it in the Aurora Turner Hall in Chicago.

Ibsen disliked Archer's use of the word 'Ghosts' as a title, but there is no English equivalent for the Norwegian title, which means roughly 'Those-Who-Walk-Again'. The French *Les Revenants* is more accurate.

1. p. 20. *Chamberlain*: After the hereditary nobility has been abolished in Norway in 1821, Chamberlain (*Kammerherre*) was a title that the King bestowed on prominent men, rather like our own Knighthood. It entailed certain duties and privileges at Court.

2. p. 21. *half-hidden by continual rain*: When a friend asked Ibsen about the play he was working on, Ibsen answered, 'It's a family story, as grey and gloomy as this rainy day.' He set the play in the country round Bergen – the rainiest part of Norway.

3. p. 23. *Fi donc!*: When the Ibsens lived in Munich they had a Bavarian maid who, as Ibsen noticed with interest, spoke dialect with her own people, but talked good unaccented German with the gentry, garnishing it with French words and phrases.

4. p. 27. *Miss Engstrand*: Pastor Manders addresses her as *jomfru*, but in English the word 'Miss' has to serve both for this and for *frøken*.

5. p. 33. *I quite agree*: Here, in the first draft, Manders had a long and rather pompous speech which ended 'Unless one is above suspicion, one never attains one's goal'. In the fair copy

Ibsen altered this to 'Unless one is *looked upon* as above suspicion ...', etc., but he must have felt that this was too obvious even for Pastor Manders, because he then deleted the whole speech.

6. p: 39. *a light overcoat*: This was an afterthought; in the first draft, *overfrakke* (overcoat) is crossed out and *høstfrakke* (literally 'autumn coat') put in its place. As Northam notes in his masterly book on Ibsen's symbolism, Osvald wasn't equipped for the northern winter.

7. p. 41. *high spirits*: There is no exact English equivalent to *livsglede* – the French *joie-de-vivre* comes nearest to it.

8. p. 50. *come up from the garden*: In the first draft, the girl was clearing the table.

9. p. 55. *Let's sit here*: *Velbekomme* is untranslatable – in England we don't say 'May it do you good'! Presumably Ibsen only wants to show that the meal is just over, so I've used a colourless phrase more in keeping with our usage.

10. p. 58. *your two aunts*: Originally Ibsen made them her sisters.

11. p. 59. *Captain Alving*: Here, as elsewhere, Ibsen has 'Chamberlain Alving', but, like Manders in Act One, 'I have chosen Captain rather than Chamberlain – Captain sounds less pretentious.'

12. p. 61. *all over the country*: Norway is a peculiarly 'haunted' land; the old legends and the belief in trolls are very near the surface.

13. p. 62. *chain-stitch*: Literally 'machine-sewn' but that would have no derogatory implication today. When the play was produced in Berlin in 1887, these lines were cut. When Ibsen asked why, the producer told him: 'Sewing-machines these days are so efficient that one cannot unpick the stitches.' Ibsen replied: 'You can be quite sure that Mrs Alving up at Rosenvold still used her old-fashioned machine.'

14. p. 63. *particularly well-developed*: Ibsen could never forgive the Church for its attacks on him after *Love's Comedy*. It was the Church Department that quashed his application to the Storthing for a Poet's Stipend on the Civil List, and

so condemned him to further years of desperate poverty. In fact he eventually got the stipend three years later only by the fortunate accident that a certain cleric was too ill to attend the meeting. Ibsen had, too, a more recent grievance against the Norwegian Church, since they had stopped his son, who was studying law in Munich, from going on to the University at Christiania. In 1880 Ibsen wrote to Hegel, his publisher, that when he got the chance he would 'deal appropriately with those black-coated theologians!'

15. p. 63. *there weren't any servants about*: This seems unlikely – another of Engstrand's lies – till we remember that Mrs Alving had sent Regina down to the wash-house to help with the decorations.

16. p. 69. *a sort of Orphanage*: Ibsen uses the same word *asyl* ('refuge') that he always uses for the Orphanage.

17. p. 71. *without a glimpse of the sun*: Ibsen is preparing us for the terrible final scene.

18. p. 74. *vermoulu*: Literally 'worm-eaten'.

19. p. 76. *pulls the bell rope*: Though there were 'no servants about' when Engstrand arrived. In fact she was justified; perhaps she knew that Regina wouldn't stay at the wash-house longer than she could help.

20. p. 79. *splendidly healthy*: Regina obviously hasn't inherited the disease.

21. p. 85. *a dreadful calamity*: When a German playgoer asked Ibsen if it was really Engstrand who set fire to the Orphanage, Ibsen, who usually resented questions about his plays, gave a sly smile and answered: '*Es wäre ihm schon zuzutrauen* [Trust him for that!].'

22. p. 91. *so formal*: The English translator's hurdle; what Osvald actually asks is 'Why don't you call me "thou"?'

23. p. 95. *Oh ... 'my father'!*: Osvald's outburst against filial piety is a reflection of Ibsen's old hatred of his own father, whom he had caricatured as the egregious Daniel Hejre in *The League of Youth*.

24. p. 95. *an old superstition*: Ibsen was obsessed with the burden of the past; he felt that though men seemed outwardly

to be progressing, their minds were not advancing at the same pace. 'I think,' he wrote, 'that we are sailing with a corpse in the cargo.' And in his verse letter *From Far Away* to Georg Brandes in 1875, he wrote of the ghosts of dead ideas and beliefs that haunt the youth of the Scandinavian countries:

> Ghosts of the long dead times and peoples
> That walk in our young folk again.

25. p. 102. *Yes! No no . . .*: Archer once asked Ibsen if Mrs Alving eventually gave Osvald the helping hand. 'I should never dream of answering such a difficult question,' said Ibsen, 'What do *you* think?' Archer answered that if she didn't, it might be because there was still a 'ghost' within her – namely that perhaps the illness was not definitely incurable. 'Yes,' said Ibsen, 'probably that is the answer – that a mother would always postpone the helping hand with the idea that where there was life there was hope.'

A Public Enemy

This play was written in 1882, in half the time that Ibsen usually took over a play, and was his reaction to the outcry caused by *Ghosts*. It was published in November 1882.

26. p. 103. *A Public Enemy*: The usual translation of the title *En Folkefiende* is Archer's *An Enemy of the People*. I have broken with this tradition out of regard for the small-part actors in Act Four. I simply cannot believe in an angry crowd shouting 'Enemy of the People, Enemy of the People!' and even the 'capable actors' whom Ibsen demanded for these walk-on parts would have difficulty in making the phrase sound convincing. 'Public Enemy' comes more easily off the tongue.

27. p. 104. *Dr Stockmann*: The name is a memory of Ibsen's childhood – he was born in Stockmann's Court in Skien, in sight of the town prison and the pillory. Though *Stockmann*

means 'Chastiser', the first bearer of the name – an ancestor of Ibsen's mother – was a priest who took the name from his parish of Stokne in Vestfold.

28. p. 104. *Aslaksen*: This character first appeared in Ibsen's earlier comedy *The League of Youth*. He has matured since those days; he no longer whines and cringes, and he seems to have had a merciful release from his ailing wife.

29. p. 106. *the Mayor comes in*: This is rather confusing for the audience who have been led to expect Mr Hovstad, and who haven't the advantage of a stage direction. Ibsen corrects this impression to some extent by making the Mayor say 'Good evening, sister-in-law', which, though it sounds somewhat stilted in English, is thoroughly in keeping with his pomposity.

30. p. 106. *hot meat at night*: Mrs Stockmann doesn't correct him, though what she gave Billing was cold. Perhaps it doesn't occur to the Mayor that he could possibly be offered anything but a hot meal.

31. p. 107. *The People's Herald*: Hovstad's paper is *Folkebudet* – literally *The People's Messenger*. Perhaps *Courier* would have been a more accurate translation of *bud*, but *Herald* still has an appropriately left-wing sound to English ears.

32. p. 110. *you don't wear one*: As Northam points out, it is revealing that while the other guests wear overcoats – the Mayor keeping his on and the rest hanging theirs in the hall – Captain Horster is hardier and never wears one.

In December 1882, Ibsen wrote from Rome to the Producer at the Theatre Royal, Copenhagen: 'A Copenhagen paper in its account of the plot speaks of Captain Horster as an old man and an old friend of the Doctor's. That is wrong. Horster is young – one of the young people whom the Doctor says he likes to see in his house. ... In the short scene with Petra in Act Five, he must suggest the beginning of a warm and intimate friendship between them.'

33. p. 112. *county magistrate*: *Amptmand* – literally 'county man' – can mean bailiff, local officer, or even the Lieutenant of a County.

34. p. 115. *sneaks a cigar*: Thirteen is surely rather young for Eylif to take to cigars.

35. p. 120. *an enormous dining-room*: Ibsen is preparing us for the setting of Act Four.

36. p. 127. *Old Morten Kiil*: The 'Badger's name is another memory of Ibsen's early days in Skien. In 1881 Ibsen had amused himself by writing down his childhood memories, so these names were fresh in his mind.

37. p. 127. *Ah ... good morning*: Here, and elsewhere, Stockmann addresses Kiil as 'father-in-law', but we in England haven't arrived at any consistent or comfortable form of address for our in-laws.

38. p. 133. *temperately*: *Mådehold* means both 'moderation' and 'temperance'. Though Aslaksen might more reasonably say 'with moderation', it would spoil the joke about the Temperance Society that keeps cropping up all through the play. I have tried to keep the balance by using 'moderation' in the Doctor's speech.

39. p. 143. *an old habit of yours*: While he was working on the play, Ibsen wrote to Hegel, his publisher: 'Dr Stockmann and I get on very well together, and often see eye to eye, but he's more muddle-headed than I am!'

40. p. 150. *The Editor's office*: A familiar scene to Ibsen; in 1851 he had some connexion with a left-wing paper the *Workers' Union*. Later he helped to found a satirical journal *The Man* which survived for thirty-nine issues. Its rather obstructive printer was the model for Aslaksen.

41. p. 156. *Councillor Stensgård*: He was the leading character in Ibsen's successful comedy *The League of Youth*, written thirteen years earlier, so that his name would be as familiar to Scandinavian audiences as that of, say, Lady Bracknell would be to us.

42. p. 159. *down in the bottom corner*: Provincial papers often printed a short story at the bottom of their front pages.

43. p. 162. *Let me take your things*: The Mayor seems inordinately fond of wearing his official gold-braided hat – just

as Ibsen loved to wear all the orders and decorations that he collected so assiduously.

44. p. 173. *Eylif'll do whatever Morten does*: Had Ibsen forgotten for the moment that Eylif is the elder by three years?

45. p. 174. *A large gathering of townspeople*: In his letter to the producer when the play was first produced at Copenhagen, Ibsen wrote: 'Please give the walk-on parts in Act Four to capable actors.'

46. p. 181. *incomprehensibly*: *Ubegribelige*. Probably the man means *ubevægelige* – 'inflexibly'. In English he could perhaps be trying to say 'incontrovertibly'.

47. p. 182. *like an eider duck*: In Ibsen's early poem *The Eider Duck*, the bird, on a northern fjord, plucks the down from her breast to line her nest, but a fisherman steals it to sell. Twice more the duck strips her breast, only to have the down taken each time. At last (in the final version) she flies away

> To the South, to the South, to the sunlit coast,

just as Stockmann had at last come south from his northern exile.

48. p. 183. *I can't ... stand Leading Citizens*: Perhaps this is another boyhood memory. Although Ibsen's parents had lost their money and were desperately poor, they were of good family and were accepted as such in Skien, Ibsen's birthplace; but when Ibsen went to work in Grimstad the leading citizens there snubbed the chemist's assistant and Ibsen felt his exclusion keenly.

49. p. 194. *You may find that expensive*: After he had sent off the MS., Ibsen wrote to his publisher: 'Please have one word in Act Four altered. A speech of Morten Kiil's reads "You'll find that expensive." I want it to read "You *may* find that expensive." It probably occurs on the 2nd page of the 43rd sheet of the MS.'

50. p. 197. *what the devil's her name?*: Ibsen himself wasn't too certain about her name; in his first draft he called her Marta, and he hit on Randina only during a later revision.

51. p. 216. *as it says somewhere*: 2 Timothy iv:2.

When We Dead Wake

This play was written between February and November 1899, and was published in December of that year. This was three years after the appearance of *John Gabriel Borkmann*, that is to say after an interval of a year longer than was usual between Ibsen's plays. It was given a first performance, for copyright reasons, at the Haymarket Theatre, London, in December 1899, a day or two before the actual publication.

Ibsen originally called it *The Resurrection Day*, but then changed the title, first to *When the Dead Wake* and then to its present form.

52. p. 222. *Professor Rubek*: In his earliest notes for the play was undecided whether to call him Stubow or Rambow; by the time he reached the first full draft, he used Stubow for the opening pages; after that, for a dozen lines or so, he called him Stubek or Stubeck. Then, just before Ulfheim's entrance, he finally settled on Rubek.

53. p. 222. *Squire Ulfheim*: *Godsejer* is literally 'landed Proprietor'.

54. p. 222. *Waiters, visitors, and children*: There is no mention of Lars, the huntsman, in the list of characters.

55. p. 224. *Aren't you glad to be home again ...?*: Ibsen had come back to Norway after twenty-seven years abroad. In a letter of Georg Brandes in June 1897 he wrote: 'Oh my dear Brandes, here, up among the fjords, is my native land, but – but – but – where do I find my true home? It is the sea that draws me most. ... For the rest, here I am in solitude, laying the plans for some new play, though I still cannot see clearly what it will turn out to be.'

56. p. 225. *Frau Professor*: Ibsen uses the German form instead of the Norwegian *Fru*. Like Ibsen himself, Rubek had won his greatest fame abroad.

57. p. 228. *portrait-busts*: Ibsen called his later plays, *The Master Builder*, *Little Eyolf*, and *John Gabriel Borkmann*, 'portrait plays'. Like Rubek he had a feeling of guilt about

them, since he thought that they only reiterated aspects of his 'message' that he had dealt with already.

58. p. 229. *the dear old farmyard*: By his desk Ibsen kept a tray of little animals – dogs and cats, wooden bears, a rabbit playing a fiddle, and so on. He once said: 'I never write a single line of my plays without that tray and its occupants in front of me on the table. I couldn't write without them. . . .' Then he went on thoughtfully: 'That may seem odd – it probably is . . . but how I use them is my own secret.' And then he gave a quiet chuckle. As a child, he used to draw caricatures of his brothers and sisters as animals.

59. p. 230. *all the glory of the world*: The phrase also occurs in Act Five of *The Pretenders*.

60. p. 231. *Is the Frau Professor offended?*: Here Ibsen uses the feminine form *professorinde*; as we in England have not yet found the need to evolve a word for a female professor, I have borrowed *'Frau Professor'* from page 225.

61. p. 231. *The Manager*: In the earlier drafts he had a name: Brager. Though Archer calls him 'Inspector', the Norwegian work *Inspektør* also implies 'overseer'; I have used 'Manager' as evoking a more familiar picture to an English reader.

62. p. 233. *A Nun*: Ibsen calls her 'Deaconess'.

63. p. 233. *her dress hangs down to her feet*: Tennant claims that Irena's dress was exactly what Laura Kieler had worn on her last visit to Ibsen. It was her marriage that he had used as a model for *A Doll's House*: she always reproached him for this, just as Irena reproaches Rubek. Originally Ibsen dressed her in flannel, not 'creamy white cashmere'.

64. p. 236. *unkempt hair*: At first Ibsen gave him close-cropped (*kortklippet*) hair.

65. p. 240. *Irena*: Until this speech Ibsen has called her 'The Lady'. Cf. 'The Lady' in Strindberg's *To Damascus* which had appeared the year before, in 1898.

66. p. 243 *Herr von Satoff*: An unlikely name for Rubek to suppose that a South American would have. Originally this husband was another Russian, but Ibsen crossed this out and made him a Bulgarian, which would have made Rubek's mis-

take more likely. Later Ibsen rewrote much of the scene, changing him to South American, but keeping the Slavonic name. Incidentally, although the only time that Rubek had heard the name was when the Manager said that Irena had registered as 'Madame de Satoff', here he calls him 'Herr von Satoff'.

67. p. 243. *a fine sharp dagger*: Ibsen originally wrote 'that I had with me in bed'. The change to 'that I always have ...' makes the implication clearer, and the reference a few lines later to the stillborn children underlines it.

68. p. 247. *What poems have you written since?*: At the end of his life, Ibsen reproaches himself for having abandoned poetry after *Peer Gynt*, and turned to the prose of realistic drama.

69. p. 251. *a mountain health-resort*: In a conversation with Gunnar Heiberg, Ibsen identified it as Hardangervidda.

70. p. 264. *I've been waiting for you for years*: Heiberg once asked Ibsen how old Irena was (the actress who created the part had played her as quite young). Ibsen answered: 'She is twenty-eight.' 'But that's not possible,' said Heiberg. 'Oh,' said Ibsen, 'so you know better than I do, eh?' 'Yes, I do,' said Heiberg, and showed how, with the years that must have passed since she first met Rubek, she would be at least forty. 'She is twenty-eight,' insisted Ibsen. 'If you know so much, why do you ask?' The next day there came a letter from him:

Dear Gunnar Heiberg,

You are right and I was wrong. I have looked up my notes: Irena is about forty.

Yours,

Henrik Ibsen

But twenty-eight was the age of Rosa Fitinghoff, with whom Ibsen, at seventy, had fallen in love.

71. p. 268. *a thin sharp knife*: The symbolic knife has now become real.

72. p. 272. *episode*: This was the word that Ibsen used to describe Goethe's relationship with Marianne von Willemer.

73. p. 276. *bear-hunter*: Literally 'bear-shooter'. In his first draft, Ibsen here calls him 'eagle-shooter'.

74. p. 277. *the hillside*: There is no single English word for *vidda* – the rough, waste, mountainside. There is an echo here of Ibsen's long early poem *On the Vidda*, where the lover leaves his betrothed to live on the *vidda* at the bidding of a Strange Hunter.

75. p. 282. *Bear-killer*: Ibsen uses four forms of the nickname: *Bjørne-jæger* = 'bear-hunter'; *Bjørnedræber* = 'bear-slayer'; *Bjørneskytte* = 'bear-shooter'; and *Bjørnemorder* = 'bear-murderer'.

76. p. 286. Originally Ibsen had a long, and rather lame, scene here, with Ulfheim producing a somewhat unlikely bottle of champagne from the hut, so that all four could drink to freedom. Ulfheim and Maia go, and Irena says: 'She has awakened ... from life's deep, heavy sleep.' The play ends with Rubek crying: 'Through the mists I can see the mountain-tops, glowing in the sunrise. We must go up there, through the mists of night, up into the morning light!'

[*The mists fall thicker and thicker over the scene.* RUBEK *and* IRENA *climb into them and are gradually lost to sight. The head of the* NUN, *searching for them, becomes visible in a gap in the mists.*

High above the clouds, the mountain peaks gleam in the morning sun.]

MORE ABOUT PENGUINS
AND PELICANS

Penguinews, which appears every month, contains details of all the new books issued by Penguins as they are published. From time to time it is supplemented by *Penguins in Print*, which is a complete list of all titles available. (There are some five thousand of these.)

A specimen copy of *Penguinews* will be sent to you free on request. For a year's issues (including the complete lists) please send £1 if you live in the British Isles, or elsewhere. Just write to Dept EP, Penguin Books, Harmondsworth, Middlesex, enclosing a cheque or postal order, and your name will be added to the mailing list.

In the U.S.A.: For a complete list of books available from Penguin in the United States write to Dept CS, Penguin Books Inc., 7110 Ambassador Road, Baltimore, Maryland 21207.

In Canada: For a complete list of books available from Penguin in Canada write to Penguin Books Canada Ltd, 41 Steelcase Road West, Markham, Ontario.

THE PENGUIN CLASSICS

Some Recent and Forthcoming Volumes